# THE COLLECTOR'S ENCYCLOPEDIA OF
# DEPRESSION GLASS

## ELEVENTH EDITION

### BY GENE FLORENCE

**COLLECTOR BOOKS**
*A Division of Schroeder Publishing Co., Inc.*

The current values in this book should be used only as a guide. They are not intended to set prices, which vary from one section of the country to another. Auction prices as well as dealer prices vary greatly and are affected by condition as well as demand. Neither the Author nor the Publisher assumes responsibility for any losses that might be incurred as a result of consulting this guide.

*On the Cover:*
Mayfair Pink Cookie Jar, $47.50
Cherry Blossom Green Tumbler, $30.00
Royal Lace Cobalt Blue Pitcher, $150.00

## *Searching For A Publisher?*

We are always looking for knowledgeable people considered to be experts within their fields. If you feel that there is a real need for a book on your collectible subject and have a large comprehensive collection, contact us.

COLLECTOR BOOKS
P.O. Box 3009
Paducah, Kentucky 42002-3009

# ACKNOWLEDGMENTS

Thanks to all you readers and collectors who keep me informed with your letters, cards and reports of new information! Thanks for bringing newly discovered pieces to shows so that I can verify them and for sending measurements and photographs confirming new discoveries! Photographs are invaluable when authenticating a new piece. (If you have trouble photographing glass, take it outside in natural light, place the glass on a neutral surface and forget the camera has a flash attachment. A cloudy bright day works best.) Please enclose a **SASE** (self addressed stamped envelope) that is **large** enough to send back your pictures, if you wish them returned!

There have been approximately **forty-five newly discovered pieces added to the listings** since the tenth edition! (Those of you who feel that nothing new is ever found had better look closely at your favorite pattern!) Similarly, there have been nine deletions from the book of pieces that have never been found that were listed in catalogues or had mysteriously appeared in my listings.

Too, over eighty measurements have been corrected in this book. These corrections have occurred due to original catalogue misinformation, entry mistakes or errors in measurement in the past. Realize, too, that the size of the **same patterned** plate or tumbler can vary from each moulding generation, especially if the pattern was made for a long time. Be sure to read about measurements on page 4.

Thanks to all the Depression Glass Clubs and show promoters who invited me to be a guest at their shows. I have enjoyed them, gained knowledge from them, and hopefully contributed to them.

A special thanks is always due my family. Cathy, my wife, is chief editor, critic and proofreader and spends days trying to make sure you understand what I meant to say. Marc, my son, is taking over shipping my book orders from Lexington while he attends the University of Kentucky. Chad, my eldest, who has now married, is still available to help load boxes for photography sessions. (There was a dealer who offered Cathy money for photographs of me in a tux at that Spring wedding.)

Thanks to "Grannie Bear," my Mom, who spent hours packing and listing the abundant glass for photography sessions we had for this book. She, along with my Dad, has continued to keep records and new listings of measurements since the last book. She has also recorded prices that items sold for in the shop. All of this helps make my writing easier.

Thanks, too, to Cathy's Mom, Sibyl, who helped Cathy sort and pack glass for days and days! My gratitude to Dad, Charles and Sibyl who kept everything under control at home while we travelled.

Glass and information for this book were furnished by Earl and Beverly Hines, Dick and Pat Spencer, Sam and Becky Collings, Dan Tucker and Lorrie Kitchen, Calvin and Gwen Key, Matt and Angela Koester, Kevin and Barbara Kiley, Mary and Dean Watkins, Ken and Sharee Pakula, Steven Cagle, Dave Periord, Gladys Florence and numerous readers from across the U.S.A., Puerto Rico, Canada, England, New Zealand and Australia!

Photographs for this book were made at Curtis and Mays Studio in Paducah by Tom Clouser and by a new cameraman, Richard Walker of New York who provided numerous photographs during a six day session that about "wiped out" our working crew from Collector Books. Glass arranging, unpacking, sorting, carting and repacking was accomplished by Dick and Pat Spencer, Earl and Beverly Hines, Lisa Cash, Sherry Kraus, Lisa Stroup and Cathy Florence. Our two van loads of glass and additional glassware brought in by friends filled a double room with boxes. Even I had a hard time figuring out how we could get all these pictures done in the time available without someone losing sanity (or perhaps gaining some since one of that crew has already left Collector Books). I haven't spoken to the new photographer since those six twelve-hour days last October; I hope he will be up to it again this year!

In addition, Jane White and many of the crew mentioned previously helped on other photography shoots over the two year period since the tenth edition. There is no way anyone could believe what we have to do to get you these photographs. Thanks to the special people in the Editorial Department at Collector Books; Lisa Stroup, who is working as Editor, and Sherry Kraus who transferred all my computer disks into a book and caught some mistakes that Cathy and I missed!

I recently received a letter from someone who was working on a collectible book. He said he had not realized that there was so much work involved and that his editor had suggested (rightly so) that he might need a spelling checker for his writing. He also needs months of sixteen hour days, or so I have found!

This eleventh book was again written in Florida (as all my books have been in the last two years). Sitting here writing and glancing at the alligators and fishing boats floating by sure beats looking at the wall in my Kentucky office. I am finally free to be at our home in Florida which is mostly a pleasant experience. (I am discounting chasing down my roofing shingles in my neighbors' yards after the recent 50 mph winds.) The fishing has been sporadic at best, but I wouldn't be doing any fishing in Kentucky at this time. As it is, I have Shellcrackers in my basket to clean and fresh fish for tomorrow's menu. Who could ask for more?

The phone rings less here although, today, I have talked to two magazine writers who are working on articles on Depression glass and verifying their facts. Depression Glass has been a popular subject in both women's and collecting magazines recently. (I used to get a polite thank you for my help, but candy seems to be the latest form of thanks - as if my expanding waistline needs a box of candy every few weeks!)

Most of the previous books' glitches have been ironed out in my Macintosh II computer, but a few items always seem to end up in the "missing" category. Can anyone ever explain to me how a listing can be in one book and totally disappear in the next one? Sharp eyed readers are kind enough to notify me of the omission.

I do my best; but there is no way I could accomplish any of this without you! As we go to press with the Eleventh Edition, thank you for making this America's #1 Best Selling Glass Book!

# FOREWORD

Depression Glass as defined in this book is the colored glassware made primarily during the Depression years in the colors of amber, blue, black, crystal, green, pink, red, yellow and white. There are other colors and some glass made before, as well as after, this time; but primarily, the glass within this book was made from the 1920's through the end of the 1930's. This book is mostly concerned with the inexpensively made dinnerware turned out by machine in quantity and sold through smaller stores or given away as promotional or premium items for other products of that time. Depression glass was often packed in cereal boxes, flour sacks or given as gifts at the local movie theaters, gasoline stations and grocery stores.

There have been changes in the collecting of Depression Glass since my first book was released in 1972. Prices have soared; seemingly plentiful patterns have been assembled into vast collections and removed from the market. Smaller Depression patterns and previously ignored crystal colors have attracted buyers; actually, anything that is Depression Glass, whether it is a known pattern or not, suddenly has added value and collectability. Collectors have become more knowledgeable and sophisticated in their collecting. Many collectors are enhancing their collections of "A to W" (Adam to Windsor) with patterns of hand-made glassware produced during the same time. This broadening interest of collectors prompted me to research and write five more books in the field of Depression Glass, one on ELEGANT glassware of the time, one on the glass KITCHENWARE items of the Depression and three others on the VERY RARE glassware of the Depression era. Additionally, collectors have been acquiring later made patterns encompassing the 1940's through the early 1960's that have led to my latest book Collect*ible Glassware from the 40's, 50's, 60's...* which is now in its second edition. To correctly date glassware from that later period, it was necessary to move some patterns previously exclusive to this book into the newer book's time frame. All patterns manufactured after 1940 are now in the newer book covering the period after the Depression years.

Information for this book comes through research, experience, fellow dealers, collectors and over 1,000,000 miles of travel pursuant to glassware. However, some of the most exciting information has come from benevolent readers who shared catalogues, magazines, photographs of glass and their specific knowledge with me. These kindnesses I especially value.

# PRICING

**All prices in this book are retail prices for mint condition glassware. This book is intended to be only a guide to prices as there are some regional price differences that cannot reasonably be dealt with herein!**

You may expect dealers to pay from 30% to 50% less than the prices quoted. Glass that is in less than mint condition, i.e., chipped, cracked, scratched or poorly molded, will bring only a **small percentage** of the price of glass that is in mint condition.

Prices have become fairly well standardized due to national advertising by dealers and Depression Glass Shows that are held from coast to coast. Several nationally known dealers have assisted in update pricing for this book. However, there **are still some regional differences in prices due partly to glass being more readily available in some areas than in others.** Companies distributed certain pieces in some areas that they did not in others. Generally speaking, however, prices are about the same among dealers from coast to coast.

Prices **tend to increase dramatically** on rare items and, in general, they have increased as a whole due to more and more collectors entering the field and people becoming more aware of the worth of Depression Glass. However, I receive letters daily from new collectors who have just "discovered" Depression Glass!

One of the more important aspects of this book is the attempt made to illustrate as well as realistically price those items that are in demand. The desire was to give you the most accurate guide to collectible patterns of Depression Glass available.

# MEASUREMENTS

To illustrate why there are discrepancies in measurements, I offer the following sample from just two years of Hocking's catalogue references:

| Year | | Ounces | | Ounces | | Ounces |
|------|---------|----------|--------------|---------|----------------|--------|
| 1935 | Pitcher | 37,58,80 | Flat Tumbler | 5,9,13½ | Footed Tumbler | 10,13 |
| 1935 | Pitcher | 37,60,80 | Flat Tumbler | 5,9,10,15 | Footed Tumbler | 10,13 |
| 1936 | Pitcher | 37,65,90 | Flat Tumbler | 5,9,13½ | Footed Tumbler | 10,15 |
| 1936 | Pitcher | 37,60,90 | Flat Tumbler | 5,9,13½ | Footed Tumbler | 10,15 |

All measurements in this book are exact as to some manufacturer's listing or to actual measurement. You may expect variance of up to ½" or 1-5 ounces. This may be due to mould variations or changes by the manufacturer as well as rounding off measurements for catalogue listings.

# INDEX

# ADAM JEANNETTE GLASS COMPANY, 1932-1934

Colors: Pink, green, crystal, some yellow and Delphite blue. *(See Reproduction Section)*

There continue to be more collectors of pink Adam than there are for the more costly green. Since green Adam pieces are less plentiful, those prices remain higher than similar items in pink. However, larger numbers searching for the pink are presently causing these prices to increase faster than for green. Most pink prices have quite a way to go to catch up to those of the green; but individual items such as tumblers and serving pieces, are selling equally well as green. Undoubtedly, the pink vase is the most elusive piece of Adam unless you include the Adam/Sierra butter dish. Many pink vases lean or sit lopsided. Because some collectors are unwilling to pay a high price for these less than first quality vases, you can sometimes find a bargain if you decide to accept less than "perfect."

Speaking of the Adam/Sierra butter dish, the Sierra design is on the top along with the Adam design. The top has both designs. Adam is on the outside of the top and Sierra is on the inside of the top only. These tops have been found on both Adam and Sierra butter bottoms, but those bottoms contain only one pattern. To be a real Adam/Sierra combination butter it has to have both patterns on that top! Many times I have seen an Adam butter top on a Sierra bottom or a Sierra top on an Adam bottom priced as the rare butter.

As I said before, green Adam is much harder to find than the pink. Still, green prices have been rather steady for years. An increase in prices for butter dishes, candy jars, candlesticks and shakers would not be surprising if a few more collectors were to begin stashing away green. If you start collecting green Adam, buy those pieces first!

As with a few other Jeannette patterns, the sugar and candy lids are interchangeable. This was a production savings idea for Jeannette then and a blessing for collectors today.

Adam lamps are not being found in any quantity. In the Floral pattern on page 81, you can see a pink lamp that is designed the same way Adam lamps were. A sherbet was frosted in order to hide the wiring and a notch was cut into the top edge of the sherbet to accommodate a switch. A metal cover was applied to the top of the frosted sherbet holding a tall bulb that was connected to a switch that fits through the notch. The prices listed are for working lamps. It is the **bulb assembly** that is hard to find. The notched, frosted sherbets are available.

Inner rims of cereal bowls and other Adam pieces need to be carefully checked. They have become damaged from both using and stacking over the years. If you buy pieces that are rough inside do not pay mint condition prices. Damaged glass has become a problem in collecting. You have to decide if you are willing to accept less than perfect glass. When it comes time to resell, I guarantee you will be happier with the prices obtained for mint glassware. Prices in this book are for mint (like new) condition glass. Some damaged glass can be repaired by competent workmen (but should be so labeled). I might add that many glass grinders and glass repairmen are not competent! Ask to see examples of their work before you entrust your glass to them.

The butter dish is the **only** piece that has been reproduced! Do not use the information given in the Reproduction Section in the back of the book for any other pieces in a pattern. You can not apply the directions of the arrows on the butter to any other pieces in Adam. **It only applies to the butter.** This goes for all reproductions I have listed in the back. Only apply the telltale clues I have listed for the piece I am describing. Transferring information to some other item will not work!

| | Pink | Green | | Pink | Green |
|---|---|---|---|---|---|
| Ash tray, ¾" | 26.00 | 22.50 | ** Cup | 22.00 | 20.00 |
| Bowl, 4¾" dessert | 14.00 | 14.00 | Lamp | 240.00 | 265.00 |
| Bowl, 5¾" cereal | 37.50 | 37.50 | Pitcher, 8", 32 oz. | 37.50 | 42.50 |
| Bowl, 7¾" | 20.00 | 21.00 | Pitcher, 32 oz. round base | 46.00 | |
| Bowl, 9", no cover | 24.00 | 38.00 | Plate, 6" sherbet | 7.50 | 8.00 |
| Bowl, cover, 9" | 21.00 | 38.00 | *** Plate, 7¾" square salad | 14.00 | 15.00 |
| Bowl, 9" covered | 52.50 | 82.50 | Plate, 9" square dinner | 25.00 | 22.00 |
| Bowl, 10" oval | 25.00 | 25.00 | Plate, 9" grill | 17.00 | 16.00 |
| Butter dish bottom | 22.50 | 62.50 | Platter, 11¾" | 22.00 | 25.00 |
| Butter dish top | 52.50 | 217.50 | Relish dish, 8" divided | 17.50 | 21.00 |
| Butter dish & cover | 75.00 | 280.00 | Salt & pepper, 4" ftd. | 65.00 | 95.00 |
| Butter dish combination | | | ****Saucer, 6" square | 7.00 | 6.00 |
| with Sierra Pattern | 795.00 | | Sherbet, 3" | 27.50 | 36.00 |
| Cake plate, 10" ftd. | 21.00 | 24.00 | Sugar | 16.00 | 18.00 |
| * Candlesticks, 4" pr. | 80.00 | 90.00 | Sugar/candy cover | 25.00 | 36.00 |
| Candy jar & cover, 2½" | 80.00 | 90.00 | Tumbler, 4½" | 27.50 | 25.00 |
| Coaster, 3¼" | 19.00 | 17.00 | Tumbler, 5½" iced tea | 55.00 | 45.00 |
| Creamer | 17.00 | 19.00 | Vase, 7½" | 227.50 | 46.00 |

* Delphite $200.00     ** Yellow $85.00     *** Round pink $50.00; yellow $85.00     **** Round pink $50.00; yellow $65.00

# AMERICAN PIONEER LIBERTY WORKS, 1931-1934

Colors: Pink, green, amber and crystal.

Green American Pioneer is still the most desired color, but you should realize that there are three distinct shades of green available. Drastic color vicissitudes do not seem to bother collectors of American Pioneer as much as they do collectors of most other patterns. So few pieces are found that they are happy to acquire any new item no matter if it is slightly different from some of their collection.

There are few collectors of crystal or amber. Those few collectors of amber pieces have told me that there is little being found except basic luncheon pieces. To date, only one set of amber covered pitchers (urns) has ever been found! The liners for these pitchers are the regular 6" and 8" plates. Now you will be able to find liners easier except for the 6" pink plate for the small urn, which is also rare.

The newly discovered cocktails in two different sizes have only been found in amber! One holds 3 oz. and stands 3¹³⁄₁₆" while the other holds 3½ oz. and stands 3¹⁵⁄₁₆".

The dresser set remains the most valuable article in this set. Only one has been found in pink and few in green. These sets have become a hot property due, in part, to the many perfume and cologne bottle collectors searching for these. Many times items in a Depression glass pattern become more valuable because collectors from some other collecting field start searching for that particular item also. It makes for heated competition, and sometimes, frustration, if you are looking for that piece in your Depression glass pattern.

There are two styles of American Pioneer cups being found. Some cups have more rim flair than others which makes one style have a 4" diameter being 2¼" tall while the other has a 3⅝" diameter and is 2⅜" tall.

The mayonnaise has been misidentified in the past. It is the bowl near the center of the bottom photograph behind the two handled bowl. You may also have difficulty in matching lids for the covered bowls. One collector just told me that he believes there are three different bowl sizes instead of the two I have mentioned previously. In any case, you may find three varieties of the 9¼" covered bowl if you are lucky enough to find even one!

There may be additional items in American Pioneer that I do not have listed; so if you find one, be sure to let me know. I do appreciate the information that you take time to share with me; and I'm making a point to pass that information along to readers.

| | Crystal, Pink | Green | | Crystal, Pink | Green |
|---|---|---|---|---|---|
| *Bowl, 5" handled | 14.50 | 17.00 | Lamp, 5½" round, ball shape (amber $80.00) | 67.50 | |
| Bowl, 8¾" covered | 87.50 | 115.00 | Lamp, 8½" tall | 85.00 | 100.00 |
| Bowl, 9" handled | 18.00 | 24.00 | Mayonnaise, 4¼" | 57.50 | 90.00 |
| Bowl, 9¼" covered | 87.50 | 110.00 | Pilsner, 5¾", 11 oz. | 95.00 | 95.00 |
| Bowl, 10¾" console | 50.00 | 60.00 | **Pitcher, 5" covered urn | 130.00 | 200.00 |
| Candlesticks, 6½" pr. | 62.50 | 82.00 | ***Pitcher, 7" covered urn | 150.00 | 210.00 |
| Candy jar and cover, 1 lb | 77.50 | 92.00 | Plate, 6" | 12.50 | 15.00 |
| Candy jar and cover, 1½ lb. | 85.00 | 115.00 | *Plate, 6" handled | 12.50 | 15.00 |
| Cheese and cracker set (indented platter and comport) | 47.50 | 57.50 | *Plate, 8" | 10.00 | 11.00 |
| Coaster, 3½" | 26.00 | 28.00 | *Plate, 11½" handled | 16.00 | 18.00 |
| Creamer, 2¾" | 25.00 | 20.00 | *Saucer | 5.00 | 6.50 |
| *Creamer, 3½" | 19.00 | 21.00 | Sherbet, 3½" | 16.00 | 19.00 |
| *Cup | 10.00 | 12.00 | Sherbet, 4¾" | 30.00 | 35.00 |
| Dresser set (2 cologne, powder jar, on indented 7½" tray) | 350.00 | 300.00 | Sugar, 2¾" | 20.00 | 21.00 |
| Goblet, 3¹³⁄₁₆", 3 oz., cocktail | 34.00 | 36.00 | *Sugar, 3½" | 18.00 | 21.00 |
| Goblet, 3¹⁵⁄₁₆", 3½ oz., cocktail | 34.00 | 36.00 | Tumbler, 5 oz. juice | 25.00 | 32.00 |
| Goblet, 4", 3 oz. wine | 34.00 | 45.00 | Tumbler, 4", 8 oz. | 25.00 | 45.00 |
| Goblet, 6", 8 oz. water | 40.00 | 42.00 | Tumbler, 5", 12 oz. | 36.00 | 45.00 |
| Ice bucket, 6" | 45.00 | 55.00 | Vase, 7", 4 styles | 72.00 | 92.00 |
| Lamp, 1¾", w/metal pole 9½" | | 50.00 | Vase, 9", round | | 195.00 |
| | | | Whiskey, 2¼", 2 oz. | 42.50 | |

*Amber - Double the price of pink unless noted
**Amber $250.00
***Amber $300.00

**Please refer to Foreword for pricing information.**

8

# AMERICAN SWEETHEART MacBETH-EVANS GLASS COMPANY, 1930-1936

Colors: Pink, Monax, red, blue; some Cremax and color trimmed Monax.

The photograph below was originally scheduled to be on the cover; but there was a problem with sizing limitations for it to fit. In any case, I hope you enjoy seeing this table setting by Pat Spencer. She works with flowers to show off the beauty of the colored glassware. The red American Sweetheart pieces are accented with Heisey stems and candlesticks.

Red and blue American Sweetheart were sold in fifteen piece settings consisting of four each cups, saucers and 8" plates with a creamer, sugar and 12" salver. Any additional pieces found in these colors were **very limited** in distribution. You may notice some price advances on the console bowls. The few bowls that have been offered recently have had large prices on them and a few have been sold at the prices listed below.

For those who are not familiar with terminology, Cremax is a beige-like color when compared to the Monax which is the name of the white color made by MacBeth-Evans. The Monax with the grayish-blue edge pictured on the bottom of page 12 is called "Smoke" by collectors. Much of Monax American Sweetheart has a bluish cast to its edges, but to be "Smoke" it will always have a black trim at the edge. Notice the flat soup that I have never shown before. This time I have tried to show many color trimmed and decorated pieces of Monax (page 13) rather than the plainer Monax. You will find pieces trimmed in pink, green, yellow or black. I hope you enjoy the effort to show you these!

Blue American Sweetheart continues to attract more collectors than red. There are several reasons for this including the abundance of red found in comparison to blue that intrigues most avid collectors. Likewise, today, more people seem to prefer blue glass to red. Over the years that has remained true in all Depression glass patterns that include a blue color.

Note the red sherbet shown on the left in the bottom picture. This sherbet was made from the mould shape of American Sweetheart, but does not carry that design as we know it. As with the pink pitchers discussed on page 14, these are not considered to be American Sweetheart but are only **shaped** like American Sweetheart. You will also find 8" plates and 6" cereal bowls without the design in both red and blue. Not long ago, I saw a plain red console bowl in Columbus, Ohio. This bowl was water stained and too highly priced for a bowl with that kind of damage. Maybe there is also a blue one available without the design.

Real 22K gold is found as a trim on Monax. Gold was often used as a glass "trim" at the time. Unfortunately, there is no premium for the gold trim; in fact, many dealers have difficulty selling it because it is hard to find a full set with gold that is not worn. The gold, and only the gold, can be removed by using a pencil eraser on it or Ajax in a wet paste form. Don't try to use a scouring pad since you may damage the glass! I only point this out because badly worn gold trimmed items will not sell, but plain Monax will.

All the decorated Monax items pictured on the bottom of page 13 have a new home in California, but I felt you should see them one more time. The 8" Monax plate with the "Indian Park, Mohawk Trail" advertisement is the only one I have owned, but I have heard of other ads on these plates. So far, no collector has contacted me to tell me **what** other ads they have found, however. So, if you have any other advertising plates, let me know what they advertise.

| | Red | Blue | Cremax | Smoke & Other Trims |
|---|---|---|---|---|
| Bowl, 6" cereal | | | 8.00 | 35.00 |
| Bowl, 9" round berry | | | 30.00 | 120.00 |
| Bowl, 9½" soup | | | | 95.00 |
| Bowl, 18" console | 750.00 | 900.00 | | |
| Creamer, ftd. | 80.00 | 95.00 | | 75.00 |
| Cup | 65.00 | 95.00 | | 65.00 |
| Lamp shade | | | 425.00 | |
| Lamp (floor with brass base) | | | 650.00 | |
| Plate, 6" bread and butter | | | | 15.00 |
| Plate, 8" salad | 40.00 | 65.00 | | 25.00 |
| Plate, 9" luncheon | | | | 35.00 |
| Plate, 9¾" dinner | | | | 65.00 |
| Plate, 12" salver | 125.00 | 165.00 | | 85.00 |
| Plate, 15½" server | 225.00 | 300.00 | | |
| Platter, 13" oval | | | | 150.00 |
| Saucer | 18.00 | 22.50 | | 15.00 |
| Sherbet, 4¼" ftd. (design inside or outside) | | | | 65.00 |
| Sugar, open ftd. | 80.00 | 95.00 | | 75.00 |
| Tid-bit, 2 tier, 8" & 12" | 175.00 | 225.00 | | |
| Tid-bit, 3 tier, 8", 12" & 15½" | 500.00 | 600.00 | | |

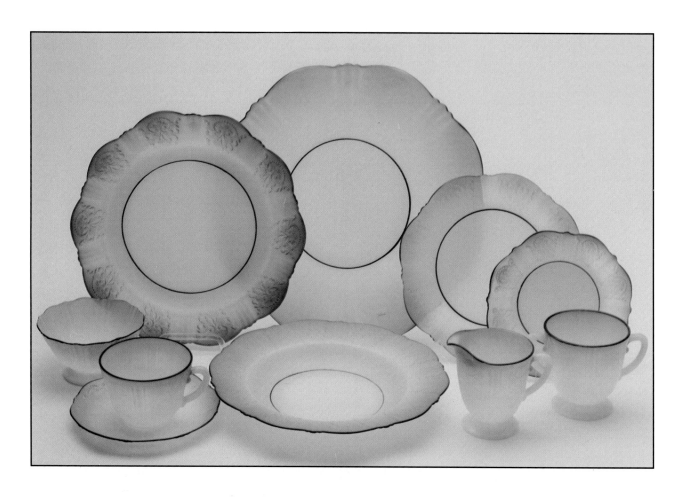

**Please refer to Foreword for pricing information**

# AMERICAN SWEETHEART (Cont.)

American Sweetheart continues to rise in price. Pink shakers and both flat and cream soup bowls have had major price adjustments. For the novice, a cream soup is two handled and was used for consomme or creamed soups. A pink cream soup can be seen in the center of the bottom picture. Neither soup was a part of basic sets. Today, that means that there are fewer of these to be found. At least there is no sugar lid in pink to find, so collectors of pink get off easier in that respect.

I sold a pair of shakers recently to a collector of Dogwood. Since no Dogwood shakers were made, he added an expensive touch to his Dogwood collection. However, shakers continue to be an albatross for most collectors of pink American Sweetheart.

One collector who bought a pair of pink shakers from Grannie Bear had only come to that show hoping to find those shakers. She bought them immediately. Not gone thirty minutes, another collector came back to get them and they were gone. She had waited to "decide" on the price. She couldn't believe she'd lost out on getting them. As she travelled the seventy-five miles back home, I bet she resolved to buy the next pair when she sees them!

Pink pitchers come in two sizes and tumblers in three. Many collectors settle for the water tumbler without adding juice and iced tea tumblers. The smaller pitcher, shown at the bottom of page 15, is not as plentiful as its larger counterpart; however, not all collectors try to find two pitchers. Please note that there are pitchers **shaped like** American Sweetheart that do not have the moulded design of American Sweetheart. You can see one of these on the right in the top photograph on page 15. It is **not** American Sweetheart (or even Dogwood which has to have the silk screened Dogwood design), but is the blank made by MacBeth-Evans to go with the plain, no design tumblers they made. The pattern has to be moulded into the pitcher for it to be American Sweetheart. I hope that solves some of the problems arising from these "no design" pitchers!

There are many reasons for price increases, such as availability, one of the major assets for this pattern. Beginning collectors see the numerous colors and learn that it has not been reproduced. Then, too, there has been an abundant supply of Monax (white color) in basic pieces such as cups, saucers, plates, sugar and creamers that can still be found at reasonable prices. Monax plates were widely distributed, and can be found in almost all parts of the country, making them an excellent starting point for new collectors. Additional rare Monax and pink pieces offer a challenge to collectors who have already bought all the basic pieces.

Be sure to notice the price increase in some of the harder to find Monax items. Most notable advances include sugar lids, cream soups, flat soups and shakers. The sugar lids have almost doubled in price in two years after staying nearly the same price for ten years. I only record what the prices are doing, but I wish I had a few lids stashed away.

Shakers have just begun to be scarce for the same reasons, but their price rise seems to be slower. I can remember the "early days" when $15.00 for a pair of **rare** Depression shakers seemed like a fortune! Of course, I was a Kentucky school teacher and that $15.00 was about 10% of a week's wages. Over $100.00 each, now, seems like a fair price for many hard to find shakers.

Complete sets of pink and Monax can still be accumulated with patience and money. Both colors have tid-bit sets consisting of two or three plates drilled with center holes and joined with a metal handle. The origin of many of these sets has been questioned over the years. Although a few of these may have been made at the factory, others were newly made by someone in the St. Louis area in the early 1970's. If you wish to buy a tid-bit, remember that it can be almost impossible to tell newly made from old. Because of this, I do not list a price for tid-bits unless they are made up of hard to find plate sizes. Most original tid-bits sell in the $50.00 range for two tiers and $75.00 for three.

There are two sizes of sherbets. Although the sherbet on the right in the top picture looks much larger than the one on the left, there is only ½" difference in diameter. The smaller, 3¾", is more difficult to find than the larger; but many collectors only buy one size, making prices closer than rarity indicates. Rarity does not always determine price. Demand does! If few collectors desire a rarely found item, then the price remains reasonable because no one is buying it!

| | Pink | Monax | | Pink | Monax |
|---|---|---|---|---|---|
| Bowl, 3¾" flat berry | 35.00 | | Plate, 15½" server | | 195.00 |
| Bowl, 4½" cream soup | 70.00 | 97.50 | Platter, 13" oval | 45.00 | 60.00 |
| Bowl, 6" cereal | 14.00 | 12.00 | Pitcher, 7½", 60 oz. | 595.00 | |
| Bowl, 9" round berry | 37.50 | 55.00 | Pitcher, 8", 80 oz. | 495.00 | |
| Bowl, 9½" flat soup | 55.00 | 67.50 | Salt and pepper, ftd. | 395.00 | 300.00 |
| Bowl, 11" oval vegetable | 55.00 | 70.00 | Saucer | 4.00 | 3.00 |
| Bowl, 18" console | | 365.00 | Sherbet, 3¾" ftd. | 18.00 | |
| Creamer, ftd. | 12.00 | 10.00 | Sherbet, 4¼" ftd. | | |
| Cup | 15.00 | 10.00 | (design inside or outside) | 15.00 | 17.00 |
| Lamp shade | | 430.00 | Sherbet in metal holder | | |
| Plate, 6" or 6½" bread & butter | 5.00 | 4.00 | (crystal only) | 3.50 | |
| Plate, 8" salad | 10.00 | 8.00 | * Sugar, open, ftd. | 11.00 | 8.00 |
| Plate, 9" luncheon | | 10.00 | Sugar lid | | 290.00 |
| Plate, 9¾" dinner | 35.00 | 20.00 | Tid-bit, 2 tier, 8" & 12" | 55.00 | 55.00 |
| Plate, 10¼" dinner | | 20.00 | Tid-bit, 3 tier, 8", 12" & 15½" | | 225.00 |
| Plate, 11" chop plate | | 15.00 | Tumbler, 3½", 5 oz. | 70.00 | |
| Plate, 12" salver | 18.00 | 15.00 | Tumbler, 4¼", 9 oz. | 65.00 | |
| | | | Tumbler, 4¾", 10 oz. | 90.00 | |

*Two style knobs.

# AUNT POLLY U.S. GLASS COMPANY, Late 1920's

Colors: Blue, green and iridescent.

Aunt Polly's collectability continues to be affected by its lack of cups or saucers. Prices would ascend if any were ever found. That lack of cup and saucers causes the same concerns for other U. S. Glass patterns such as Strawberry, Cherryberry and Swirl.

It has now been fifteen years since I discovered that U. S. Glass was the manufacturer of Aunt Polly and her sister patterns mentioned above. In all that time, not one additional piece has been discovered. That doesn't count the two-handled, open candy, in front of the sugar and tumbler in the top photograph that was inadvertently left out of my listing. The covered candy is shown in green on the bottom right. This candy lid is interchangeable with the sugar lid making this an expensive candy dish since perfect lids are so difficult to find today. These candy dishes have only been found in green and iridescent colors.

There is an Aunt Polly "look-alike" shown in both pictures. At least they are assumed to be "look-alikes," but they may be variations of the tumbler mould. The blue tumbler on the outside left and the vaseline colored tumbler in the bottom photo are slightly different from the normally found tumblers. The panelled lines are wider and there is no design in the bottom. The ground bottoms on these items may indicate early prototypes that were reworked, because the vaseline colored tumbler is a typical U. S. Glass color of the late 1920's. In any case, they make interesting additions to any collection! There has been no additional information found on these tumblers since I included them in my last book.

Similarly, there are two variations of the creamer shown. One has a more pronounced lip than the other. Originally these lips were formed by hand using a wooden tool; so that probably accounts for these irregularities.

Aunt Polly collectors are still finding several pieces extremely difficult to obtain. The oval vegetable, sugar lid, shakers and butter dish have always been a problem. The blue butter top or bottom creates a headache; on the other hand, the bottoms in green or iridescent are plentiful. This occurs because all the U.S. Glass butter bottoms are interchangeable. The bottom has a starred design and fits Cherryberry, Strawberry and U. S. Swirl as well as Aunt Polly tops. That is the reason that the butter top prices are so much more than the bottoms in the green and iridescent. There is no blue color in other U.S. Glass patterns, however; so there always were fewer butter bottoms to be obtained in blue.

Many collectors are having trouble finding **mint** condition sherbet plates. This pattern is very inclined to mould imperfections such as irregular finished seams on almost all pieces. If you are adamant about mint condition, I advise you to look for some other pattern.

Blue is still **the** color most collected, but a few collectors of the iridized and green sets remain. The primary difficulty in collecting green is the diversity of shades. Green is found from almost yellow in appearance to a vivid green as you can see in the photograph on the next page. If color variations bother you, then green Aunt Polly is not for you.

| | Green, Iridescent | Blue | | Green, Iridescent | Blue |
|---|---|---|---|---|---|
| Bowl, 4¾" berry | 8.00 | 17.50 | Creamer | 26.00 | 42.00 |
| Bowl, 4¾", 2" high | 10.00 | 19.00 | Pitcher, 8" 48 oz. | | 160.00 |
| Bowl, 5½" one handle | 14.00 | 20.00 | Plate, 6" sherbet | 6.00 | 12.00 |
| Bowl, 7¼" oval, handled pickle | 11.00 | 37.50 | Plate, 8" luncheon | | 18.00 |
| Bowl, 7⅞" large berry | 17.00 | 40.00 | Salt and pepper | | 195.00 |
| Bowl, 8⅜" oval | 36.00 | 85.00 | Sherbet | 9.00 | 12.00 |
| Butter dish and cover | 210.00 | 185.00 | Sugar | 23.00 | 30.00 |
| Butter dish bottom | 75.00 | 80.00 | Sugar cover | 45.00 | 130.00 |
| Butter dish top | 135.00 | 105.00 | Tumbler, 3⅝", 8 oz. | | 26.00 |
| Candy, cover, 2-handled | 60.00 | | Vase, 6½" ftd. | 27.50 | 38.00 |

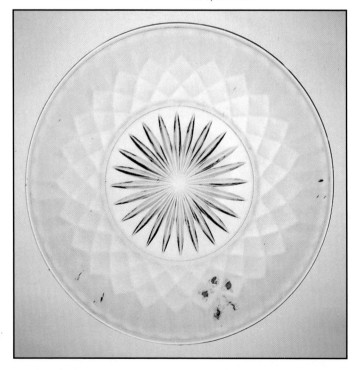

**Please refer to Foreword for pricing information**

# "AURORA" HAZEL ATLAS GLASS COMPANY, Late 1930's

Colors: Cobalt blue, pink, green and crystal.

As soon as I wrote that "Aurora was a delightful addition to any collection that will not completely drain your budget," the little 4½" deep bowl went soaring in price! Regardless of how many of these little bowls I have found, not one has lasted in Grannie Bear's booth beyond the first day of a show! Usually, it is some dealer who buys it before the doors even open to the public. Cobalt blue attracts collectors in ways that no other color seems to do. Even with the price of the little bowl now being $35.00, an eight place setting would not involve borrowing against the house as some other cobalt blue sets will; so, if you like cobalt blue, here is a smaller pattern to check out!

Several readers have suggested that patterns that have only a tall creamer and no sugar should have the creamer listed as a milk pitcher. If you prefer calling it that, do so.

Most pieces have been found in pink, but these command as high a price as the blue due to scarcity of the pink. You will not be able to put a complete set together in pink since the small bowl, creamer and tumbler have so far never been seen in that color. Recently, a Canadian reader wrote to tell me of finding green Aurora cereal bowls.

Both green and crystal cereal bowls, cups and saucers have been found; but, so far, only collectors of cup and saucers have been very excited over them. Only time will tell; if you find any other Aurora pieces in these (or other) colors, please let me know.

|  | Cobalt, Pink |  | Cobalt, Pink |
|---|---|---|---|
| Bowl, 4½" deep | 35.00 | Plate, 6½" | 11.00 |
| * Bowl, 5⅜" cereal | 15.00 | *** Saucer | 6.00 |
| Creamer, 4½" | 20.00 | Tumbler, 4¾", 10 oz. | 19.00 |
| ** Cup | 15.00 | | |

*Green $7.00 or crystal $5.00          **Green $7.50          ***Green $2.50

---

# "AVOCADO," NO. 601 INDIANA GLASS COMPANY, 1923-1933

Colors: Pink, green, crystal and white. *(See Reproduction Section)*

As previously shown, all sixteen pieces made in Avocado are illustrated this time. Avocado is expensive, and in my experience, usually sells in large lots rather than a piece here and there. Prices for pitcher and tumblers in green have escalated even more. A crystal pitcher was recently found and three different white sets have surfaced in the last two years. These white items were a part of Indiana's experimenting with that color in the mid-1950's. You will also find Pyramid and Sandwich pieces in white.

I have included prices on the crystal since several readers were kind enough to send me listings of what they had paid for their collections.

Unless someone breaks up a collection, finding Avocado is a problem. For some reason this pattern has tended to stay in group settings more than any other pattern has. Rarely do you see a single piece.

Green is still the predominant color collected. Green tumblers have jumped over the $200.00 mark with hardly a stumble. Reproduced green items are much darker than the original green shown here. I have preached since 1974 about the reproductions and how to tell the differences so that you will not be taken in by a fake. (On the positive side are reports that that particular glass selling scheme is collapsing.)

Pink reproduced items have an orange cast to the color, but this does vary. Buyer beware! Know your dealer and his reputation for integrity. Pink prices have finally recovered from those reproduced pitchers and tumblers that were introduced in 1974.

If you spot any pieces in yellow, they are of **recent** vintage!

|  | Crystal | Pink | Green |  | Crystal | Pink | Green |
|---|---|---|---|---|---|---|---|
| Bowl, 5¼" 2-handled | 10.00 | 25.00 | 30.00 | *Pitcher, 64 oz. | 3.50 | 700.00 | 900.00 |
| Bowl, 6" ftd. relish | 9.00 | 23.00 | 25.00 | ***Plate, 6⅜" sherbet | 5.00 | 13.50 | 16.00 |
| Bowl, 7" 1 handle preserve | 8.00 | 18.00 | 25.00 | **Plate, 8¼" luncheon | 7.00 | 17.00 | 19.00 |
| Bowl, 7½" salad | 12.00 | 32.00 | 50.00 | Plate, 10¼" 2-handled cake | 14.00 | 35.00 | 50.00 |
| Bowl, 8" 2-handled oval | 9.00 | 19.00 | 26.00 | Saucer, 6⅜" | | 25.00 | 28.00 |
| Bowl, 9½", 3¼" deep | 22.00 | 90.00 | 125.00 | ***Sherbet | | 50.00 | 55.00 |
| ***Creamer, ftd. | 12.00 | 30.00 | 35.00 | ***Sugar, ftd. | 12.00 | 32.00 | 34.00 |
| Cup, ftd., 2 styles | | 29.00 | 32.00 | *Tumbler | 25.00 | 150.00 | 250.00 |

*Caution on pink. The orange-pink is new!
*White: Pitcher $400.00; Tumbler $30.00.
**Apple design $10.00. Amber has been newly made.
***Remade in dark shade of green.

# BEADED BLOCK IMPERIAL GLASS COMPANY, 1927-1930's

Colors: Pink, green, crystal, ice blue, vaseline, iridescent, amber, red, opalescent and milk white.

Beaded Block is one of those patterns that collectors of other patterns buy to add an additional serving or display piece of Depression glass. The multitude of colors of Beaded Block is matched by few other patterns in this book. It is the one Depression pattern that gets priced by unknowledgeable antique dealers as "Carnival," "Vaseline" or "Pattern" glass. It was originally made in the late 1920's and early 1930's. I say "originally" because Imperial had a reissue of the pink and iridized pink in the late 1970's and early 1980's. Pieces are easily spotted since they are marked IG in the bottom. Only a few other marked pieces are found but they include the white lily bowl shown in the bottom photograph. When I visited the factory in 1981, I was told that the white was made in the early 1950's and the IG mark (for Imperial Glass) was first used about that time.

An interesting piece of Beaded Block is appearing occasionally. It is a two-part candy in the shape of a large pear. I was told by a collector that it was an apple but it looks like a pear to me. These have been found in yellow and green. Lately one of these sold for $150.00 and another for $350.00. The last one I saw priced was $650.00. It didn't sell at that show! Prices are obviously unstable at the moment, and it will take time to establish a general market for this item.

There remains an abundance of square plates, but most of the round plates must have been turned into bowls, which was how bowls were made in Beaded Block. The edges of plates were turned up to make a bowl. That makes the size variances in this pattern a major headache for collectors. Sizes listed in the Imperial catalogues vary greatly as to actual sizes found today. **The sizes listed here were all obtained from actual measurements and not from the catalogue.** You may find some differences in your measurements, so don't get too alarmed. The 2-handled jelly which most companies called a cream soup measures from 4¾" to 5". Be sure to read the section on measurements at the bottom of page 4!

A few pink Beaded Block pitchers have finally been found! Like the white pitcher, pink ones are surfacing after I mentioned they were rare in the last book. I have had reports of seven white pitchers now, but only four pink ones!

Red lily bowls are still being found in the central Ohio area and that seems to be the only place they were distributed. In fact, no other red Beaded Block pieces have appeared except that 4½" lily bowl.

The 6" vases shown in cobalt and pink are not Beaded Block, but are often sold as such. They have no beading and no scalloped edge as do all the other pieces except the white lily bowl previously discussed. Imperial called these tall pieces "footed jellies." These were attained at groceries with a product inside. One found with the original label still attached reads "Good Taste Mustard Seed, 3½ oz., Frank Tea & Spice Co., Cin., O." I imagine the edge had to be smooth to take a lid, but why change the sides to a "zipper-like" design? Remember, these are a "go-with" piece and not truly Beaded Block.

Collecting a set of Beaded Block in one color is a challenge. Maybe that is why most collectors buy all colors instead of only one. I rarely attend a show with glass that I am not asked if I have any pieces of Beaded Block.

| | *Crystal, Pink, Green, Amber | Other Colors |
|---|---|---|
| Bowl, 4⅞"-5" 2-handled jelly | 7.50 | 16.00 |
| **Bowl, 4½" round lily | 9.50 | 19.00 |
| Bowl, 5½" square | 7.50 | 11.00 |
| Bowl, 5½" 1 handle | 7.50 | 12.00 |
| Bowl, 6" deep round | 11.00 | 19.00 |
| Bowl, 6¼" round | 8.00 | 16.50 |
| Bowl, 6½" round | 8.00 | 16.50 |
| Bowl, 6½" 2-handled pickle | 13.00 | 19.00 |
| Bowl, 6¾" round, unflared | 11.50 | 17.00 |
| Bowl, 7¼" round, flared | 11.50 | 18.00 |
| Bowl, 7½" round, fluted edges | 21.00 | 25.00 |
| Bowl, 7½" round, plain edge | 18.50 | 23.00 |
| Bowl, 8¼" celery | 13.00 | 18.50 |
| Creamer | 16.00 | 27.50 |
| ***Pitcher, 5¼", pint jug | 95.00 | |
| Plate, 7¾" square | 7.00 | 10.00 |
| Plate, 8¾" round | 15.50 | 19.00 |
| Stemmed jelly, 4½" | 9.50 | 18.00 |
| Stemmed jelly, 4½", flared top | 11.00 | 19.00 |
| Sugar | 14.50 | 25.00 |
| Vase, 6" bouquet | 12.00 | 24.00 |

\* All pieces 25% to 40% lower.
\*\* Red $100.00
\*\*\* White $160.00, pink $150.00

**Please refer to Foreword for pricing information**

# BLOCK OPTIC, "BLOCK" HOCKING GLASS COMPANY, 1929-1933

Colors: Green, pink, yellow, crystal and some amber and blue.

For several years new collectors have asked about the 5¾" blown vase that has not been pictured since an early book. It took years to round up one to show again, but you can see it at the bottom of page 24. This vase is shaped just like the Cameo one, as I have written before; but you can now see it again.

A new discovery is the 2" tall, 11¾" diameter, rolled edge console bowl in amber. This was found with the amber candlesticks; so perhaps one will show up in pink or green someday.

The 4¼" diameter bowl with a height of 1½" is the one shown in the middle of the top photograph on page 23. This bowl is difficult to find and appears to be made thicker than most Block Optic.

Many new collectors have started collecting Depression glass with Block Optic pattern since it was widely distributed and a piece or two seems to have remained in everyone's family. I used to recommend Block Optic to new collectors because it was economically priced and a beginner could afford to start with it. Today, the price is no longer as economical as it once was! Of course, nothing else is either! As far as collectability goes, Block remains high on the list of collector demand. There is yet an abundant supply of almost all basic pieces, and infrequently found items are not completely "out of sight" as is the case in many other green Depression patterns.

Add to the five styles of cups shown that there are **four different shapes of creamer and sugars**. While looking at the bottom of page 23 mentally number the cup and saucers from one to five starting on the left. Number 1 and 3 are the rounded cups that come with plain or fancy handles as do the cups in Cameo. Number 1, which has the fancy handle, fits the 6⅛" saucer with cup ring. Number 2 is the only cup that will fit the 5¾" saucer with cup ring. Number 4 is a flat bottomed cup that fits on a combination saucer/sherbet plate. Number 5 has a pointed handle. I will not make price distinctions now; but pricing patterns are beginning to emerge on the different styles of cups! (Several rabid collectors state that there are even more varieties than these, but this will be enough to make you stagger now.)

There are variations in handles and slight differences in style to make **a total of five different styles of creamers and sugars** that can be collected in Block Optic.(There are four shapes but five styles.) In yellow, only the fancy handled, rounded type shown on page 25 has been found. There are three styles of pink creamer/sugar sets, flat bottomed and two styles of cone shaped pairs. One of the cone shaped styles has a base that is plain whereas the other type has a rayed base. (This is true of many of Hocking's patterns. Some tumblers or stems also show variations of plain and ribbed bases.) In green creamers/sugars, there are the two cone shaped styles with one of these having pointed handles, the flat bottomed variety, and the rounded with plain handles evidenced by the frosted pair in the top photo. I have never seen a green Block Optic fancy handled set. Let me know if you have such a pair!

Regarding the frosted green creamer and sugar shown in the top picture, Hocking, as well as other companies, satinized (frosted by using camphoric acid) many of their dinnerware lines. Evidently, these were special orders or special promotions since many were hand decorated with flowers or fruit. Today, many collectors shy away from these pieces for some reason. Frosted items only bring a fraction of the price of their unfrosted counterparts. Even though these pieces are more scarce, there is so little demand that the price is lessened. That is one of the lessons beginners need to learn as soon as possible about collectibles. Rarity does not always determine price! Demand is the major determining factor of price!

Note the Deco decorated pink candy on the bottom of page 25. I have seen more than one of these in my travels; thus these candies may have been a special order or promotional item at one time. Speaking of pink, no more of the 3½" short wines have surfaced and many of the stems in this pattern have had large price increases in the last few years. New collectors and the scarcity of these items have both contributed to this. Not only are stems scarce, but when have you seen any serving pieces in pink?

A tumble-up set has been found that explains how they were sold. A stopper in a bottle was marked "Baree' Fragrant Bath Salts Paris, New York." That is how the decanter in Mayfair was also sold years ago. It, too, contained bath salts and the stopper was used as a measuring device!

Some green Block is found with a black foot or stem. Collecting a set of this would be nigh impossible unless you find it all at one time. As far as I can determine, that black is fired-on and can not be removed! Few pieces of crystal Block can be found. Only the butter dish has a premium value. Other crystal pieces sell for half the prices of green **if** a buyer can be found.

A reader in California sent some interesting information about the green butter dish top. In the twenty years I have been buying Depression glass, I have seen 15 to 20 green Block butter tops for every bottom. I had assumed that the heavy top had destroyed many of the bottoms over the years since it is difficult to grasp when trying to pick it up. It seems that the tops were also sold as a butter holder for ice boxes. This top slid into a metal holder eliminating the need for a glass bottom! It is amazing the ideas that glass companies had to market their glass.

# BLOCK OPTIC, "BLOCK" (Cont.)

| | Green | Yellow | Pink |
|---|---|---|---|
| Bowl, 4¼" diam., 1⅜" tall | 7.50 | | 7.00 |
| Bowl, 4½" diam., 1½" tall | 26.00 | | |
| Bowl, 5¼" cereal | 12.00 | | 22.50 |
| Bowl, 7" salad | 22.50 | | |
| Bowl, 8½" large berry | 24.00 | | 22.00 |
| *Butter dish and cover, 3" x 5" | 45.00 | | |
| Butter dish bottom | 26.50 | | |
| Butter dish top | 18.50 | | |
| **Candlesticks, 1¾" pr. | 97.50 | | 70.00 |
| Candy jar & cover, 2¼" tall | 50.00 | 55.00 | 45.00 |
| Candy jar & cover, 6¼" tall | 47.50 | | 110.00 |
| Comport, 4" wide mayonnaise | 28.00 | | 60.00 |
| Creamer, 3 styles: cone shaped, round, rayed-foot & flat (5 kinds) | 13.00 | 13.00 | 12.00 |
| Cup, four styles | 7.00 | 8.00 | 7.00 |
| Goblet, 3½" short wine | | | 350.00 |
| Goblet, 4" cocktail | 32.00 | | 30.00 |
| Goblet, 4½" wine | 32.00 | | 30.00 |
| Goblet, 5¾", 9 oz. | 20.00 | | 26.00 |
| Goblet, 7¼", 9 oz. thin | | 32.00 | |
| Ice bucket | 35.00 | | 40.00 |
| Ice tub or butter tub, open | 40.00 | | 85.00 |
| Mug | 32.00 | | |
| Pitcher, 7⅝", 54 oz., bulbous | 70.00 | | 65.00 |
| Pitcher, 8½", 54 oz. | 38.00 | | 38.00 |
| Pitcher, 8", 80 oz. | 70.00 | | 75.00 |
| Plate, 6" sherbet | 3.00 | 3.00 | 3.00 |
| Plate, 8" luncheon | 5.00 | 5.00 | 5.00 |
| Plate, 9" dinner | 20.00 | 38.00 | 30.00 |
| Plate, 9" grill | 12.00 | 38.00 | 17.00 |
| Plate, 10¼" sandwich | 23.00 | | 21.00 |
| Salt and pepper, ftd. | 35.00 | 70.00 | 70.00 |
| Salt and pepper, squatty | 80.00 | | |
| Sandwich server, center handle | 60.00 | | 45.00 |
| Saucer, 5¾", with cup ring | 10.00 | | 7.50 |
| Saucer, 6⅛", with cup ring | 9.50 | | 6.00 |
| Sherbet, non-stemmed (cone) | 4.00 | | |
| Sherbet, 3¼", 5½ oz. | 6.00 | 9.00 | 7.50 |
| Sherbet, 4¾", 6 oz. | 14.00 | 15.00 | 14.00 |
| Sugar, 3 styles: as creamer | 12.50 | 11.00 | 11.00 |
| Tumbler, 2⅝", 3 oz. | 19.00 | | 21.00 |
| Tumbler, 3½", 5 oz. flat | 19.00 | | 21.00 |

| | Green | Yellow | Pink |
|---|---|---|---|
| Tumbler, 9½ oz. flat, 3¹³⁄₁₆" flat | 14.00 | | 14.00 |
| Tumbler, 10 or 11 oz., 5" flat | 17.00 | | 14.00 |
| Tumbler, 12 oz., 4⅞" flat | 24.00 | | 22.00 |
| Tumbler, 15 oz., flat, 5¼", | 34.00 | | 30.00 |
| Tumbler, 3¼", 3 oz. ftd. | 22.00 | | 19.00 |
| Tumbler, 9 oz. ftd. | 16.00 | 20.00 | 13.00 |
| Tumbler, 6", 10 oz. ftd. | 24.00 | | 24.00 |
| Tumble-up night set | 60.00 | | |
| Tumbler, 3" only | 45.00 | | |
| Bottle only | 16.00 | | |
| Vase, 5¾" blown | 265.00 | | |
| Whiskey, 1⅝", 1 oz. | | | 37.50 |
| Whiskey, 2¼", 2 oz. | 25.00 | | 25.00 |

*Green clambroth $195.00 - blue $400.00
   crystal $100.00

**Amber $100.00

# "BOWKNOT" MANUFACTURER UNKNOWN, Probably late 1920's

Color: Green.

Bowknot has piqued the interest of some new collectors and this has caused some price jumps in a few items already in short supply. One of the things to watch out for is inner rim roughness on bowls and sherbets. Bowknot remains a mystery pattern as to its manufacturer and the exact dates it was made. Add to that a cup with no saucer and two different style tumblers with no pitcher and you have a real Columbo type "knot."

You can see the cereal bowl, which I had a devil of a time finding! After mentioning that last time, the price has vaulted. Many dealers do not carry some of the smaller patterns such as Bowknot to shows. To me that seems to be a mistake; whenever I take Bowknot to shows, it is among the first pieces to leave my booth. Cathy thinks this is a neat pattern. Evidently, she is not the only one as evidenced from the reactions of collectors spotting a piece or two in our show display.

I still get letters from novice collectors who feel that they have found the first creamer and sugar. The Fostoria patterns "June" and "Romance" have a bow also but neither of these patterns were made in green. If you find a green Bowknot creamer or sugar, run, don't walk, to the nearest phone and give me a call.

| | Green | | Green |
|---|---|---|---|
| Bowl, 4½" berry | 14.00 | Sherbet, low ftd. | 14.00 |
| Bowl, 5½" cereal | 18.00 | Tumbler, 5", 10 oz. | 16.00 |
| Cup | 7.50 | Tumbler, 5", 10 oz. ftd. | 16.00 |
| Plate, 7" salad | 11.00 | | |

**Please refer to Foreword for pricing information**

# CAMEO, "BALLERINA" or "DANCING GIRL" HOCKING GLASS COMPANY, 1930-1934

Colors: Green, yellow, pink and crystal w/platinum rim. (*See Reproduction Section*)

Cameo pattern as we know it was made by the Hocking Glass Company in the early 1930's, but evidently the pattern evolved from a design called "Springtime" made by Monongah Glass Company. This company was taken over by Hocking and many of their patterns were continued by Hocking. To see the Springtime pattern as it existed before being machine-made, I have shown a crystal cocktail on the bottom of this page beside the rarely seen sandwich server. Monongah's glass was plate etched and is of exceptional quality when compared to our Cameo. Thankfully, the little dancing girl was continued in another form and that has made many of today's collectors very happy.

Yellow Cameo is shown at the top of page 29. Many yellow items are quite difficult to obtain including the butter dish. However, yellow Cameo cups, saucer/sherbet plates, footed tumblers, grill and dinner plates were heavily promoted by Hocking. These five yellow pieces are still plentiful today. In fact, until the last few years, they were difficult to sell. Prices on commonly found yellow pieces have begun to rise. It's really an attractive yellow pattern; so if you like it, now may be the time to get your basic set!

I receive numerous letters and calls about Cameo saucers each year. The real Cameo saucer has an indented cup ring, but it has only been found in green. Hocking made very few of these indented saucers. They usually made a dual purpose saucer/sherbet plate for their patterns. If you will look on the bottom of page 31, the difference can be seen in green. The saucer on the right has a **distinct** indented ring (1¾" center) while the saucer/sherbet plate (2¾" center) on the left does not (although the cup may hide that fact).

I should also point out the color variations in the cups as well as the handle styles in that picture. The cups on the left have plain handles (abbreviated "ph" in ads) and the cup on the right has a fancy handle (abbreviated "fh" in ads).

Green Cameo remains one of the most desirable Depression Glass patterns. There are enough easily found pieces to obtain a set without having all the rare accessory items. Many collectors can not afford everything. They do not try to find every stem and every tumbler; instead they purchase only one or two different sizes of tumblers or stems.

Enjoy the photograph of pink Cameo on page 30. Pink is rarely seen. It is also expensive as you can tell by looking at the prices. New collectors be forewarned of the price and the difficulty in obtaining it. That footed oil lamp base with a threaded top (below the pink photograph) is the only that has ever surfaced.

Cameo has two styles of grill plates. (A grill plate is a sectioned or divided plate that keeps the food separated. They were used mostly in restaurants and "grills" of that day.) Both styles are shown on the bottom of page 30. One has tab handles and one does not. Both are common in yellow. In green, however, the grill with the tab or closed handles is harder to find. The 10½" rare, rimmed dinner or flat cake plate is just like the heavy edged grill plate only without the dividers! The regular dinner plate is shown in the center back top photo on page 31. Notice this plate has a large center as opposed to the small centered sandwich plate on the left back of the bottom photograph.

The darker green bottle on the top right of page 31 is marked underneath "Whitehouse Vinegar." These originally came from the grocery with vinegar — and a cork. Glass stoppers are found atop water bottles. These do not have a Cameo pattern on them, but are plain paneled.

All the miniature pieces in Cameo are new! No smaller Cameo was ever made during the Depression era. See the Reproduction Section in the back of the book for information on this and the reproduced Cameo shakers. A new importer is making a sometimes weakly patterned shaker in pink, cobalt blue and a darker shade of green than the original color. If new tops are the first thing you notice — beware!

# CAMEO, "BALLERINA" or "DANCING GIRL" (Cont.)

| | Green | Yellow | Pink | Crystal, Plat |
|---|---|---|---|---|
| Bowl, 4¼" sauce | | | | 5.50 |
| Bowl, 4¾" cream soup | 105.00 | | | |
| Bowl, 5½" cereal | 29.00 | 27.00 | 150.00 | 6.50 |
| Bowl, 7¼" salad | 50.00 | | | |
| Bowl, 8¼" large berry | 32.00 | | 130.00 | |
| Bowl, 9" rimmed soup | 45.00 | | 90.00 | |
| Bowl, 10" oval vegetable | 22.00 | 38.00 | | |
| Bowl, 11", 3-legged console | 65.00 | 80.00 | 40.00 | |
| Butter dish and cover | 180.00 | 1,500.00 | | |
| Butter dish bottom | 110.00 | 500.00 | | |
| Butter dish top | 70.00 | 1,000.00 | | |
| Cake plate, 10", 3 legs | 19.00 | | | |
| Cake plate, 10½" flat | 90.00 | | 130.00 | |
| Candlesticks, 4" pr. | 93.00 | | | |
| Candy jar, 4" low and cover | 65.00 | 70.00 | 450.00 | |
| Candy jar, 6½" tall and cover | 145.00 | | | |
| Cocktail shaker (metal lid) appears in crystal only | | | | 475.00 |
| Comport, 5" wide mayonnaise | 27.00 | | 175.00 | |
| Cookie jar and cover | 47.50 | | | |
| Creamer, 3¼" | 20.00 | 17.00 | | |
| Creamer, 4¼" | 25.00 | | 97.50 | |
| Cup, 2 styles | 13.50 | 7.50 | 70.00 | 5.50 |
| Decanter, 10" with stopper | 135.00 | | | 175.00 |
| Decanter, 10" with stopper, frosted (stopper represents ⅓ value of decanter) | 30.00 | | | |
| Domino tray, 7" with 3" indentation | 120.00 | | | |
| Domino tray, 7" with no indentation | | | 225.00 | 110.00 |
| Goblet, 3½" wine | 675.00 | | 750.00 | |
| Goblet, 4" wine | 60.00 | | 198.00 | |
| Goblet, 6" water | 47.00 | | 160.00 | |
| Ice bowl or open butter, 3" tall x 5½" wide | 145.00 | | 600.00 | 230.00 |

| | Green | Yellow | Pink | Crystal, Plat |
|---|---|---|---|---|
| Jam jar, 2" and cover | 150.00 | | | 155.00 |
| Pitcher, 5¾", 20 oz. syrup or milk | 195.00 | 1,750.00 | | |
| Pitcher, 6", 36 oz. juice | 55.00 | | | |
| Pitcher, 8½", 56 oz. water | 47.50 | | 1,300.00 | 455.00 |
| Plate, 6" sherbet | 4.00 | 4.00 | 85.00 | 2.0 |
| Plate, 7" salad | | | | 3.50 |
| Plate, 8" luncheon | 10.00 | 11.00 | 30.00 | 4.00 |
| Plate, 8½" square | 37.50 | 200.00 | | |
| Plate, 9½" dinner | 16.00 | 9.00 | 65.00 | |
| Plate, 10" sandwich | 13.00 | | 40.00 | |
| Plate, 10½" rimmed dinner | 90.00 | | 130.00 | |
| Plate, 10½" grill | 8.00 | 6.00 | 45.00 | |
| Plate, 10½" grill with closed handles | 62.50 | 6.00 | | |
| Plate, 10½" with closed handles | 11.00 | 11.00 | | |
| Platter, 12", closed handles | 18.00 | 38.00 | | |
| Relish, 7½" ftd., 3 part | 26.00 | | | 130.00 |
| *Salt and pepper, ftd. pr. | 65.00 | | 750.00 | |
| Sandwich server, center handle | 4,500.00 | | | |
| Saucer with cup ring | 165.00 | | | |
| Saucer, 6" (sherbet plate) | 4.00 | 3.50 | 78.00 | |
| Sherbet, 3⅛" molded | 12.50 | 37.50 | 65.00 | |
| Sherbet, 3⅛" blown | 14.00 | | 65.00 | |
| Sherbet, 4⅞" | 32.00 | 40.00 | 90.00 | |
| Sugar, 3¼" | 17.00 | 13.00 | | |
| Sugar, 4¼" | 21.00 | | 98.00 | |
| Tumbler, 3¾", 5 oz. juice | 26.00 | | 80.00 | |
| Tumbler, 4", 9 oz. water | 24.00 | | 75.00 | 9.00 |
| Tumbler, 4¾", 10 oz. flat | 25.00 | | 90.00 | |
| Tumbler, 5", 11 oz. flat | 26.00 | 45.00 | 85.00 | |
| Tumbler, 5¼", 15 oz. | 60.00 | | 120.00 | |
| Tumbler, 3 oz. ftd. juice | 55.00 | | 120.00 | |
| Tumbler, 5", 9 oz. ftd. | 24.00 | 14.00 | 98.00 | |
| Tumbler, 5¾", 11 oz. ftd. | 55.00 | | 115.00 | |
| Tumbler, 6⅜", 15 oz. ftd. | 425.00 | | | |
| Vase, 5¾" | 165.00 | | | |
| Vase, 8" | 32.50 | | | |
| Water bottle (dark green) Whitehouse vinegar | 16.00 | | | |

* Beware Reproductions

**Please refer to Foreword for pricing information**

# CHERRYBERRY U.S. GLASS COMPANY, Early 1930's

Colors: Pink, green, crystal; some iridized.

Collecting sets of Cherryberry began to develop from collectors searching for Strawberry. Very few collectors took notice of this pattern for years, except those who were buying Strawberry and were continually running into cherries instead of strawberries. Now, Cherryberry has become a valuable Depression glass pattern with a few "Carnival" glass collectors raiding our ranks to grab the iridescent pitchers, tumblers and butter dishes, the most desirable iridized pieces. Not only do collectors of Cherryberry and Carnival Glass explore for these, but collectors of butters and pitchers hunt them, also.

Crystal is much rarer than pink or green; as yet, there are fewer collectors looking for it.

Note the color variances in the green in the photograph. This is the other problem beside finding it. The green can be found from a very yellowish shade to a bluish one. It will drive you out on a limb of that Cherry tree if you search for perfectly matched shades of green.

This is another of the U.S. Glass patterns that has no cup or saucer and has a plain butter base. If all these U.S. Glass patterns are "sister" patterns, then Strawberry and Cherryberry are twins. You can only tell them apart by the fruit.

| | Crystal, Iridescent | Pink, Green | | Crystal, Iridescent | Pink, Green |
|---|---|---|---|---|---|
| Bowl, 4" berry | 6.50 | 8.50 | Olive dish, 5" one-handled | 9.00 | 15.00 |
| Bowl, 6¼", 2" deep | 37.50 | 50.00 | Pickle dish, 8¼" oval | 9.00 | 15.00 |
| Bowl, 6½" deep salad | 16.00 | 20.00 | Pitcher, 7¾" | 155.00 | 150.00 |
| Bowl, 7½" deep berry | 17.00 | 20.00 | Plate, 6" sherbet | 6.00 | 9.00 |
| Butter dish and cover | 145.00 | 155.00 | Plate, 7½" salad | 8.00 | 14.00 |
| Butter dish bottom | 77.50 | 87.50 | Sherbet | 6.50 | 9.00 |
| Butter dish top | 67.50 | 67.50 | Sugar, small open | 12.00 | 17.00 |
| Comport, 5¾" | 16.00 | 24.00 | Sugar, large | 15.00 | 24.00 |
| Creamer, small | 12.00 | 17.00 | Sugar cover | 28.00 | 50.00 |
| Creamer, 4⅝" large | 15.00 | 35.00 | Tumbler, 3⅝", 9 oz. | 17.50 | 32.00 |

# CHERRY BLOSSOM JEANNETTE GLASS COMPANY, 1930-1939

Colors: Pink, green, Delphite (opaque blue), crystal, Jadite (opaque green) and red. *(See Reproduction Section)*

A few years ago reproductions had dealers refusing to handle Cherry Blossom since you couldn't give it away. What a difference time and education about the differences in old and new has made for collecting Cherry Blossom! All pieces in all colors have increased in price since the last book! Even the Delphite color, an opaque light blue has seen some escalation.

Prices have increased to ante-repro days except for the shakers which still have a long way to go. The problem with shakers is not only the large number of reproductions made, but that many collectors are willing to purchase these fakes to have a pair of shakers for their set so as to not have to pay the high price of the rarely found older ones. I still get many calls and letters on the pink shakers. Only two pairs of original pink shakers were ever found; so the likelihood of your finding another old pair is fairly remote, at best, particularly at a bargain price. I've learned never to say "never," however. People **are** still uncovering rare Depression glass even at this late date!

A 9" platter finally surfaced in green! Measure this platter outside edge to outside edge. The 11" platter measures only 9" on the inside rims. To be a 9" platter the measurements have to be from outside to outside. I said a green 11" platter had surfaced in the Tenth edition and everyone must have known I meant 9" since I didn't get stacks of letters pointing it out.

Other pieces of Cherry Blossom are becoming harder to acquire. The aforementioned 9" platter, mugs, soup and cereal bowls and the 10" green grill plate have all been troublesome for collectors to procure, especially in mint condition. Now the three-footed bowl and flat iced teas have joined the roster. Be sure to check all inner rims of Cherry Blossom pieces since there is a proclivity for them to have chips and nicks. This was caused by stacking as much as from utilization. You can safely stack dishes with proper sized paper plates between them.

Crystal Cherry Blossom appears at times. Normally, it is the two-handled bowl that sells in the $15.00 range. It is scarce, but there is not enough crystal found to be collectible as a set. A few red pieces have been found, but the reproduction red wiped out the demand for those.

The letters AOP stand for "all over pattern" on the footed tumblers and rounded pitcher. The footed large tumblers and the AOP pitcher come in two styles. One style has a scalloped or indented foot while the other is round with no indentations. PAT stands for "pattern at the top" illustrated by the flat bottomed tumblers and pitchers.

There are some known experimental pieces of Cherry such as a pink cookie jar, pink five-part relish, orange with green trim slag bowl and amber children's pieces. That five-part round relish recently sold for $900.00. Pricing on experimental items is difficult to determine; but keep your eye out for any of these pieces, and don't pass them up if the price is right - for you! There is always some market demand for rare items of Depression glassware.

# CHERRY BLOSSOM JEANNETTE GLASS COMPANY, 1930-1939 (Cont.)

| | Pink | Green | Delphite |
|---|---|---|---|
| Bowl, 4¾" berry | 14.00 | 16.00 | 14.00 |
| Bowl, 5¾" cereal | 30.00 | 33.00 | |
| Bowl, 7¾" flat soup | 50.00 | 50.00 | |
| * Bowl, 8½" round berry | 42.50 | 42.50 | 40.00 |
| Bowl, 9" oval vegetable | 35.00 | 35.00 | 45.00 |
| Bowl, 9" 2-handled | 28.00 | 30.00 | 23.00 |
| ** Bowl, 10½", 3 leg fruit | 75.00 | 75.00 | |
| Butter dish and cover | 70.00 | 80.00 | |
| Butter dish bottom | 15.00 | 22.50 | |
| Butter dish top | 55.00 | 57.50 | |
| Cake plate (3 legs) 10¼" | 25.00 | 25.00 | |
| Coaster | 14.00 | 12.00 | |
| Creamer | 17.00 | 17.00 | 18.00 |
| Cup | 16.00 | 18.00 | 16.00 |
| Mug, 7 oz. | 185.00 | 155.00 | |
| ***Pitcher, 6¾" AOP, 36 oz. scalloped or round bottom | 47.50 | 50.00 | 80.00 |
| Pitcher, 8" PAT, 42 oz. flat | 50.00 | 50.00 | |
| Pitcher, 8" PAT, 36 oz. footed | 50.00 | 50.00 | |
| Plate, 6" sherbet | 7.00 | 7.00 | 10.00 |
| Plate, 7" salad | 17.00 | 20.00 | |
| ****Plate, 9" dinner | 20.00 | 22.00 | 18.00 |
| Plate, 9" grill | 24.00 | 23.00 | |

| | Pink | Green | Delphite |
|---|---|---|---|
| Plate, 10" grill | | 65.00 | |
| Platter, 9" oval | 760.00 | 910.00 | |
| Platter, 11" oval | 35.00 | 38.00 | 40.00 |
| Platter, 13" and 13" divided | 60.00 | 60.00 | |
| Salt and pepper (scalloped bottom) | 1,225.00 | 925.00 | |
| Saucer | 6.00 | 6.00 | 6.00 |
| Sherbet | 15.00 | 17.00 | 14.00 |
| Sugar | 12.00 | 15.00 | 18.00 |
| Sugar cover | 15.00 | 16.00 | |
| Tray, 10½" sandwich | 20.00 | 22.00 | 18.00 |
| Tumbler, 3¾", 4 oz. footed AOP | 14.00 | 18.00 | 18.00 |
| Tumbler, 4½", 9 oz. round foot AOP | 30.00 | 32.00 | 18.00 |
| Tumbler, 4½", 8 oz. scalloped foot AOP | 28.00 | 30.00 | 18.00 |
| Tumbler, 3½", 4 oz. flat PAT | 17.00 | 26.00 | |
| Tumbler, 4¼", 9 oz. flat PAT | 17.00 | 21.00 | |
| Tumbler, 5", 12 oz. flat PAT | 50.00 | 65.00 | |

*Yellow - $350.00      **Jadite - $275.00      ***Jadite - $300.00

****Translucent green - $175.00      Jadite - $40.00

## CHERRY BLOSSOM - CHILD'S JUNIOR DINNER SET

| | Pink | Delphite |
|---|---|---|
| Creamer | 45.00 | 45.00 |
| Sugar | 45.00 | 45.00 |
| Plate, 6" | 10.00 | 13.00 (design on bottom) |
| Cup | 35.00 | 35.00 |
| Saucer | 6.00 | 7.00 |
| 14 Piece set | 295.00 | 310.00 |

Original box sells for $15.00 extra with pink sets.

**Please refer to Foreword for pricing information**

# CHINEX CLASSIC MacBETH-EVANS DIVISION OF CORNING GLASS WORKS, Late 1930's - Early 1940's

Colors: Ivory, ivory w/decal decoration.

Chinex devotees are having a rough time finding several decorated patterns of Chinex. My favorite is the blue trimmed castle decal. The blue and pink trimmed pieces with a red flower are not being found regularly, nor is the brown trimmed castle scene. More of this pattern is found in the Pittsburgh area than any other part of the country. Undoubtedly, the fact that MacBeth-Evans was just down the road has a great deal to do with this.

This pattern "grows" on you. I have enjoyed finding the many pieces shown on page 37. Eliminating the 1950's patterns from this book has allowed me to expand upon some of these minor patterns that can be collected.

A few collectors got upset with me for disclosing the beauty of the pastel trimmed, red flower design in an earlier book. I was blamed for the higher prices caused by new collectors buying it before the long time collectors could find it. They were right in the respect that more collectors did start to search and it disappeared more quickly into new collections. What they should have realized is that the **value** of their already collected glassware was increasing with each new person searching for it!

This undecorated Chinex is great in the microwave according to a Midwestern collector. I must admit that I have never tried it in the microwave, so remember to test it first by putting it in for a **short** time (a few seconds - not the major thirty my wife disintergated her contacs with!) and checking for "hot" spots just as you would any other dish not designed specifically for the microwave.

Plainer, undecorated beige pieces are still awaiting collectors to notice them. So far, not many have taken on this challenge. Castle decal items are the most desirable, but the darker blue is more popular than the lighter blue or brown trimmed.

Remember, butter bottoms look like Cremax instead of Chinex. The butter tops have the "scroll like" design that distinguishes Chinex, but this scroll design is missing from the butter bottoms. The bottom has a plain pie crust edge. Also, the floral or castle designs will be inside the base of the butter. See the butter bottom on the right in the castle decorated picture. I have never found a top to this butter; so I do not know if there is a castle scene on the top around the knob or not.

| | Browntone or Plain Ivory | Decal Decorated | Castle Decal |
|---|---|---|---|
| Bowl, 5¾" cereal | 5.50 | 8.00 | 15.00 |
| Bowl, 7" vegetable | 14.00 | 22.00 | 32.00 |
| Bowl, 7¾" soup | 12.50 | 17.50 | 30.00 |
| Bowl, 9" vegetable | 11.00 | 22.00 | 32.50 |
| Bowl, 11" | 17.00 | 32.00 | 42.00 |
| Butter dish | 55.00 | 75.00 | 115.00 |
| Butter dish bottom | 12.50 | 27.50 | 42.50 |
| Butter dish top | 42.50 | 47.50 | 72.50 |
| Creamer | 5.50 | 10.00 | 18.00 |
| Cup | 4.50 | 6.50 | 13.00 |
| Plate, 6¼" sherbet | 2.50 | 3.50 | 7.50 |
| Plate, 9¾" dinner | 4.50 | 8.50 | 16.00 |
| Plate, 11½" sandwich or cake | 7.50 | 13.50 | 22.50 |
| Saucer | 2.50 | 4.50 | 6.50 |
| Sherbet, low ftd. | 7.00 | 11.00 | 22.00 |
| Sugar, open | 5.50 | 9.00 | 17.50 |

**Please refer to Foreword for pricing information**

# CIRCLE HOCKING GLASS COMPANY, 1930's

Colors: Green, pink and crystal.

Sets of green Circle can be gathered, but it will take the patience of Job to put a set together in pink. Let me know if you have managed to do so. Notice that I have only gathered four pieces in pink in my travels and one of those was a gift from a collector. For some reason it has not been in the areas where I have looked; maybe you will have better luck than I.

Circle is more noticed by collectors of kitchenware (especially reamer collectors) than it is by Depression glass enthusiasts. The 80 oz. pitcher made by Hocking with a reamer top is highly desired by reamer enthusiasts. There are probably more of these pitchers sitting with reamer tops in reamer collections than there are in Circle accumulations. The major problem with the pitcher and reamer is that color variations of these pitchers make it difficult to find a reamer that matches the green shade of the pitcher. The pitcher shown here is very yellow when compared to the other green pieces. (Hopefully, that yellowish tint will show when the book is printed.)

Two styles of cups add to the mystique of this pattern. The flat bottomed style fits a saucer/sherbet plate while the rounded cup takes an indented saucer. I still have not found the indented saucer for my pink cup, but a collector found me the pink saucer/sherbet plate this time. I have never heard of tumblers, pitchers or bowls in pink. I believe only a luncheon set was made in the pink, but two styles of cups make you wonder....

Both of the bowls, 9⅜" and 5¼", have ground bottoms. I have previously said that I doubted the existence of a 9½" dinner plate, but a 10" sandwich plate is pictured. I have received a letter from a lady who says she has three 9½" plates.

You can find green colored stems with crystal tops easier than you can find plain green stems; however, few buy crystal topped items at present. I, personally, like two toned variations in glass.

| | Green, Pink | | Green, Pink |
|---|---|---|---|
| Bowl, 4½" | 8.00 | Plate, 6" sherbet/saucer | 1.50 |
| Bowl, 5¼" | 10.00 | Plate, 8¼" luncheon | 4.00 |
| Bowl, 5" flared, 1¾" deep | 10.00 | Plate, 10" sandwich | 12.00 |
| Bowl, 8" | 15.00 | Saucer w/cup ring | 1.50 |
| Bowl, 9⅜" | 16.00 | Sherbet, 3⅛" | 4.00 |
| Creamer | 9.00 | Sherbet, 4¾" | 6.00 |
| Cup (2 styles) | 5.00 | Sugar | 7.00 |
| Decanter, handled | 37.50 | Tumbler, 3½", 4 oz. juice | 8.00 |
| Goblet, 4½" wine | 12.50 | Tumbler, 4", 8 oz. water | 9.00 |
| Goblet, 8 oz. water | 11.00 | Tumbler, 5", 10 oz. tea | 16.00 |
| Pitcher, 60 oz. | 32.00 | Tumbler, 15 oz. flat | 18.00 |
| Pitcher, 80 oz. | 27.50 | | |

# CLOVERLEAF HAZEL ATLAS GLASS COMPANY, 1930-1936

Colors: Pink, green, yellow, crystal and black.

Arrangements of Cloverleaf collections are always well received by collectors and the public when displays are exhibited at shows. Cloverleaf is a pattern easily recognized by non collectors.

There seem to be equal numbers of collectors for yellow, black and green. Very few are turning to pink or crystal since they are limited to a luncheon set. Only a pink flared 10 oz. tumbler exists besides the basic luncheon pieces. That pink tumbler is quite sparsely distributed and is not found in crystal at all. Crystal makes a pleasant table display with colored accoutrements.

At present all Cloverleaf colors are selling well with yellow leading the way. In yellow, the candy dish, shakers and bowls do not seem to be available at any price. In green, the 8" bowl and tumblers are selling briskly.

Black Cloverleaf prices have slowed somewhat with the ash trays suddenly being ignored. I have noticed that this is true in many patterns. Evidently, the non-smokers are being heard for a change or the smokers are finally "wising up"; and it is affecting the sale of smokers' items even in the glassware business. However, one man at a show recently told me that since he read of the virtual shunning of smoking accessories in my book, he made up his mind right then he was going to start a collection of them! The black sherbet plate and saucer are the same size. The saucer has no "Cloverleaf" pattern in the center. These sherbet plates still turn up in stacks of saucers occasionally; so keep your eyes open!

Some black Cloverleaf pieces in the photograph on page 41 are gold decorated, probably for a special promotion. I have included these hoping the Cloverleaf pattern will show better in the picture. In my first book in 1972, we highlighted the designs with Bon Ami; but that made for unnatural white clover leaves.

Actually, Cloverleaf was to some extent limited in distribution nationally. In 1978, I bought a large collection of Cloverleaf in Ohio. It had been gathered from dealers all over the country, but major portions of the accumulation had come from Ohio and Pennsylvania. A yellow candy bottom marked "large sherbet – $2.00" became my favorite piece of this collection since the tag had been left on it when it was bought. (Someone buying my New Era plates with the "flower pot saucer" labels will get a laugh years from now - if those tags are not removed.)

I have been reminded to point out that the Cloverleaf pattern comes on both the inside and outside of the pieces. That does not seem to make a difference in value or collectability. In order for the black to show the pattern, moulds had to be designed with the pattern on the outside. On transparent pieces, the pattern could be on the bottom or the inside and it would still show. In black, the pattern on the bottom of a plate makes it look like a plain black plate; so it was moved to the top. Over the years, transparent pieces also were made using the moulds designed for the black; so, you now find these pieces with designs on both sides.

| | Pink | Green | Yellow | Black |
|---|---|---|---|---|
| Ash tray, 4", match holder in center | | | | 67.50 |
| Ash tray, 5¾", match holder in center | | | | 77.50 |
| Bowl, 4" dessert | 12.00 | 18.00 | 24.00 | |
| Bowl, 5" cereal | | 25.00 | 30.00 | |
| Bowl, 7" deep salad | | 37.50 | 47.50 | |
| Bowl, 8" | | 50.00 | | |
| Candy dish and cover | | 47.50 | 98.00 | |
| Creamer, 3⅝" ftd. | | 10.00 | 16.00 | 17.00 |
| Cup | 7.00 | 8.00 | 10.00 | 16.00 |
| Plate, 6" sherbet | | 5.00 | 7.00 | 35.00 |
| Plate, 8" luncheon | 7.00 | 8.00 | 14.00 | 15.00 |
| Plate, 10¼" grill | | 18.00 | 20.00 | |
| Salt and pepper, pr. | | 30.00 | 98.00 | 78.00 |
| Saucer | 4.00 | 4.00 | 5.00 | 7.00 |
| Sherbet, 3" ftd. | 6.00 | 7.00 | 11.00 | 19.00 |
| Sugar, 3⅝" ftd. | | 10.00 | 16.00 | 17.00 |
| Tumbler, 4", 9 oz. flat | | 47.50 | | |
| Tumbler, 3¾", 10 oz. flat flared | 19.00 | 34.00 | | |
| Tumbler, 5¾", 10 oz. ftd. | | 21.00 | 30.00 | |

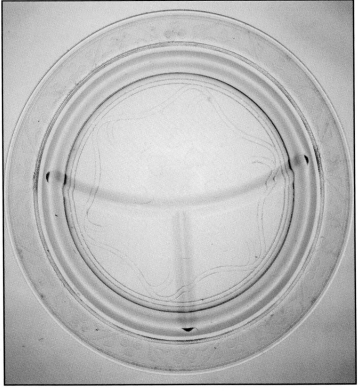

# COLONIAL, "KNIFE AND FORK" HOCKING GLASS COMPANY, 1934-1936

Colors: Pink, green, crystal and opaque white.

Pink and crystal Colonial are presently outselling green. For years there was little demand for any color except green. The tide has turned and it is the green that is taking up dealer inventory. Color preference in collecting has been cyclical for the twenty-four years that I have been watching Depression glass. Now, the green is slightly out of favor!

Prices for crystal stems are approaching prices of their green counterparts. There is a **true** scarcity of crystal stems. There are no stems in pink. Only footed tumblers are found in pink; do not confuse them with stems. Each of the three sizes of footed tumblers can be seen in the bottom photograph on page 44.

There is some difficulty in finding out the manufacturer of the white Colonial pieces that are found occasionally. So far, luncheon plates, cups, saucer/sherbet plates, creamer, sugar without lid and shakers have been found. There is speculation that these may have been run by Corning for Hocking; but I doubt if records will ever show this. Meanwhile, you can keep your eyes open for these rarely found mystery pieces.

Soup bowls (both cream and regular), cereals, unclouded shakers and dinners are still difficult to discover in all colors of Colonial. Cereal bowls may be the most difficult cereals to obtain in all of Depression glass. They are not the most expensive, but they are even harder to find than ones that are.

Mugs surface in pink; but only three have been found in green. These were found in Washington Court House, Ohio, for $1.00 each in the early 1970's. Bargains still turn up, but not as often as they once did. More education about glassware today means higher priced "bargains." I get letters every week of bargain "finds" somewhere in the world. Depression glass does turn up in Canada, Mexico, England, Australia, New Zealand and even the Philippines; I have letters and pictures to prove it!

The 11 oz. tumbler measures 2¾" across the top while the 12 oz. measures exactly 3" across the top. These two tumblers are often confused. It is easier to measure across the top than to measure the contents! The spooner stands 5½" tall while the sugar without a lid is only 4½". I bought the last pink spooner I saw at a large flea market marked as a $15.00 sugar bowl!

The 15 oz. lemonade rarely turns up in pink or crystal. The once abundant supply of green lemonade tumblers has all but dried up.

The cheese dish lid is ¼" shorter than the butter top. The cheese dish is a wooden board with a raised grooved spot on which the lid rests. I will show it to you again in the Twelfth edition since I just repurchased the one that was first shown in my third book. The butter top is 4" tall and the cheese top is only 3¾" tall. It took a level and some ingenuity to discover that there was not the ½" difference that I have previously recorded. The cheese top has a more flattened look when you have the two tops together. So far, the cheese has only been found in green; but the pink butter is already impossible to find without looking for a cheese dish also! The 3" pink sherbet is more than twice as difficult to find as the normally found 3⅜" sherbet, but it only sells for twice as much. So far, no 3" green or crystal sherbets have surfaced. Keep looking!

| | Pink | Green | Crystal | | Pink | Green | Crystal |
|---|---|---|---|---|---|---|---|
| Bowl, 3¾" berry | 42.50 | | | Plate, 6" sherbet | 6.00 | 7.00 | 4.00 |
| Bowl, 4½" berry | 14.00 | 15.00 | 7.00 | Plate, 8½" luncheon | 9.00 | 9.00 | 4.50 |
| Bowl, 5½" cereal | 50.00 | 80.00 | 22.50 | Plate, 10" dinner | 45.00 | 57.50 | 25.00 |
| Bowl, 4½" cream soup | 57.50 | 57.50 | 60.00 | Plate, 10" grill | 23.00 | 23.00 | 13.00 |
| Bowl, 7" low soup | 55.00 | 55.00 | 22.00 | Platter, 12" oval | 30.00 | 21.00 | 15.00 |
| Bowl, 9" large berry | 24.00 | 27.00 | 20.00 | Salt and pepper, pr. | 130.00 | 130.00 | 55.00 |
| Bowl, 10" oval vegetable | 30.00 | 33.00 | 18.00 | Sauce/sherbet plate (white 3.00) | 6.00 | 6.00 | 4.00 |
| Butter dish and cover | 580.00 | 55.00 | 40.00 | Sherbet, 3" | 20.00 | | |
| Butter dish bottom | 377.50 | 32.50 | 25.00 | Sherbet, 3⅜" | 10.00 | 14.00 | 6.50 |
| Butter dish top | 177.50 | 22.50 | 15.00 | Spoon holder or celery | 120.00 | 115.00 | 70.00 |
| Cheese dish | | 200.00 | | Sugar, 5" | 24.00 | 14.00 | 10.00 |
| Cream/milk pitcher, 5", 16 oz. | 50.00 | 20.00 | 15.00 | Sugar cover | 50.00 | 20.00 | 15.00 |
| Cup (white 7.00) | 11.00 | 11.00 | 8.00 | Tumbler, 3", 5 oz. juice | 16.00 | 24.00 | 13.00 |
| Goblet, 3¾", 1 oz. cordial | | 27.00 | 18.00 | **Tumbler, 4", 9 oz. water | 20.00 | 20.00 | 15.00 |
| Goblet, 4", 3 oz. cocktail | | 25.00 | 15.00 | Tumbler, 5⅛" high, 11 oz., | 34.00 | 40.00 | 20.00 |
| Goblet, 4½", 2½ oz. wine | | 25.00 | 15.00 | Tumbler, 12 oz. iced tea | 42.00 | 47.50 | 24.00 |
| Goblet, 5¼", 4 oz. claret | | 25.00 | 16.00 | Tumbler, 15 oz. lemonade | 60.00 | 70.00 | 40.00 |
| Goblet, 5¾", 8½ oz. water | 37.50 | 28.00 | 20.00 | Tumbler, 3¼", 3 oz. ftd. | 14.00 | 21.00 | 12.00 |
| Mug, 4½", 12 oz. | 455.00 | 765.00 | | Tumbler, 4", 5 oz. ftd. | 28.00 | 38.00 | 16.00 |
| + Pitcher, 7", 54 oz. | 45.00 | 50.00 | 28.00 | ***Tumbler, 5¼", 10 oz. ftd. | 42.00 | 42.00 | 25.00 |
| *+ Pitcher, 7¾", 68 oz. | 60.00 | 65.00 | 30.00 | Whiskey, 2½", 1½ oz. | 11.00 | 14.00 | 10.00 |

*Beaded top in pink $1,000.00     **Royal ruby $100.00     ***Royal ruby $150.00     +With or without ice lip

44

# COLONIAL BLOCK HAZEL ATLAS GLASS COMPANY, Early 1930's

Colors: Green, crystal, black and pink; white in 1950's.

Pink Colonial Block is not seen as often as green. I have talked to several collectors who tried to put sets of pink together, and they are having a diffiicult time! One collector who had put an eight place set of green together in two years said he was stymied by finding only thirteen pieces of pink in over a year. He had found some of the goblets that are rarely seen. Pink might be a challenging set if you need another task in life.

The candy dish, butter tub (shown in the foreground) and pitcher are the most coveted items of green. The few pink Colonial Block collectors report that they have never seen a pink pitcher. That goblet by the pitcher is Colonial Block and not Block Optic as I see it often mislabeled. Many Block Optic collectors use these goblets with their sets since they are less costly. The heavier Colonial Block goblets are definitely more durable when compared to the thinner Block Optic.

Most pieces of Colonial Block are marked HA, but not all are so marked. The **H** and **A** are atop each other confusing some novice collectors into believing that this is the symbol for Anchor Hocking. The anchor is a symbol used by Anchor Hocking and that was not used until after the 1930's.

U.S. Glass made a similar pitcher to the one shown here. There is little difference in them except most Hazel Atlas pitchers are marked. Collectors today are not as rigid in their collecting standards as they once were. Many collectors will buy either pitcher to go with their set. That is why I call items that are similar to a pattern but not actually a part of it, "go-with" or "look-alike" pieces. Usually, these items are more reasonably priced.

A few black and frosted green Colonial Block powder jars are being found. You can see a black lid which is all I have found! No other black pieces have been seen. Let me hear what you find. The white creamer, sugar and lid are the only white pieces available so far. Some more sherbets have been found recently. How a piece like that can go undiscovered all these years is one of those astounding things that keep me enjoying and writing about glass!

| | Pink, Green | White | | Pink, Green | White |
|---|---|---|---|---|---|
| Bowl, 4" | 6.50 | | Creamer | 11.00 | 7.00 |
| Bowl, 7" | 16.00 | | Goblet | 11.00 | |
| Butter dish | 45.00 | | Pitcher | 38.00 | |
| Butter dish bottom | 12.50 | | *Powder jar with lid | 17.50 | |
| Butter dish top | 32.50 | | Sherbet | 8.00 | |
| Butter tub | 37.50 | | Sugar | 10.00 | 5.50 |
| Candy jar w/cover | 35.00 | | Sugar lid | 10.00 | 4.50 |

*Black $22.50

# COLONIAL FLUTED, "ROPE" FEDERAL GLASS COMPANY, 1928-1933

Colors: Green and crystal.

Colonial Fluted is a pattern that was used extensively initially; so you will find many pieces with heavy wear marks. Knives will scratch the surface of most glassware; you need to choose your menus carefully, today, if you serve on your collection. I wouldn't suggest a hearty grilled steak and **Ginsu**™ knives on any of your glassware or china.

Colonial Fluted is still priced moderately enough that it can be used today without fear of a piece or two being broken by guests. Experience has shown me that most guests recognize this old glass as "antique" and treat it very gently. Many times they are hesitant to use it. For heavens' sakes don't tell them how much it's worth if they ask - until after the meal. When asked, I once told my mother-in-law the goblet she was drinking from cost $65.00 - and I thought she would drop it from the shock before replacing it on the coaster.

The "F" in a shield found in middle of many Colonial Fluted pieces is the trademark used by the Federal Glass Company. Not all pieces are marked.

Colonial Fluted is another set of Depression glass that is usually a starter set for beginning collectors. There is no dinner plate in Colonial Fluted; but there is a dinner sized plate having the roping effect around the outside of the plate (without the fluting) made by Federal that goes very well with this if you are willing to overlook the missing flutes. It is shown in the back of the photograph.

Colonial Fluted can be blended with other sets or used for occasions such as card parties or small gatherings. In fact, much of the original advertising for this pattern was for bridge sets. Crystal is seldom collected, but there is a demand for the crystal decal pieces with hearts, spades, diamonds and clubs that make up a bridge set. I received a photo not too long ago from a collector who was delighted to have found a single piece of the bridge set! She was now embarking on a search for the other pieces.

|  | Green |  | Green |
|---|---|---|---|
| Bowl, 4" berry | 5.50 | Plate, 6" sherbet | 2.50 |
| Bowl, 6" cereal | 8.00 | Plate, 8" luncheon | 5.00 |
| Bowl, 6½", deep (2½") salad | 18.00 | Saucer | 2.00 |
| Bowl, 7½" large berry | 16.00 | Sherbet | 6.00 |
| Creamer | 6.50 | Sugar | 5.00 |
| Cup | 5.00 | Sugar cover | 16.00 |

# COLUMBIA FEDERAL GLASS COMPANY, 1938-1942

Colors: Crystal, some pink.

One piece of Columbia that was over produced was the butter dish. You can find these with all sorts of multicolored, flashed decorations and floral decals. Some have even been satinized and then flashed with color and others have only the satinized finish. Federal must have tried everything to sell these and it must have worked since there are so many found today! It is the only butter dish in this book that has not increased at least twenty percent in the last ten years.

Columbia tumblers come in two sizes. The 2⅞", 4 ounce juice and 9 ounce water are all I am sure about at this time. Both are pictured. I have had numerous reports of other sizes and have had others shown to me at Depression Glass shows. So far, these have all turned out to be Duncan and Miller pieces and not Columbia. You can find the water tumblers with advertisements of dairy products on them. Keep watching!

Pink Columbia sells very well! This was surprising to me since there are only four different pieces to be found and they are scarce. I had often wondered why it sold so well, but a collector of crystal said she mixes in a few pieces of pink "for color." Maybe others do the same!

I hope you can see the elusive snack tray shown behind the pink cup and saucer on the right. Many collectors have not known what to look for since it is an unusual piece and shaped differently than most Columbia. These were found with Columbia cups in a boxed set about twenty years ago in northern Ohio. The box was labeled "Snack Sets" by Federal Glass Company. The trays are also being found with Federal cups **other than Columbia**. I have been told that they turn up regularly in the Denver area.

Prices continue to increase for the bowls, tumblers and the snack plate.

You will find many decorated pieces besides the butter dish. Luncheon sets have been found with pastel bands and floral decals. These are difficult to sell, today, unless you find a complete matching set. It is nearly impossible to find these sets piece by piece.

|  | Crystal | Pink |  | Crystal | Pink |
|---|---|---|---|---|---|
| Bowl, 5" cereal | 15.00 |  | Cup | 8.50 | 18.00 |
| Bowl, 8" low soup | 18.00 |  | Plate, 6" bread & butter | 3.50 | 13.00 |
| Bowl, 8½" salad | 17.00 |  | Plate, 9½" luncheon | 9.50 | 27.50 |
| Bowl, 10½" ruffled edge | 19.00 |  | Plate, 11" chop | 9.00 |  |
| Butter dish and cover | 20.00 |  | Saucer | 3.50 | 9.00 |
|   Ruby flashed (22.00) |  |  | Snack plate | 35.00 |  |
|   Other flashed (21.00) |  |  | Tumbler, 2⅞", 4 oz., juice | 17.50 |  |
| Butter dish bottom | 7.50 |  | Tumbler, 9 oz., water | 25.00 |  |
| Butter dish top | 12.50 |  |  |  |  |

# CORONATION, "BANDED RIB," "SAXON" HOCKING GLASS COMPANY, 1936-1940

Colors: Pink, green, crystal and Royal Ruby.

Coronation tumblers have received most of the fame for this pattern since they have been regularly confused with the seldom found Old Colony ("Lace Edge") tumblers. Note the fine ribs above the middle of the Coronation tumbler. These ribs are missing on a "Lace Edge" glass. Look on the bottom of page 109 or in the store display photographs following to see the differences. (I might point out here that the real name of the pattern we have called "Lace Edge" is shown in those store displays as OLD COLONY. Get used to the name since after this book Old Colony will be listed in the "O" section alphabetically and not in the "L" section as it now is.)

It has been ten years since I first discovered green Coronation. The green pieces at the bottom of page 49 are in Anchor Hocking's morgue and the ones in the top picture are ones I have been able to uncover. The larger green tumbler in the lower photograph is 5⁷⁄₁₆" tall and holds 14¼ oz. For new readers the lower photo was taken by Anchor-Hocking of glassware in their morgue. The morgue is so called since it has examples of past (dead production) patterns made by the Company. Unfortunately, this was not well kept. Many examples have "walked out" over the years. It is now under lock, but the disappearance of items began long ago. Who knew Depression glass was going to be so meaningful?

Notice that the handles on the Royal Ruby bowls are open; handles on the pink are closed and handles on the green are nonexistent. If you should find another style of handle on a different color than these combinations, let me know.

Dealers uneducated about Depression glass still mark big prices on those commonly found, red, handled berry bowls. They have always been plentiful and some years ago a large accumulation was discovered in an old warehouse. They are hard to sell; yet, I see them priced for two to three times their worth. They are usually marked "rare" or "old" or "pigeon blood." That "pigeon blood" terminology comes from old time collectors who used that term to describe dark red glass. Royal Ruby is the name of the red glass that was made by Hocking and only their red glassware can be called Royal Ruby.

Many collectors buy Coronation tumblers and use them with Old Colony since they cost a third as much. Both are the same shape and color since both were made by Hocking. Just don't confuse the two since there is quite a price discrepancy!

Red cups were sold on crystal saucers. In fact, those crystal saucer/sherbet plates are the only crystal pieces that I have seen in this pattern. No red saucer/sherbet plates have ever been seen. I would not go so far as to say that red saucers were never made. If I have learned anything in the last 20 years, it is never to say some piece of glass was never made.

|  | Pink | Royal Ruby | Green |
| --- | --- | --- | --- |
| Bowl, 4¼" berry | 4.50 | 6.50 |  |
| Bowl, 4¼", no handles |  |  | 25.00 |
| Bowl, 6½" nappy | 6.00 | 12.00 |  |
| Bowl, 8" large berry, handled | 8.50 | 15.00 |  |
| Bowl, 8", no handles |  |  | 125.00 |
| Cup | 5.50 | 6.50 |  |
| Pitcher, 7¾", 68 oz. | 400.00 |  |  |
| Plate, 6", sherbet | 2.00 |  |  |
| Plate, 8½" luncheon | 4.50 | 8.00 | 35.00 |
| * Saucer (same as 6" plate) | 2.00 |  |  |
| Sherbet | 4.50 |  | 55.00 |
| Tumbler, 5", 10 oz. ftd. | 20.00 |  | 125.00 |

*Crystal $.50

# CREMAX MacBETH-EVANS DIVISION OF CORNING GLASS WORKS, Late 1930's-Early 1940's

Colors: Cremax, Cremax with fired-on color trim.

Cremax with the green castle decal must be fairly hard to find, because no one has written about having a set (or even a few pieces) since I first showed it in the last book. I had never seen that decal in green. Besides the red floral decorations, it is the first decoration on Cremax that I have actually liked! A few months ago I did find an 11½" Cremax sandwich plate decorated with the same red floral design as is found on Petalware. If you have pieces with additional decorations, let me hear about those!

Demitasse sets are being found in sets of eight. Some have been found on a wire rack. The usual make-up of these sets has been two sets each of four colors: pink, yellow, blue and green. I have finally obtained some of these to show you.

Cremax continues to be an orphan that few collectors want. Its sister pattern, Chinex, has numerous collectors, while Cremax goes practically unnoticed. It is not readily found. There are several different floral patterned decals that can be collected. Maybe it is the scarcity that keeps collectors from buying Cremax the way they do Chinex.

Regularly the bottom to the butter dish in Chinex is thought to be Cremax. The scalloped edges of the butter bottom are just like the edges on Cremax plates; however, the only tops to the butter ever found have the Chinex scroll-like pattern. If you find only the bottom of a butter, it is a Chinex bottom!

An additional problem surrounds the name Cremax. The beige-like **color** made by MacBeth-Evans is also called cremax. Be aware of that.

| | Cremax | Decal Decorated | | Cremax | Decal Decorated |
|---|---|---|---|---|---|
| Bowl, 5¾" cereal | 3.50 | 7.50 | Plate, 9¾" dinner | 4.50 | 9.50 |
| Bowl, 9" vegetable | 6.50 | 13.00 | Plate, 11½" sandwich | 5.00 | 11.00 |
| Creamer | 4.50 | 8.00 | Saucer | 2.00 | 3.50 |
| Cup | 4.00 | 5.00 | Saucer, demitasse | 5.00 | 9.00 |
| Cup, demitasse | 13.00 | 22.00 | Sugar, open | 4.50 | 8.00 |
| Plate, 6¼" bread and butter | 2.00 | 4.00 | | | |

# "CROW'S FOOT," PADEN CITY GLASS COMPANY, LINE 412 & LINE 890, 1930's

Colors: Ritz blue, Ruby red, amber, amethyst, black, pink and yellow.

Crow's Foot is the commonly used blank for Paden City etchings as is the Fairfax blank for Fostoria etchings. The squared shape is Line #412, and the round is Line #890.

| | Red | Black/ Blue | Other Colors | | Red | Black/ Blue | Other Colors |
|---|---|---|---|---|---|---|---|
| Bowl, 4⅞", square | 25.00 | 30.00 | 12.50 | Cup, ftd. or flat | 10.00 | 12.50 | 5.00 |
| Bowl, 6" | 30.00 | 35.00 | 15.00 | Gravy boat, flat | 85.00 | 100.00 | 40.00 |
| Bowl, 6½", rd., 2½" high, 3½" base | 45.00 | 50.00 | 22.50 | Gravy boat, pedestal | 125.00 | 140.00 | 65.00 |
| Bowl, 8½", square, 2 hdld | 50.00 | 60.00 | 27.50 | Mayonnaise, 3 ftd. | 45.00 | 55.00 | 22.50 |
| Bowl, 10", ftd. | 65.00 | 75.00 | 32.50 | Plate, 5¾" | 2.25 | 3.50 | 1.25 |
| Bowl, 10", square, 2 hdld. | 65.00 | 75.00 | 32.50 | Plate, 8", round | 9.00 | 11.00 | 4.50 |
| Bowl, 11", oval | 35.00 | 42.50 | 17.50 | Plate, 8½", square | 7.00 | 9.00 | 3.50 |
| Bowl, 11", square | 60.00 | 70.00 | 30.00 | Plate, 9¼", round, small dinner | 30.00 | 35.00 | 15.00 |
| Bowl, 11", square, rolled edge | 65.00 | 75.00 | 32.50 | Plate, 9½", rd., 2-hdld. | 65.00 | 75.00 | 32.50 |
| Bowl, 11½", 3 ftd., round console | 85.00 | 100.00 | 42.50 | Plate, 10⅜", rd., 2 hdld. | 50.00 | 60.00 | 25.00 |
| Bowl, 11¾", console | 75.00 | 85.00 | 37.50 | Plate, 10⅜", sq., 2 hdld. | 40.00 | 50.00 | 20.00 |
| Bowl, cream soup, ftd./flat | 20.00 | 22.50 | 10.00 | Plate, 10½", dinner | 90.00 | 100.00 | 40.00 |
| Bowl, Nasturtium, 3 ftd. | 175.00 | 200.00 | 90.00 | Plate, 11", cracker | 45.00 | 50.00 | 22.50 |
| Bowl, whipped cream, 3 ftd. | 55.00 | 65.00 | 27.50 | Platter, 12" | 27.50 | 32.50 | 15.00 |
| Cake plate, sq., low pedestal ft. | 85.00 | 95.00 | 42.50 | Relish, 11", 3 pt. | 85.00 | 100.00 | 45.00 |
| Candle, round base, tall | 75.00 | 85.00 | 37.50 | Sandwich server, rd., center hdld. | 65.00 | 75.00 | 32.50 |
| Candle, square, mushroom | 37.50 | 42.50 | 20.00 | Sandwich server, sq., center hdld. | 35.00 | 40.00 | 17.50 |
| Candlestick, 5¾", | 25.00 | 30.00 | 12.50 | Saucer, 6", round | 2.50 | 3.00 | 1.00 |
| Candy w/cover, 6½", 3 part (2 styles) | 50.00 | 60.00 | 25.00 | Saucer, 6", square | 3.00 | 3.50 | 1.50 |
| Candy, 3 ftd., rd., 6⅛" wide, 3¼" high | 150.00 | 185.00 | 75.00 | Sugar, flat | 11.00 | 13.50 | 5.50 |
| Cheese stand, 5" | 25.00 | 30.00 | 12.50 | Sugar, ftd. | 11.00 | 13.50 | 5.50 |
| Comport, 3¼" tall, 6¼" wide | 27.50 | 32.50 | 15.00 | Tumbler, 4¼" | 75.00 | 85.00 | 37.50 |
| Comport, 6⅝" tall, 7" wide | 60.00 | 75.00 | 30.00 | Vase, 10¼", cupped | 85.00 | 100.00 | 45.00 |
| Creamer, flat | 12.50 | 15.00 | 6.50 | Vase, 10¼", flared | 65.00 | 75.00 | 32.50 |
| Creamer, ftd. | 12.50 | 15.00 | 6.50 | Vase, 11¾", flared | 125.00 | 175.00 | 65.00 |

**Please refer to Foreword for pricing information**

# CUBE, "CUBIST" JEANNETTE GLASS COMPANY, 1929-1933

Colors: Pink, green, crystal, amber, white, ultramarine, canary yellow and blue.

Cube is a pattern design that catches the eye of non-collectors. Fostoria's American pattern is also recognized by non-collectors for the same reason. Cube is often mistaken for American by beginning collectors. Cube is very dull and wavy in appearance when compared to the bright, clearer quality of Fostoria's American pattern. The crystal 3⁹⁄₁₆" creamer and 3" sugar on the 7½" round tray are the most often confused pieces.

Prices for pink pitcher and tumblers continue to increase. Though both colors are hard to find, green seems to be disappearing faster than pink. Because most collectors are looking for four, six or eight tumblers, it usually takes longer to find these than the pitcher. Be sure to check the sides of tumblers and pitchers inasmuch as they damaged on the sides before the heavy rims did!

Many pieces of cube-like pink and a darker shade of green are now being marketed under the name Whitehall by Indiana. If you have a pitcher or some other colored piece with a cubed pattern in a shape not shown here, you likely have Whitehall. No pink pitcher or tumblers are found in American either.

Green Cube is more difficult to find than the pink, but there are more collectors of the pink. The major difficulty in collecting pink is not in finding it, but in finding it with the right tint of pink. The pink varies from a light pink to an orange-pink. This only shows how difficult it was for glass factories in the Depression era to consistently produce the same quality of glassware. As the glass tanks got hotter, the color got lighter. The orange shade of pink is difficult to sell. I have also depicted two distinct shades of green using the butter dish as an example. The darker shade of green is not as desirable as the normally found green. Both colors of Cube make for difficulties when ordering by mail if you want your glass to match. That is why it is preferable to attend shows and see what you are getting. You might even be willing to pay a little more for that convenience!

The powder jar is three legged and shown to the left of the pink butter dish in the top picture. Occasionally, these jars are found with celluloid or some other lid. Powder jars were not made with those lids at the factory. These were possibly replacements when tops were broken. Another possibility is that powder bottoms were bought from Jeannette and non-glass lids were made up elsewhere to fit the bottoms. In any case, prices below are for intact, original glass lids. The powder jars with other types of lids sell for half or less. As with most lidded items, it was the top that was most often obliterated, leaving far too many bottoms.

Lack of a dinner size plate is the only drawback for collecting this pattern besides the aforementioned color tints. At least Cube has a pitcher for the tumblers (and all the other basic pieces including cups and saucers)!

|  | Pink | Green |
|---|---|---|
| Bowl, 4½" dessert | 6.50 | 7.00 |
| * Bowl, 4½" deep | 7.00 | |
| ** Bowl, 6½" salad | 9.50 | 14.00 |
| Butter dish and cover | 60.00 | 60.00 |
| Butter dish bottom | 20.00 | 20.00 |
| Butter dish top | 40.00 | 40.00 |
| Candy jar and cover, 6½" | 27.50 | 30.00 |
| Coaster, 3¼" | 7.00 | 7.50 |
| *** Creamer, 2⅝" | 2.00 | |
| Creamer, 3⁹⁄₁₆" | 6.00 | 9.00 |
| Cup | 7.50 | 9.00 |
| Pitcher, 8¾", 45 oz. | 185.00 | 210.00 |
| Plate, 6" sherbet | 3.50 | 4.00 |
| Plate, 8" luncheon | 6.50 | 7.00 |
| Powder jar and cover 3 legs | 23.00 | 23.00 |
| Salt and pepper, pr. | 35.00 | 35.00 |
| Saucer | 3.00 | 3.00 |
| Sherbet, ftd. | 7.00 | 7.50 |
| *** Sugar, 2⅜" | 2.00 | |
| Sugar, 3" | 7.00 | 8.00 |
| Sugar/candy cover | 14.00 | 14.00 |
| Tray for 3⁹⁄₁₆" creamer and sugar, 7½" (crystal only) | 4.00 | |
| Tumbler, 4", 9 oz. | 60.00 | 65.00 |

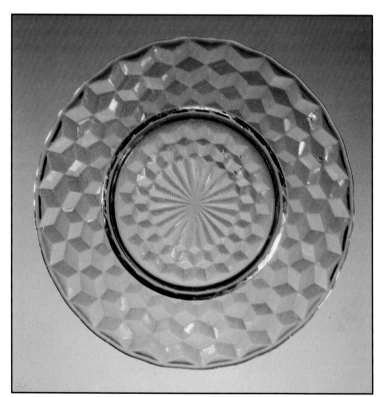

*Ultramarine - $25.00
**Ultramarine - $50.00
***Amber or white - $3.00; crystal $1.00

**Please refer to Foreword for pricing information**

# "CUPID" PADEN CITY GLASS COMPANY, 1930's

Colors: Pink, green, light blue, peacock blue, black, canary yellow, amber and crystal.

Cupid collecting keeps you searching! I finally found a green creamer and sugar set at the recent Houston Depression glass show. Unfortunately, all the photographs were long since made; so it will be a while before you will be able to see them. However, I believe I have included enough to whet your appetite.

The only piece of black Cupid known is the covered casserole shown previously in the ninth edition. The silver decorated edges give this an elegance all its own.

Samovars are rarely found, but are fetching "big bucks" when they are! You can see one on page 55 and another on page 57. So far, these had only been reported in green and blue until a fired-on orange one was found near Pittsburgh and brought for me to look at last year. It was the ugliest piece of glass I have had the chance to own. I asked the owner to have it photographed for me. The pictures did not turn out well enough for the book. Maybe you should be glad! (Yes, I told the owner just what I said above.)

Paden City is a company where new discoveries are the norm rather than unusual! Most pieces are shown in catalogues with no etchings; and until a piece shows up with a Paden City etching, there is no way to know that it does exist in that pattern. Thus, Cupid "discoveries" continue to be made.

An unusual cobalt vase with silver overlay was brought to me in Miami a few years ago. It was the wrong color and shape to be Cupid, so I looked at the bottom and saw the words "Made in Germany" there. The collector was shocked when I showed him since he had never noticed those words. Hold on! This is not the only piece. Cathy and I have found two other vases since then. One is yet a different shaped cobalt vase and the other is a stately lavender. They both have silver overlays of the exact Cupid pattern found on the Paden City pieces. You can see the cobalt blue vase on page 57. The cobalt lamp with silver overlay reported from Arizona is probably German also. How this happened is beyond me, but with Europe's doors opening wider, we may see some other mysteries unveiled in the future. I asked if anyone knew anything about these pieces last time and so far, there have been no answers forthcoming.

Prices on this Paden City pattern continue to ascend. I heard first hand from a West coast dealer who sold a green cake stand for $200.00. **Keep in mind that one sale at a high price does not mean that everyone would be willing to pay that price.** People have been known to buy **one** piece of Cupid just to own a attractive piece of glass. After a while this one little purchase creates a Cupid collector. You do not have to own a large number of Cupid pieces to enjoy using what you have!

Those center-handled pieces were called sandwich trays and the odd, center-handled bowls of Paden City were called candy trays.

I finally received a report of another blue plate! I have been asking about this lovely color for fourteen years and finally another piece has been found! Let me know what **you** find in Cupid!

| | Green/Pink | | Green/Pink |
|---|---|---|---|
| Bowl, 8½" oval-ftd. | 145.00 | Creamer, 5" ftd. | 80.00 |
| Bowl, 9¼" ftd. fruit | 150.00 | Ice bucket, 6" | 140.00 |
| Bowl, 9¼" center-handled | 125.00 | Ice tub, 4¾" | 150.00 |
| Bowl, 10¼", fruit | 115.00 | * Lamp, silver overlay | 350.00 |
| Bowl, 10½", rolled edge | 105.00 | Mayonnaise, 6" diameter, | |
| Bowl, 11" console | 105.00 | fits on 8" plate | 115.00 |
| Cake plate, 11¾" | 127.50 | Plate, 10½" | 85.00 |
| Cake stand, 2" high, ftd. | 130.00 | Samovar | 795.00 |
| Candlestick, 5" wide, pr. | 135.00 | Sugar, 4¼" ftd. | 80.00 |
| Candy w/lid, ftd., 5¼" high | 175.00 | Sugar, 5" ftd. | 80.00 |
| Candy w/lid, 3 part | 160.00 | Tray, 10¾" center-handled | 85.00 |
| Casserole, covered (black) silver overlay | 350.00 | Tray, 10⅞" oval-ftd. | 115.00 |
| Comport, 6¼" | 67.50 | Vase, 8¼" elliptical | 325.00 |
| Creamer, 4½" ftd. | 80.00 | Vase, fan-shaped | 200.00 |

* possibly German

**Please refer to Foreword for pricing information**

# DELLA ROBBIA #1058 WESTMORELAND GLASS COMPANY, LATE 1920's-1940's

Colors: Crystal w/ applied lustre colors, milk glass.

Della Robbia has been collected for years by a few people, but in the last five years it has grown in popularity to the point that I am now including it in my book. This listing is only a beginning from catalogue information that I own. Hopefully, you will let me know of additional pieces or of other catalogue information that I am now missing.

You will find Della Robbia in crystal, milk glass and crystal with applied lustre colors. Notice that the fruits on each piece are apples, pears and grapes. A similar pattern made by someone else has bananas in the design; do not confuse the patterns.

There are two different color variations in the fruit decorations. All the apples are red; pears, yellow; and grapes, purple; but the intensity of the colors applied is different. Look at the pictures on page 59 and compare them to the pieces at the bottom of page 60. The darker colored fruits shown are the pieces that are most in demand. One of the problems with this deeper color is that the applied lustre scratches off very easily. Supposedly there is no difference in these color varieties, but most collectors will not mix the two.

I have a collector in Kentucky that only wants the lighter color because it does not rub off easily. All the pieces on the bottom of page 60 are in that collection; she says that even though it is lighter to begin with, it does not scratch off with use. That collector had a chance to buy the pieces photographed on page 59 and turned them down because they did not match the rest of her set. That made several other collectors ecstatic when the pieces became available for sale.

For the listings, I should discuss some terminology of Westmoreland. Cupped means turned in from the outside as opposed to belled which is turned out from the inside. The flanged pieces have an edge that is parallel to the base of the piece.

The sweetmeat is the comport shown to the right rear of the bottom photograph on page 59. In the same picture is the 14" footed salver or cake plate. The indentation in the center must have made for interesting cakes. I guess they had bundt pans before I was aware of them! The two-part candy with the ruffled bottom is the one shown on the left in that same shot. Its catalogue description is "candy jar, scalloped edge, w/cover."

One collector said that punch cups are harder to find than the regular cups, but all the dealers who helped me price this pattern did not price the punch cups for more than the regular cups. That punch set is a beauty; but if you ever tried to pack an 18" plate, you will understand why you see so few of these for sale at shows.

The moulds of a Della Robbia pitcher and tumbler were used to make some carnival colored water sets. These were made for Levay just as were pieces of red English Hobnail. In any case, they were made in light blue and amethyst carnival and maybe another color. If you have more information than this, please let me know!

| | | | |
|---|---:|---|---:|
| Basket, 9" | 165.00 | Cup, punch | 15.00 |
| Basket, 12" | 225.00 | Pitcher, 32 oz. | 195.00 |
| Bowl, 4½", nappy | 27.50 | Plate, 6", finger liner | 10.00 |
| Bowl, 5", finger | 30.00 | Plate, 6⅛", bread & butter | 10.00 |
| Bowl, 6", nappy, bell | 32.50 | Plate, 7¼", salad | 20.00 |
| Bowl, 6½", one hdld. nappy | 27.50 | Plate, 9", luncheon | 30.00 |
| Bowl, 7½", nappy | 37.50 | Plate, 10½", dinner | 65.00 |
| Bowl, 8", bell nappy | 42.50 | Plate, 14", torte | 80.00 |
| Bowl, 8", bell, hdld. | 55.00 | Plate, 18" | 165.00 |
| Bowl, 8", heart, hdld. | 75.00 | Plate, 18", upturned edge, punch bowl liner | 165.00 |
| Bowl, 9", nappy | 65.00 | Platter, 14", oval | 125.00 |
| Bowl, 12", ftd. | 100.00 | Punch bowl set, 15 pc. | 550.00 |
| Bowl, 13", rolled edge | 95.00 | Salt and pepper, pr. | 50.00 |
| Bowl, 14", oval, flange | 145.00 | Salver, 14", ftd., cake | 125.00 |
| Bowl, 14", punch | 175.00 | Saucer | 10.00 |
| Bowl, 15", bell | 145.00 | Stem, 3 oz., wine | 22.00 |
| Candle, 4" | 27.50 | Stem, 3¼ oz., cocktail | 20.00 |
| Candle, 4", 2-lite | 65.00 | Stem, 5 oz., 4¾", sherbet, high foot | 22.50 |
| Candy jar w/cover, scalloped edge | 75.00 | Stem, 5 oz., sherbet, low foot | 18.00 |
| Candy, round, flat, chocolate | 65.00 | Stem, 6 oz., champagne | 25.00 |
| Comport, 6½", 3⅝" high, mint, ftd. | 25.00 | Stem, 8 oz., 6", water | 28.00 |
| Comport, 8", sweetmeat, bell | 95.00 | Sugar, ftd. | 15.00 |
| Comport, 12", ftd., bell | 110.00 | Tumbler, 5 oz., ginger ale | 25.00 |
| Comport, 13", flanged | 110.00 | Tumbler, 8 oz., ftd. | 27.50 |
| Creamer, ftd. | 15.00 | Tumbler, 8 oz., water | 20.00 |
| Cup, coffee | 17.50 | | |

*Westmoreland's Handmade,*
*Hand-Decorated Crystal*

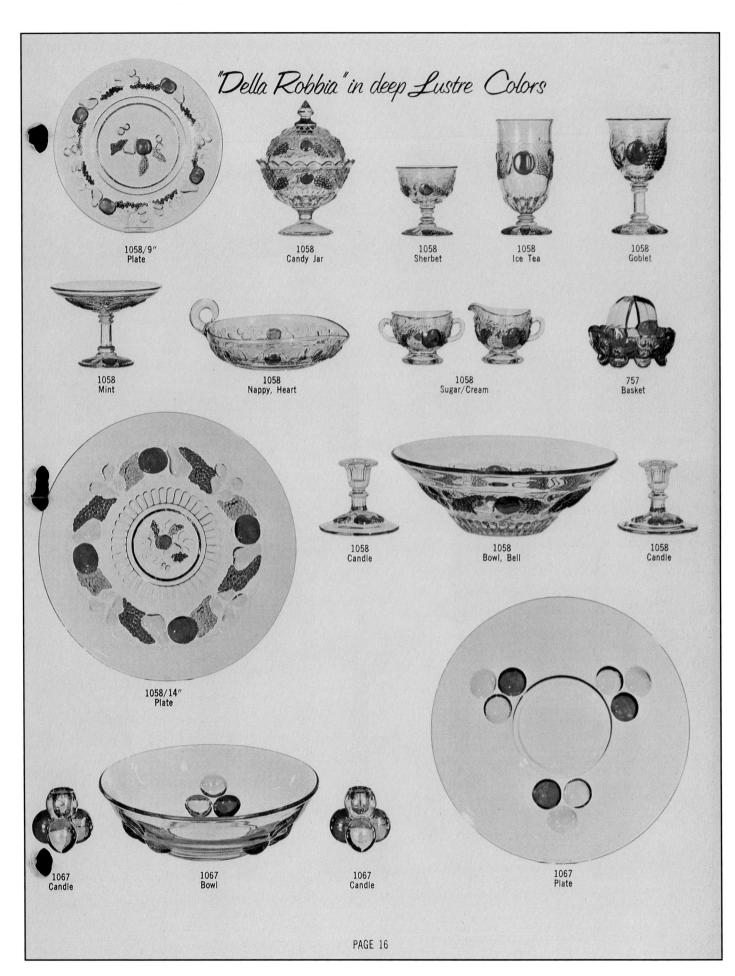

# "Della Robbia" in deep Lustre Colors

1058/9"
Plate

1058
Candy Jar

1058
Sherbet

1058
Ice Tea

1058
Goblet

1058
Mint

1058
Nappy, Heart

1058
Sugar/Cream

757
Basket

1058/14"
Plate

1058
Candle

1058
Bowl, Bell

1058
Candle

1067
Candle

1067
Bowl

1067
Candle

1067
Plate

# "Della Robbia" Pattern in Crystal with Applied Lustre Colors.

### "Della Robbia"

### "Zodiac" Plate

**TOP ROW:** 1058/9"/L126. Plate, Luncheon.
1058/7½"/L126. Plate, Salad.
1058/8 oz./L126. Goblet.
1058/11 oz./L126. Ice Tea, Footed.
1058/8 oz./L126. Tumbler, Footed.
1058/L126/3¼ oz. Cocktail.
1058/L126. Sherbet, Low Foot.

**SECOND ROW:** 1058/L126. Sugar and Cream

Set, Individual. "Della Robbia."
1058/L126. Salt, with Chrome Top.
1058/L126. Pepper, with Chrome Top.
1058/L126. Cup and Saucer.
1058/8 oz./L126. Tumbler.
1058/6½"/L126. Nappy, Cupped, Handled.

**THIRD ROW:** 1058/6½"/L126. Mint, Footed.
1058/4"/L126. Candlestick.

1058/12"/L126. Bowl, Bell.
1058/½ lb./L126. Candy Jar and Cover.
1058/4½"/L126. Nappy, Round.

**BOTTOM ROW:** 1058/14"/L126. Plate, Torte.
1058/8"/L126. Nappy, Heart Shape, Handled.
25/15"/L126. Plate, "Zodiac." Pictures the
twelve signs of the Zodiac. An attractive serving piece for sandwiches or canapes.

# DIAMOND QUILTED, "FLAT DIAMOND" IMPERIAL GLASS COMPANY, Late 1920's-Early 1930's

Colors: Pink, blue, green, crystal, black; some red and amber.

Pink and green Diamond Quilted are the only colors that can be collected in a large set. Unfortunately, there is no dinner plate unless you have teenagers who would be happy with the 14" sandwich plate as a standard sized eating plate. Lack of a dinner plate stops some collectors from further pursuing any pattern. I have always said that you should collect what you like to look at and don't let the missing dinner plate or whatever stop you from putting the rest of the set together.

I have tried to show you as much Diamond Quilted in colors besides pink and green this time. This will give you an idea of the other colors and items that are available for making a smaller set.

The candle shown in the catalogue ad at the bottom of the page is sometimes confused as Windsor Diamond. Console sets at 65¢ and a dozen candy dishes in assorted colors for $6.95 would be quite a bargain today. No, I do not have any for sale at that price. This ad is from a 1930's catalogue and not my store. I mention that since I get letters every year from people trying to order glass from these old catalogue ads placed throughout the book! They even send their Visa or MasterCard number and ask that I send several sets. Nobody ever orders just **one** set. It has to be multiples! One said she understood if I had to add postage. Considering the ad states the six sets weigh thirty pounds, she was being generous!

There is a Hazel Atlas quilted diamond pitcher and tumbler set made in pink, green, cobalt blue and a blue similar to the blue shown here that is confused with Imperial's Diamond Quilted. The quilting on Hazel Atlas pieces ends in a straight line around the top of each piece. Notice this *Imperial* Diamond Quilted pattern ends unevenly in points. You may also notice that the diamond designs on Diamond Quilted pieces are flat as opposed to those Imperial ones that are curved.

Diamond Quilted punch bowls are still **the** elusive part to this puzzle of collecting. I have not seen one at a show since both pink and green sets were in Chicago four years ago. I had never before seen both sets at the same show. As more and more of the harder to find pieces are disappearing into collections, there are fewer rare pieces being offered for sale. Until these collections are sold, those rarely found items are not seen again. Believe me, they're just becoming increasingly valuable as they remain in those collections, too!

Black pieces have the design on the bottom. Thus, the design on the plate can only be seen if it is turned over. A black creamer is shown satinized with painted flowers. It is the only piece I have seen with such treatment.

Blue is the color many people would like to collect, but there is very little of that color being found. Amber and red are found even less often.

| | Pink, Green | Blue, Black | | Pink, Green | Blue, Black |
|---|---|---|---|---|---|
| Bowl, 4¾" cream soup | 8.00 | 18.00 | Pitcher, 64 oz. | 47.50 | |
| Bowl, 5" cereal | 6.50 | 13.00 | Plate, 6" sherbet | 4.00 | 5.00 |
| Bowl, 5½" one handle | 6.50 | 16.00 | Plate, 7" salad | 6.00 | 9.00 |
| Bowl, 7" crimped edge | 7.00 | 16.00 | Plate, 8" luncheon | 6.00 | 12.00 |
| Bowl, 10½", rolled edge console | 18.00 | 53.00 | Punch bowl and stand | 400.00 | |
| Cake salver, tall 10" diameter | 52.00 | | Plate, 14" sandwich | 12.50 | |
| Candlesticks (2 styles), pr. | 22.50 | 47.50 | Sandwich server, center handle | 24.00 | 45.00 |
| Candy jar and cover, ftd. | 57.50 | | Saucer | 3.00 | 5.00 |
| Compote, 6" tall, 7¼" wide | 40.00 | | Sherbet | 5.00 | 14.00 |
| Compote and cover, 11½" | 67.50 | | Sugar | 8.00 | 15.00 |
| Creamer | 8.00 | 16.50 | Tumbler, 9 oz. water | 9.00 | |
| Cup | 9.50 | 15.00 | Tumbler, 12 oz. iced tea | 9.00 | |
| Goblet, 1 oz. cordial | 11.00 | | Tumbler, 6 oz. ftd. | 8.50 | |
| Goblet, 2 oz. wine | 11.00 | | Tumbler, 9 oz. ftd. | 12.50 | |
| Goblet, 3 oz. wine | 11.00 | | Tumbler, 12 oz. ftd. | 15.00 | |
| Goblet, 6", 9 oz. champagne | 10.00 | | Vase, fan, dolphin handles | 47.50 | 67.50 |
| Ice bucket | 45.00 | 83.00 | Whiskey, 1½ oz. | 8.00 | |
| Mayonnaise set: ladle, plate, comport | 36.00 | 56.00 | | | |

# DIANA FEDERAL GLASS COMPANY, 1937-1941

Colors: Pink, amber and crystal.

Almost all the activity in Diana has been in the color pink. A little amber and some crystal sell occasionally, but it is the pink that drives dealers crazy trying to keep it in stock.

Pink is still making some price jumps but not anything as drastic as from the Ninth to the Tenth editions. This was one of the used-to-be less expensive patterns! It is not as available as it once was and collectors have been paying through clenched teeth to finish sets that they have started. Of course that goes for many other Depression glass patterns as well. The prices listed below are **actual selling** prices and **not advertised prices.** There is a **major difference** between an advertised price for an item and the price actually accepted by both buyer and seller. Rarely have I heard of something selling for more than advertised, but often I've heard of less! Not only does my shop, Grannie Bear, sell a lot of glass, but dealers coast to coast are willing to share prices obtained on glassware with you and me. I thank them for that!

No, I do not use auction results either. Pieces at auctions rarely sell for realistic figures. Rare items will bring small prices if only one person knows it is rare. Common items will fetch astronomical prices if two people want it or two "bidders" try to keep each other from owning it. My personal feeling is that auction results are the **worst indicators of true prices.**

There are very few pink demitasse sets being found. These sets in crystal seem to be more plentiful (as well as the sprayed-on cranberry or red sets.) Flashed red sets are selling in the $10.00 to $12.00 range. So far, there is little demand for the frosted or satinized pieces that have shown up in crystal or pink. Some crystal frosted pieces have been trimmed in colors, predominantly red. Finding any of these specialty items is a problem unless you buy a whole set at one time.

Collectors of crystal Diana have found out what collectors of the other colors noticed years ago. There are very few tumblers available. Tumblers, candy dishes, shakers, sherbets and even platters are rarely being found in any of Diana's colors. Only pink has made the big price advances recently, but that could be a gauge that other colors are soon to adopt that upward swing.

New collectors often confuse Diana with other swirled patterns such as Swirl and Twisted Optic. The centers of Diana's pieces are swirled where the centers of the other patterns are plain. The elusive sherbet is shown in amber behind the sugar. The spirals on this sherbet are often mistaken for Spiral by Hocking. This is the only sherbet shown in original advertisements for this pattern.

| | Crystal | Pink | Amber |
|---|---|---|---|
| * Ash tray, 3½" | 2.50 | 3.50 | |
| Bowl, 5" cereal | 4.00 | 8.50 | 12.00 |
| Bowl, 5½" cream soup | 5.00 | 20.00 | 15.00 |
| Bowl, 9" salad | 6.00 | 19.00 | |
| Bowl, 11" console fruit | 5.50 | 35.00 | 15.00 |
| Bowl, 12" scalloped edge | 7.00 | 24.00 | 16.00 |
| Candy jar and cover, round | 15.00 | 35.00 | 32.00 |
| Coaster, 3½" | 2.50 | 7.00 | 10.00 |
| Creamer, oval | 3.50 | 11.00 | 9.00 |
| Cup | 3.00 | 12.00 | 7.00 |
| Cup, 2 oz. demitasse and 4½" saucer set | 13.00 | 45.00 | |
| Plate, 6" bread & butter | 1.50 | 4.00 | 2.00 |
| Plate, 9½" | 5.00 | 14.00 | 9.00 |
| Plate, 11¾" sandwich | 5.00 | 22.50 | 10.00 |
| Platter, 12" oval | 5.50 | 25.00 | 13.00 |
| Salt and pepper, pr. | 24.00 | 65.00 | 92.00 |
| Saucer | 1.50 | 5.00 | 2.00 |
| Sherbet | 3.00 | 11.00 | 9.00 |
| Sugar, open oval | 3.00 | 11.00 | 8.00 |
| Tumbler, 4⅛", 9 oz. | 22.00 | 42.00 | 26.00 |
| Junior set: 6 cups and saucers with round rack | 90.00 | 270.00 | |

* Green $3.00

**Please refer to Foreword for pricing information**

# DOGWOOD, "APPLE BLOSSOM," "WILD ROSE" MacBETH-EVANS GLASS COMPANY, 1929-1932

Colors: Pink, green, some crystal, Monax, Cremax and yellow.

Dogwood is continuing to sell in my shop as fast as I can find it. Green is catching up to pink in desirability, but it is in far shorter supply! I haven't owned a Dogwood pink large bowl or platter in three years. A set of green I purchased last year is gone except for the omnipresent 8" luncheon plates. There is still an adequate supply of pitchers and most sizes of tumblers in both colors. Only the pink juice tumbler is rarely found, but the price has gotten so high on that piece that few collectors are willing to buy more than one.

A few items in the top picture on page 69 need discussing. The four items on the left in front of the grill plate are all "go-with" items and not actually Dogwood. The champagne has a moulded dogwood-like design but was not made by MacBeth-Evans. This usually sells in the $12.00 to $15.00 range. The ash tray was packed with many MacBeth-Evans patterns and was once erroneously thought to be Royal Lace. This one has an advertisement for the glass company itself. I also have one of these in red, but it is so dark that we have not been able to show this design embossed on it with a photograph. The center handled mint tray is a Mt. Pleasant piece but has etched dogwood blossoms and these sell around $25.00 to Dogwood collectors desiring a new item. The little shot glass has the same shape as all the Dogwood tumblers, but is missing the Dogwood silk screening. It is **not** Dogwood without the design! The same goes for the larger tumblers like it. There are pitchers shaped like Dogwood that do not have the silk screen design of Dogwood. These are **not** Dogwood, but are the blanks made by MacBeth-Evans to go with the plain, no design tumblers (like the shot glass shown) they made. The pattern has to be silk screened onto the pitcher to be Dogwood and command those prices. Several collectors have bought these blanks to use with their sets, however; and that's perfectly fine.

Few pieces of yellow are being found, but there is not much demand for it either.

Cremax is another rare color of Dogwood that does not excite many collectors. You can see four pieces of Cremax in the top picture including the 8½" berry, 5½" cereal, cup and 6" plate. I have never found a saucer for the cup. The Monax salver (12" plate) shown in the center was once thought of as hard to find; but, over the years, it has turned out to be more of a novelty than rare. In fact, you can buy them today for less than you could fifteen years ago. I used to sell them in the $25.00 range, but have recently had a couple in my shop not sell at $15.00!

The pink sugar and creamer represent the thick footed style while the green creamer and sugar show the thin, flat style. Pink is found in both styles, but the green is only found in the thin variety. The thin creamers were made by adding a spout to the cups. Some of these thin creamers have a very undefined spout. Although there are thick and thin pink cups, the saucers for both style cups are the same.

Grill plates come in two styles. Some of these have the Dogwood pattern all over the plate as the pink one does, and others have the pattern only around the rim of the plate as on the green one. Sherbets, grill plates (rim pattern only), and the large fruit bowls are also difficult to amass in green Dogwood. Note the two distinct shades of glass on the green pitchers. I included both to show that color variations are a problem only if it bothers you!

Sherbets come in two styles. Some have a Dogwood blossom etched on the bottom; some do not. I have been told that this discrepancy drives mail order dealers to drink. Please be sure to specify which style you are trying to match if that is important to you. It really makes no difference in price since they are only from different moulds.

See the *Very Rare Glassware of the Depression Years, Second Series* for a picture of the only known Dogwood coaster!

| | Pink | Green | Monax Cremax | | Pink | Green | Monax Cremax |
|---|---|---|---|---|---|---|---|
| *Bowl, 5½" cereal | 25.00 | 25.00 | 5.00 | Plate, 9¼" dinner | 30.00 | | |
| Bowl, 8½" berry | 52.50 | 95.00 | 36.00 | Plate, 10½" grill AOP or | | | |
| Bowl, 10¼" fruit | 300.00 | 180.00 | 70.00 | border design only | 19.00 | 19.00 | |
| Cake plate, 11" heavy | | | | Plate, 12" salver | 25.00 | | 15.00 |
| solid foot | 500.00 | | | Platter, 12" oval (rare) | 395.00 | | |
| Cake plate, 13" heavy | | | | Saucer | 7.00 | 8.00 | 16.00 |
| solid foot | 85.00 | 80.00 | 160.00 | Sherbet, low footed | 30.00 | 90.00 | |
| Coaster, 3¼" | 455.00 | | | Sugar, 2½" thin, flat | 16.00 | 42.00 | |
| Creamer, 2½" thin, flat | 16.00 | 42.00 | | Sugar, 3¼" thick, footed | 16.00 | | |
| Creamer, 3¼" thick, footed | 19.00 | | | Tumbler, 3½", 5 oz. | | | |
| Cup, thick | 16.00 | | 36.00 | decorated | 255.00 | | |
| Cup, thin | 14.00 | 34.00 | | Tumbler, 4", 10 oz. decorated | 35.00 | 75.00 | |
| Pitcher, 8", 80 oz. decorated | 160.00 | 475.00 | | Tumbler, 4¾", 11 oz. | | | |
| Pitcher, 8", 80 oz. (American | | | | decorated | 40.00 | 85.00 | |
| Sweetheart Style) | 530.00 | | | Tumbler, 5", 12 oz. decorated | 50.00 | 95.00 | |
| Plate, 6" bread and butter | 8.00 | 9.00 | 21.00 | Tumbler, moulded band | 20.00 | | |
| * Plate, 8" luncheon | 7.00 | 8.00 | | | | | |

*Yellow - $55.00

# DORIC JEANNETTE GLASS COMPANY, 1935-1938

Colors: Pink, green, some Delphite and yellow.

Green Doric is more scarce, but has fewer collectors than pink. Green Doric collecting is a challenge. It probably will not break you at one time since you will need years to complete a large set unless you get extremely lucky! Prices for green continue to out distance the pink, but the pink is gradually catching up on some items. Doric pitchers, especially the footed ones, cereal and cream soup bowls, and tumblers have all become key pieces to own in Doric.

The major problem for Doric collectors is the mould seams on many pieces; it is a particular problem on the footed tumblers and cereals. This hinders some collectors who are searching for perfection. Some collectors have not seen either piece! In other words, don't let a little roughness keep you from owning these if you see them for sale! Perfection is desirable in glass collecting, but it can be carried to extremes. Carrying a magnifying glass to a coin or stamp show may be considered normal behavior; but in a glass show, it is not the norm – although I have seen it done!

Spending time in Florida, I have noticed more green Doric there than any place I have travelled. One of the major difficulties in buying glass in Florida is cloudy glass. Evidently, well water creates cloudy deposits on the glass. Nothing will remove this; you could make a fortune if you could figure out a way to easily remove these deposits. In any case, most of the Doric tumblers I've seen in Florida are cloudy or "sick" as most dealers call this condition. Don't get duped into buying cloudy glass unless it is very inexpensive or you have the magic cure!

The yellow pitcher in the bottom photo is still the only one known. Pay attention to its price! Speaking of Doric pitchers, the large footed ones come with or without an ice lip as shown in the pink. All Doric footed pitchers are difficult to find, with the green nearly impossible. Candy and sugar lids in this pattern are not interchangeable. The candy lid is taller and more domed.

I still get a lot of letters about rare Delphite (opaque blue) pieces. Actually, the sherbet and the cloverleaf candy are common in Delphite. All other Delphite pieces are rare in Doric; however, there are few collectors; thus the price is still reasonable for so rare a color.

The three-part candy can be found in a metal holder. One of these is shown in earlier editions.

An iridized, three-part candy was made in the 1970's and sold for 79 cents in our local dish barn. All other colors of the three-part candy are old.

Lids shown on the pink shakers are original nickel plated tops; those on the green are newly made aluminum tops. Original lids are preferable when available, but there are options to having no lids at all.

| | Pink | Green | Delphite | | Pink | Green | Delphite |
|---|---|---|---|---|---|---|---|
| Bowl, 4½" berry | 7.00 | 8.00 | 36.00 | Plate, 6" sherbet | 4.00 | 5.00 | |
| Bowl, 5" cream soup | | 310.00 | | Plate, 7" salad | 16.00 | 17.00 | |
| Bowl, 5½" cereal | 42.00 | 58.00 | | Plate, 9" dinner | | | |
| Bowl, 8¼" large berry | 14.00 | 17.00 | 110.00 | (serrated 100.00) | 11.00 | 15.00 | |
| Bowl, 9" 2-handled | 15.00 | 15.00 | | Plate, 9" grill | 12.50 | 16.00 | |
| Bowl, 9" oval vegetable | 25.00 | 30.00 | | Platter, 12" oval | 20.00 | 22.00 | |
| Butter dish and cover | 65.00 | 80.00 | | Relish tray, 4" x 4" | 9.50 | 8.50 | |
| Butter dish bottom | 22.50 | 30.00 | | Relish tray, 4" x 8" | 11.00 | 15.00 | |
| Butter dish top | 42.50 | 50.00 | | Salt and pepper, pr. | 32.50 | 35.00 | |
| Cake plate, 10", 3 legs | 21.00 | 21.00 | | Saucer | 3.50 | 4.50 | |
| Candy dish and | | | | Sherbet, footed | 11.00 | 13.00 | 5.00 |
| cover, 8" | 32.00 | 35.00 | | Sugar | 11.00 | 12.00 | |
| * Candy dish, 3-part | 5.50 | 6.50 | 5.00 | Sugar cover | 12.50 | 20.00 | |
| Coaster, 3" | 16.00 | 16.00 | | Tray, 10" handled | 12.50 | 15.00 | |
| Creamer, 4" | 11.00 | 12.00 | | Tray, 8" x 8" serving | 18.00 | 20.00 | |
| Cup | 8.00 | 9.00 | | Tumbler, 4½", 9 oz. | 60.00 | 90.00 | |
| Pitcher, 5½", 32 oz. flat | 32.00 | 37.00 | 950.00 | Tumbler, 4", 10 oz. | | | |
| Pitcher, 7½", 48 oz. | | | | footed | 55.00 | 80.00 | |
| footed | 410.00 | 755.00 | | Tumbler, 5", 12 oz., | | | |
| (Also in yellow | | | | footed | 67.50 | 97.50 | |
| at $1,800.00) | | | | | | | |

*Candy in metal holder - $40.00. Iridescent made recently. Ultramarine $15.00.

**Please refer to Foreword for pricing information**

# DORIC AND PANSY JEANNETTE GLASS COMPANY, 1937-1938

Colors: Ultramarine; some crystal and pink.

Discoveries of large quantities of Doric and Pansy continue to be made in Canada and England! No wonder we always thought Doric and Pansy was rare. It is in the continental United States, but not so outside these boundaries! I have now heard of at least twenty-five butter dishes found in England in the last seven years. Those are just the ones that I have heard about and I am sure there are others. The price on the butter dish has continued to slide with so many butters now on the market.

Watch out for weak patterned shakers. These should fetch less (20 or 25 percent) than the price listed. If the only way you can tell that the shaker is Doric and Pansy comes from color and shape instead of pattern, then leave it alone. Sugars and creamers are also being found along with those butter dishes; however, their price has not been as dramatically affected since they were not so highly priced as the butters. Tumblers and large and small berry bowls are not being found as often in the accumulations abroad. The tumbler pictured is rarely found. At one time there were two of these. The one shown here has been glued together due to a helper stepping in a hole as we were loading my van **after** the photography session. At least it was not before it had been photographed! There have also been no reported findings of the children's sets in England or Canada!

The other major problem facing collectors of ultramarine Doric and Pansy is color variation. Many pieces have a distinct green cast instead of blue. Few collectors buy the green shade of ultramarine. Unless you are able to buy the greener hue as a large lot, you may have trouble if you ever resell it. However, there is the plus side to this greener shade if you like it. Oft times you can purchase it at a bargain price! Who knows, with tastes in colors changing, that shade may ultimately be the one to own!

Only berry and children's sets have been found in pink. Crystal creamer and sugar sets can be found, but have few collectors. These sets are usually purchased by collectors of sugar and creamers rather than Doric and Pansy collectors.

| | Green, Teal | Pink, Crystal | | Green, Teal | Pink, Crystal |
|---|---|---|---|---|---|
| Bowl, 4½" berry | 15.00 | 8.00 | Plate, 6" sherbet | 10.00 | 7.50 |
| Bowl, 8" large berry | 72.50 | 20.00 | Plate, 7" salad | 32.50 | |
| Bowl, 9" handled | 30.00 | 14.00 | Plate, 9" dinner | 27.50 | 7.50 |
| Butter dish and cover | 465.00 | | Salt and pepper, pr. | 375.00 | |
| Butter dish bottom | 80.00 | | Saucer | 6.00 | 4.00 |
| Butter dish top | 385.00 | | Sugar, open | 110.00 | 65.00 |
| Cup | 17.50 | 9.00 | Tray, 10" handled | 22.50 | |
| Creamer | 115.00 | 70.00 | Tumbler, 4½", 9 oz. | 70.00 | |

## DORIC AND PANSY
## "PRETTY POLLY PARTY DISHES"

| | Teal | Pink | | Teal | Pink |
|---|---|---|---|---|---|
| Cup | 40.00 | 30.00 | Creamer | 40.00 | 30.00 |
| Saucer | 8.00 | 7.00 | Sugar | 40.00 | 30.00 |
| Plate | 10.00 | 8.00 | 14-Piece set | 315.00 | 240.00 |

**Please refer to Foreword for pricing information**

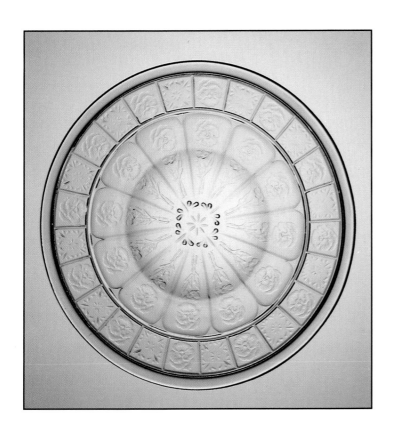

# ENGLISH HOBNAIL WESTMORELAND GLASS COMPANY, 1920's-1940's

Colors: Pink, ice blue, turquoise blue, cobalt blue, green and red.

For the purpose of breaking up English Hobnail into time periods that it best fits, I have placed crystal and amber into the *Collectible Glassware of the 40's, 50's, 60's...* and am including the other colors in this book. It may take some time to iron out all the pieces that exist in the colors, but this is a start to making it easier to identify each item. There are several pages of catalogue listings in the *Collectible Glassware of the 40's, 50's, 60's...;* refer to that for identification. I am trying to eliminate duplication; since the catalogue pages are from the later years of Westmoreland's production when only amber and crystal were being run, they were included in the later book.

For now, I will only list two columns of prices. Pink and green will make up one column and blue will make up the other. A piece in cobalt blue will be twenty-five to thirty percent more than the price listed; since few pieces were made in cobalt, a separate column would take up valuable space in the listings.

Collecting a complete set of English Hobnail in any color is difficult. This, too, is a pattern that has many color variances. Pink is the easiest color to find, but there are two distinct shades of pink. There are three different greens, from a light yellow green to a deep, dark green. Many collectors mix shades of color, but others cannot abide mixing them. That only becomes a problem when you have searched for eons for a particular piece, you find it, and the color shading is wrong.

The demise of Westmoreland has spurred many new collectors of blue, pink and green English Hobnail.

Cobalt blue pieces of English Hobnail are found very rarely. Turquoise blue has more collectors than the cobalt because so many more pieces can be found in that shade of blue. I had the privilege of viewing a large collection of turquoise English Hobnail being sold at a show I attended. En masse, it was exquisite and attracted a large crowd of "ahs" and "ohs" from the passersby. The turquoise blue vase is particularly nice as an accessory piece.

For beginning collectors, I offer the following observations to distinguish English Hobnail from Miss America. The centers of English Hobnail pieces have centered rays of varying distances. Notice the upright pieces in the photographs for this six point star effect. In Miss America, shown on page 129, the center rays all end at an equidistance from the center. The hobs on English Hobnail are more rounded and "feel" smoother to the touch; goblets flare and the hobs go directly into a plain rim area. On Miss America the hobs are sharper to touch and the goblets do not flair at the rim; both goblets and tumblers of Miss America have three sets of rings above the hobs before entering a plain glass rim.

| | Pink/Green | *Ice Blue | | Pink/Green | *Ice Blue |
|---|---|---|---|---|---|
| Ash tray, 3" | 15.00 | | Bowl, 6½", grapefruit | 18.00 | |
| Ash tray, 4½" | | 21.00 | Bowl, 6½", round nappy | 18.00 | |
| Ash tray, 4½", sq. | 22.50 | | Bowl, 7", round nappy | 20.00 | |
| Bon bon, 6½", hdld. | 25.00 | 35.00 | Bowl, 8", cupped, nappy | 30.00 | |
| Bottle, toilet, 5 oz. | 22.50 | 45.00 | Bowl, 8", ftd. | 45.00 | |
| Bowl, 3", cranberry | 15.00 | | Bowl, 8", hexagonal ftd., 2-hdld. | 65.00 | 100.00 |
| Bowl, 4", rose | 45.00 | | Bowl, 8", pickle | 27.50 | |
| Bowl, 4½", finger | 15.00 | | Bowl, 8", round nappy | 32.50 | |
| Bowl, 4½", round nappy | 13.00 | 27.50 | Bowl, 9", celery | 30.00 | |
| Bowl, 4½", sq. ftd., finger | 15.00 | 35.00 | Bowl, 10", flared | 37.50 | |
| Bowl, 5", round nappy | 15.00 | 32.50 | Bowl, 11", rolled edge | 37.50 | 75.00 |
| Bowl, 6", crimped dish | 17.50 | | Bowl, 12", celery | 32.50 | |
| Bowl, 6", round nappy | 1600 | | Bowl, 12", flange or console | 37.50 | |
| Bowl, 6", square nappy | 16.00 | | Candlestick, 3½", rd. base | 17.50 | 30.00 |

*Cobalt blue - twenty-five to thirty percent higher

| | Pink/Green | *Ice Blue | | Pink/Green | *Ice Blue |
|---|---|---|---|---|---|
| Candlestick, 9", rd. base | 32.50 | | Plate, 8", rd. | 12.50 | |
| Candy dish, 3 ftd. | 45.00 | | Plate, 8½", rd. | 12.50 | 25.00 |
| Candy, ½ lb. and cover, cone shaped | 37.50 | 75.00 | Plate, 10", rd. | 32.50 | 65.00 |
| Cigarette box and cover, 4½"x2½" | 27.50 | 45.00 | Plate, 14", rd., torte | 37.50 | |
| Cigarette jar w/cover, rd. | 22.50 | 50.00 | Puff box, w/ cover, 6", rd. | 27.50 | 77.50 |
| Compote, 5", round, rd. ftd. | 25.00 | | Saucer, demitasse, rd. | 15.00 | |
| Compote, 6", honey, rd. ftd. | 30.00 | | Saucer, rd. | 4.00 | 5.00 |
| Compote, 8", ball stem, sweetmeat | 55.00 | | Shaker, pr., rd. ftd. | 77.50 | |
| Creamer, hexagonal, ftd. | 22.50 | 45.00 | Stem, 2 oz., sq. ftd., wine | 30.00 | 60.00 |
| Creamer, sq. ftd. | 42.50 | | Stem, 3 oz., rd. ftd., cocktail | 20.00 | 35.00 |
| Cup | 18.00 | 20.00 | Stem, 5 oz., sq. ftd., oyster cocktail | 16.00 | |
| Cup, demitasse | 45.00 | | Stem, 8 oz., sq. ftd., water goblet | 30.00 | 50.00 |
| Ice tub, 4" | 47.50 | | Stem, sherbet, rd. low foot | | 12.00 |
| Ice tub, 5½" | 65.00 | 100.00 | Stem, sherbet, sq. ftd., low | 12.00 | |
| Lamp, 6¼", electric | 50.00 | | Stem, sherbet, rd. high foot | 1500 | |
| Lamp, 9¼", electric | 110.00 | | Stem, sherbet, sq. ftd., high | 15.00 | 35.00 |
| Marmalade w/cover | 35.00 | 55.00 | Sugar, hexagonal, ftd. | 22.50 | 45.00 |
| Mayonnaise, 6" | 20.00 | | Sugar, sq. ftd. | 45.00 | |
| Nut, individual, ftd. | 12.00 | | Tid-bit, 2 tier | 42.50 | 65.00 |
| Pitcher, 23 oz., rounded | 145.00 | | Tumbler, 5 oz., ginger ale | 18.00 | |
| Pitcher, 32 oz., straight side | 150.00 | | Tumbler, 8 oz., water | 22.00 | |
| Pitcher, 38 oz., rounded | 190.00 | | Tumbler, 10 oz., ice tea | 25.00 | |
| Pitcher, 60 oz., rounded | 265.00 | | Tumbler, 12 oz., ice tea | 27.50 | |
| Pitcher, 64 oz., straight side | 275.00 | | Urn, 11", w/cover (15") | 295.00 | |
| Plate, 5½", rd. | 9.50 | | Vase, 7½", flip | 65.00 | |
| Plate, 6", sq. finger bowl liner | 9.00 | | Vase, 7½", flip jar w/cover | 85.00 | |
| Plate, 6½", rd. | 10.00 | | Vase, 8½", flared top | 115.00 | 200.00 |
| Plate, 6½, rd. finger bowl liner | 9.50 | | Vase, 10" (straw jar) | 85.00 | |

*Cobalt blue - twenty-five to thirty percent higher

# FIRE-KING DINNERWARE "PHILBE" HOCKING GLASS COMPANY, 1937-1938

Colors: Blue, green, pink and crystal.

Finally, another cup in Fire-King Dinnerware has been found. Although this cup was crystal, there is cause for joy since the only other cup ever found was the blue pictured in the top photograph on page 79. That blue cup and saucer set was found in Washington Court House, Ohio, along with several other pieces in the middle 1970's. It has been a long dry spell between discoveries! I'll be able to show you that cup in the next edition since it has already been captured on film thanks to a Michigan collector (who now has my crystal saucer/sherbet plate to complete his set).

This pattern is one that few collectors have in their accumulations. Those collectors who try to have one piece of every pattern in my book, find that Fire-King Dinnerware is usually one of the very last examples they find. You can see additional pieces pictured in my *Very Rare Glassware of the Depression Years, Second Series* including the blue candy dish, tall water goblet and green cookie jar. The green cookie is the one I first owned in the early 1970's. I also bought it in Washington Court House, Ohio, for $10.00 and sold it for $10.00 to a friend who was "collecting" this pattern. She was "collecting" for a few months, that is, until she sold it for $300.00 to a collector in California! After all these years I was finally able to repurchase that cookie jar in January, 1991. Of course, it had been through a couple of dealers' inventories and the price was a lot more than the $10.00 I had paid for it originally. It is now in a large glass collection in Oregon!

The blue is very similar to Mayfair's blue. Many pieces have an added platinum trim as can be seen in the photograph. I have never seen blue Mayfair trimmed in platinum in all my travels. This seems strange since this pattern seems to have been a contemporary of Mayfair.

On my first trip to Anchor Hocking in June 1972, there was a large set of this glassware in a window display in the showroom. Until then, all I knew was that it had the same shape as Cameo and the color of blue Mayfair. I discovered that the footed tumblers and the goblet even had the Mayfair shape. Only once did I ever see several pieces for sale at one time and they are all shown here in the photograph of the blue. All of the platinum banded blue pieces, except the pitcher, turned up in 1975 at the flea market mentioned above.

Many of the pieces shown here are the only ones ever found. Of the four pitchers shown on the right, only one other pink juice and a blue water without platinum band have been found. The usually found blue items include footed tumblers of which the tea is more easily found than the water.

Oval vegetable bowls are the only commonly found piece of pink although that bowl is also common in green and crystal. Green grill plates or luncheon plates might end up in your collection with more ease than anything else in "Philbe." For once, even the 6" saucer/sherbet plates in any color are rarer than these plates.

| | Crystal | Pink, Green | Blue | | Crystal | Pink, Green | Blue |
|---|---|---|---|---|---|---|---|
| Bowl, 5½" cereal | 18.00 | 37.50 | 50.00 | Plate, 10½" salver | 22.50 | 50.00 | 70.00 |
| Bowl, 7¼" salad | 26.00 | 47.50 | 70.00 | Plate, 10½" grill | 22.50 | 42.50 | 60.00 |
| Bowl, 10" oval vegetable | 45.00 | 75.00 | 150.00 | Plate, 11⅝" salver | 22.50 | 62.50 | 95.00 |
| Candy jar, 4" low, with cover | 215.00 | 725.00 | 795.00 | Platter, 12" closed handles | 30.00 | 105.00 | 150.00 |
| Cookie jar with cover | 520.00 | 915.00 | 1,500.00 | Saucer, 6" (same as sherbet plate) | 30.00 | 55.00 | 75.00 |
| Creamer, 3¼" ftd. | 37.50 | 110.00 | 130.00 | Sugar, 3¼" ftd. | 40.00 | 110.00 | 130.00 |
| Cup | 55.00 | 110.00 | 140.00 | Tumbler, 4", 9 oz. flat water | 35.00 | 105.00 | 130.00 |
| Goblet, 7¼", 9 oz. thin | 65.00 | 165.00 | 195.00 | Tumbler, 3½" ftd. juice | 35.00 | 150.00 | 175.00 |
| Pitcher, 6", 36 oz. juice | 275.00 | 615.00 | 875.00 | Tumbler, 5¼", 10 oz. ftd. | 27.50 | 67.50 | 85.00 |
| Pitcher, 8½", 56 oz. | 365.00 | 895.00 | 1,125.00 | Tumbler, 6½", 15 oz. ftd. iced tea | 35.00 | 70.00 | 70.00 |
| Plate, 6" sherbet | 30.00 | 55.00 | 75.00 | | | | |
| Plate, 8" luncheon | 20.00 | 37.50 | 47.50 | | | | |
| Plate, 10" heavy sandwich | 22.50 | 62.50 | 95.00 | | | | |

# FLORAL, "POINSETTIA" JEANNETTE GLASS COMPANY, 1931-1935

Colors: Pink, green, Delphite, Jadite, crystal, amber, red and yellow.

Floral's small sized **reproduction shakers** are now being found in pink, cobalt blue and a very dark green color. Cobalt blue and the dark green Floral shakers are of little concern since they were originally never made in these colors. The green is darker than the original green shown here but not as deep a color as Forest Green. The new pink shakers, however, are not only a very good pink, but they are also a fairly good copy! There are many minor variations in design and leaf detail to someone who knows glassware well, but I have always tried to pick out a point that anyone can use to determine validity whether he be a novice or professional. There is one easy way to tell the Floral reproductions. Take off the top and look at the threads where the lid screws onto the shaker. On the old there are a **pair of parallel threads** on each side or at least a pair on one side that end right before the mould seams down each side. The new Floral has **one continuous line** thread that starts on one side and continues around the shaker until it ends above the beginning line on the other side. There is approximately one inch of overlapped thread making two lines for that inch; but the whole thread is **one continuous line** and not two separate ones as on the old. No other Floral reproductions have been made as of May 1993.

Rose bowls, and vases in all sizes have been found in England; so if you vacation in Europe, remember to try England for Depression glass. Also, I frequently visit the English furniture importer's shops since you can never tell what they will have shipped over here.

Floral lemonade pitchers are still being found in the Northwest, but not in the number of previous years. Pink lemonade pitchers substantially outnumber the green. There are more collectors for green than pink; so those factors cause the price differences in these colors.

Floral is one of Jeannette's patterns in which the sugar and candy lids **are** interchangeable.

There are two distinct varieties of pink Floral platters. One has a normal flat edge as shown in the back right of the top photo; the other has a scalloped edge like the platter in Cherry Blossom.

For new collectors I might point out a couple of items in the pink picture atop page 81. The 9" comport is the piece right in the center and the ice tub is the oval, tab handled piece on its immediate right. For a description of the lamp shown in the bottom photograph, be sure to read about a similarly made lamp under Adam on page 6.

Unusual Floral green pieces continue to be found in England and Canada. As with Doric and Pansy, it is the more unusual and previously thought to be rare pieces that are being found. They **were** rare in our country until collectors in Canada discovered Depression glass and started digging in the nooks and crannies up there. Many Canadians have ancestry in England who continued the search over there. The green Floral, flat bottomed pitchers and flat bottomed tumblers are continuing to be found and the prices are moderating because of these many discoveries. Floral found in Canada and England is usually a slightly lighter green color, and flat pieces all have ground bottoms which may mean that this was an early production of this pattern. This Floral is also paneled to the extent that it stands out from normally found Floral. I just purchased a green cup with a ground bottom and saucer. The saucer is the normally found one; but the cup, which is slightly ftd., will not fit this saucer's indentation! You can see this style cup in the foreground at the top of page 83!

Unusual items in Floral (so far) include the following:
   a)  an entire set of **Delphite**
   b)  a **yellow** two-part relish dish
   c)  **amber** and **red** plate, cup and saucer
   d)  green and crystal juice pitchers w/ground flat bottoms (shown)
   e)  ftd. vases in green and crystal, flared at the rim (shown); some hold **flower frogs with the Floral pattern on the frogs (**shown)
   f)  a crystal lemonade pitcher
   g)  lamps (shown in green and pink)
   h)  a green **grill** plate
   i)  an octagonal vase with patterned, octagonal foot (shown)
   j)  a **ruffled edge** berry and master berry bowl
   k)  pink and green Floral **ice tubs** (shown)
   l)  oval vegetable with cover
   m)  **rose bowl** and **three ftd. vase** (shown)
   n)  two styles of **9" comports** in pink and green
   o)  9 oz. flat tumblers in green (shown)
   p)  3 oz. ftd. tumblers in green (shown)
   q)  8" round bowl in **beige** and **opaque red**
   r)  **caramel** colored dinner plate
   s)  **cream soups** (shown in pink)
   t)  **beige** creamer and sugar
   u)  green **dresser set** (shown)
   v)  **beige**, 8½" bowl (like Cherry Blossom)

| | Pink | Green | Delphite | Jadite |
|---|---|---|---|---|
| Bowl, 4" berry (ruffled $65.00) | 15.00 | 16.00 | 32.50 | |
| Bowl, 5½" cream soup | 700.00 | 700.00 | | |
| *Bowl, 7½" salad (ruffled $125.00) | 15.00 | 16.00 | 50.00 | |
| Bowl, 8" covered vegetable | 35.00 | 42.50 | 75.00 (no cover) | |
| Bowl, 9" oval vegetable | 16.00 | 17.00 | | |
| Butter dish and cover | 80.00 | 85.00 | | |
| Butter dish bottom | 22.50 | 25.00 | | |
| Butter dish top | 57.50 | 60.00 | | |
| Canister set: coffee, tea, cereal sugar, 5¼" tall, each | | | | 45.00 |
| Candlesticks, 4" pr. | 67.50 | 77.50 | | |
| Candy jar and cover | 32.50 | 37.50 | | |
| Creamer, flat (Cremax $160.00) | 12.50 | 13.50 | 72.50 | |
| Coaster, 3¼" | 14.00 | 9.50 | | |
| Comport, 9" | 750.00 | 850.00 | | |
| ***Cup | 11.00 | 12.00 | | |
| Dresser set | | 1,050.00 | | |
| Frog for vase (also crystal $500.00) | | 650.00 | | |
| Ice tub, 3½" high oval | 800.00 | 850.00 | | |
| Lamp | 235.00 | 255.00 | | |
| Pitcher, 5½", 23 or 24 oz. | | 495.00 | | |
| Pitcher, 8", 32 oz. ftd. cone | 32.50 | 35.00 | | |
| Pitcher, 10¼", 48 oz. lemonade | 210.00 | 230.00 | | |
| Plate, 6" sherbet | 6.00 | 7.50 | | |
| Plate, 8" salad | 10.00 | 11.00 | | |
| **Plate, 9" dinner | 15.00 | 17.00 | 125.00 | |
| Plate, 9" grill | | 160.00 | | |
| Platter, 10¾" oval | 15.00 | 17.00 | 135.00 | |
| Platter, 11" (like Cherry Blossom) | 65.00 | | | |
| Refrigerator dish and cover, 5" square | | 60.00 | | 20.00 |
| ***Relish dish, 2-part oval | 15.00 | 16.00 | 150.00 | |
| ****Salt and pepper, 4" ftd. pair | 42.50 | 50.00 | | |
| Salt and pepper, 6" flat | 45.00 | | | |
| ***Saucer | 10.00 | 11.00 | | |
| Sherbet | 15.00 | 17.00 | 80.00 | |
| Sugar (Cremax $160.00) | 8.50 | 10.00 | 72.50 (open) | |
| Sugar/candy cover | 15.00 | 17.50 | | |
| Tray, 6" square, closed handles | 15.00 | 17.00 | | |
| Tray, 9¼", oval for dresser set | | 165.00 | | |
| Tumbler, 3½", 3 oz. ftd. | | 150.00 | | |
| Tumbler, 4", 5 oz. ftd. juice | 16.50 | 20.00 | | |
| Tumbler, 4½", 9 oz. flat | | 165.00 | | |
| Tumbler, 4¾", 7 oz. ftd. water | 17.50 | 20.00 | 175.00 | |
| Tumbler, 5¼", 9 oz. ftd. femonade | 42.50 | 45.00 | | |
| Vase, 3 legged rose bowl | | 475.00 | | |
| Vase, 3 legged flared (also in crystal) | | 450.00 | | |
| Vase, 6⅞" tall (8 sided) | | 425.00 | | |

*Cremax $125.00
**These have now been found in amber and red.
***This has been found in yellow.
****Beware reproductions!

**Please refer to Foreword for pricing information**

# FLORAL AND DIAMOND BAND U.S. GLASS COMPANY, Late 1920's

Colors: Pink, green; some iridescent, black and crystal.

Pink Floral and Diamond luncheon plates and sugar lids or iced tea tumblers (in both pink and green) are difficult to discover. Many Floral and Diamond butter bottoms have been borrowed to be used on other U.S. Glass patterns such as Strawberry and Cherryberry. This has transpired because all U.S. Glass butter bottoms are plain. They are all interchangeable since the patterns are found on the top only. Floral and Diamond butter dishes used to be very inexpensively priced in comparison to Strawberry and Cherryberry; so, collectors bought Floral and Diamond butter dishes to use the bottoms for those more expensive patterns. These past collecting practices have now created a shortage of butter bottoms in Floral and Diamond.

As you can see by the 1928 ads below, at times this pattern was described as "Floral and Diamond" and sometimes as "Diamond and Floral." Please! You can not order these items shown in the advertisement below from my shop. They were the prices for this pattern in 1928. I was astounded to know how many people think they can still order at these prices!

A collecting problem with all U.S. Glass patterns is the various shades of green. Some of the green is blue tinted. It is up to you to decide how serious you are about color matching. An additional fact that new collectors need to be aware of is mould roughness along the seams of pieces in this pattern. This is "normal" for Floral and Diamond and not considered a detriment by long time collectors who have come to accept **some** roughness.

Iridescent Floral and Diamond pitchers with excellent iridized color bring higher prices from "Carnival" glass collectors as a pattern called "Mayflower" than they do with Depression glass collectors. Dealers who sell both Depression and Carnival glass have been buying these pitchers at Depression glass shows and reselling them at "Carnival" glass conventions and auctions. Sometimes glassware that fits into two different categories, as does Floral and Diamond, receives more respect from one group of collectors than it does the other. It happens all the time. Prices for toys "Made in Occupied Japan" sell for higher prices to toy collectors than to collectors of "Occupied Japan" or "advertising" collectors will pay more for one ad out of a magazine than a magazine collector will pay for the whole magazine. There are many different markets available and each has its own idiosyncrasies.

Only the small creamer and sugar have been found in black. These sugars and creamers are often found with a cut flower over the top of the normally found moulded flower.

The crystal pitcher and butter dishes are rare! Notice the crystal pitcher on the right in the bottom photograph. It is yellow in appearance which is a problem in collecting crystal. You will have to take that into consideration if you search for crystal.

|  | Pink | Green |  | Pink | Green |
|---|---|---|---|---|---|
| Bowl, 4½" berry | 7.50 | 8.50 | Sherbet | 6.50 | 7.50 |
| Bowl, 5¾" handled nappy | 11.00 | 11.00 | Sugar, small | 9.50 | 11.00 |
| Bowl, 8" large berry | 12.50 | 13.50 | Sugar, 5¼" | 14.00 | 14.00 |
| * Butter dish and cover | 130.00 | 120.00 | Sugar lid | 47.50 | 57.50 |
| Butter dish bottom | 85.00 | 92.50 | Tumbler, 4" water | 18.00 | 22.00 |
| Butter dish top | 45.00 | 27.50 | Tumbler, 5" iced tea | 30.00 | 35.00 |
| Compote, 5½" tall | 15.00 | 16.00 |  |  |  |
| Creamer, small | 10.00 | 11.00 |  |  |  |
| Creamer, 4¾" | 17.50 | 19.00 |  |  |  |
| * Pitcher, 8", 42 oz. | 85.00 | 90.00 |  |  |  |
| Plate, 8" luncheon | 35.00 | 35.00 |  |  |  |

* Iridescent - $250.00; Crystal - $100.00

**Seven-Piece Berry Set**
You'll really be most satisfied with the purchase of this set. It's very attractive, and affords a fitting and stylish addition to your present pieces. In green pressed glass, with diamond and floral design. Large bowl, 8 inches in diameter, and six sauce dishes to match, 4½ inches in diameter.
**35N6838**—Weight, packed, 7 pounds. Per set......**68c**

**Seven-Piece** **Water Set**
Made from green pressed glass, with a floral and diamond design. You'll find that the sparkling scintillating pitcher and glasses are a set you'll be mighty proud to own when serving cold drinks. 3-pint pitcher. Six 8-ounce tumblers.
**35N6837**—Weight, packed, 12 pounds. Per set. **$1.18**

# FLORENTINE NO. 1, "OLD FLORENTINE," "POPPY NO. 1"
## HAZEL ATLAS GLASS COMPANY, 1932-1935

Colors: Pink, green, crystal, yellow and cobalt blue.

One of the most confusing things for new collectors is learning the difference between Florentine No. 1 and No. 2. It is simple. Notice the outlines of the pieces standing in the back of the photographs. The scalloped edges occur on all flat pieces of Florentine No. 1. All footed pieces (such as tumblers, shakers or pitchers) have the serrated edge. In Florentine No. 2 all pieces have a plain edge. Florentine No. 1 was once advertised as hexagonal and Florentine No. 2, was once advertised as round. This should also help you to remember the differences.

Pink is the hardest color to acquire. The footed tumblers, covered oval vegetable bowl and ruffled creamer and sugar are almost unavailable at any price to collectors of pink. Sets can be collected in green, crystal or yellow with much work. Serrated edges are easily damaged; that is the first place you should look when you pick up a piece to examine.

The 48 oz. flat bottomed pitcher was sold with both Florentine No. 1 and No. 2, sets. It was listed as 54 oz. in catalogues but measures six ounces less. This pitcher is shown in yellow and green on page 89. My inclination is to lean toward placing this pitcher only with Florentine No. 1 using the handle shape as my sole criteria. However, this pitcher continually is found with flat bottomed Florentine No. 2 tumblers; so I will list it with both patterns.

Speaking of flat tumblers, many with **paneled** interiors are being found in sets with Florentine No. 1 pitchers. Evidently these paneled tumblers should be considered to be Florentine No. 1 rather than Florentine No. 2. That information is for purists. Paneled flat tumblers are harder to find, but few collectors seem to make this a "must have" style. Since Hazel Atlas sold both Florentines together, why not collect them together?

There have been a multitude of fired-on colors emerging in luncheon sets, but there has also been little collector demand for these. You can find all sorts of colors and colored bands on crystal if that strikes your fancy. There are even some banded designs found on colors other than crystal.

Many 5½" yellow ash trays have a V.F.W. (Veterans of Foreign Wars) embossed in the bottom. In fact, I have seen more with this embossing than without it.

Florentine No. 1 shakers have been reproduced in pink and cobalt blue. There may be other colors to follow. No cobalt blue Florentine No. 1 shakers have ever been found; so those are no problem. The pink shaker is more difficult. I am comparing one to several old pairs from my shop. The old shakers have a major open flower on each side. There is a top circle on this blossom with three smaller circles down each side. The seven circles form the outside of the blossom. The new blossom looks more like a strawberry with no circles forming the outside of the blossom. This repro blossom looks like a poor drawing! Do not use the threading test mentioned under Floral for the Florentine No. 1 shakers, however. It won't work for Florentine although these are made by the same importing company out of Georgia. The threads are right on this reproduction pattern. The reproductions I have seen have been badly moulded, but that is not to say that it will not be corrected.

| | Crystal, Green | Yellow | Pink | Cobalt Blue | | Crystal, Green | Yellow | Pink | Cobalt Blue |
|---|---|---|---|---|---|---|---|---|---|
| Ash tray, 5½" | 22.00 | 26.00 | 26.00 | | Plate, 8½" salad | 7.50 | 12.00 | 11.00 | |
| Bowl, 5" berry | 11.00 | 14.00 | 12.00 | 15.00 | Plate, 10" dinner | 15.00 | 21.00 | 21.00 | |
| Bowl, 5", cream | | | | | Plate, 10" grill | 10.00 | 13.00 | 15.00 | |
| soup or ruffled nut | 18.00 | | 15.00 | 50.00 | Platter, 11½" oval | 14.00 | 20.00 | 19.00 | |
| Bowl, 6" cereal | 21.00 | 22.00 | 20.00 | | *Salt and pepper, ftd. | 37.50 | 55.00 | 55.00 | |
| Bowl, 8½" large berry | 21.00 | 26.00 | 26.00 | | Saucer | 3.00 | 4.00 | 4.00 | 17.00 |
| Bowl, 9½" oval vegetable | | | | | Sherbet, 3 oz. ftd. | 10.00 | 11.00 | 10.00 | |
| and cover | 47.50 | 55.00 | 55.00 | | Sugar | 9.50 | 12.00 | 12.00 | |
| Butter dish and cover | 120.00 | 155.00 | 155.00 | | Sugar cover | 16.00 | 22.00 | 22.00 | |
| Butter dish bottom | 47.50 | 82.50 | 82.50 | | Sugar, ruffled | 32.50 | | 32.50 | 50.00 |
| Butter dish top | 72.50 | 72.50 | 72.50 | | Tumbler, 3¼", 4 oz. | | | | |
| Coaster/ash tray, 3¾" | 16.00 | 18.00 | 23.00 | | ftd. | 14.00 | | | |
| Comport, 3½", ruffled | 22.00 | | 12.00 | 55.00 | Tumbler, 3¾", 5 oz. | | | | |
| Creamer | 9.50 | 18.00 | 17.00 | | ftd. juice | 14.00 | 20.00 | 20.00 | |
| Creamer, ruffled | 35.00 | | 35.00 | 60.00 | Tumbler, 4", 9 oz., ribbed | 14.00 | | 20.00 | |
| Cup | 9.00 | 10.00 | 9.00 | 75.00 | Tumbler, 4¾", 10 oz. | | | | |
| Pitcher, 6½", 36 oz. | | | | | ftd. water | 21.00 | 20.00 | 22.00 | |
| ftd. | 40.00 | 45.00 | 45.00 | 825.00 | Tumbler, 5¼", 12 oz. | | | | |
| Pitcher, 7½", 48 oz. | | | | | ftd. iced tea | 27.50 | 29.00 | 29.00 | |
| flat, ice lip or none | 65.00 | 165.00 | 110.00 | | Tumbler, 5¼", 9 oz. | | | | |
| Plate, 6" sherbet | 6.00 | 7.00 | 6.00 | | lemonade (like Floral) | | | 100.00 | |

*Beware reproductions

**Please refer to Foreword for pricing information**

# FLORENTINE NO. 2, "POPPY NO. 2" HAZEL ATLAS GLASS COMPANY 1932-1935

Colors: Pink, green, crystal, some cobalt, amber and ice blue.

Be sure to read about the differences between the Florentines in the first paragraph on page 86 (under Florentine No.1) if you are having trouble distinguishing between these patterns. Many collectors are mixing the Florentines together. Some pieces of each pattern have been found in boxed sets over the years, so the factory must have mixed them also. I have shown the ruffled nut or cream soup that seems to be a part of Florentine No. 1 in the bottom photograph of green. Would you have noticed this mixture had I not pointed it out?

Between the two patterns, the lids to the butter dishes, and also the oval vegetable tops, are interchangeable. That should mean you will have twice the chance of finding a lid for your butter or oval vegetable bowl. It doesn't! It means that twice as many collectors are looking for tops broken over the years! I have had several letters recently asking for the measurements on the candy and butter lids since they are so similar. If you buy a candy lid thinking you are getting a butter lid, you have a problem since they are not interchangeable. The candy lid measures 4¾" in diameter, but the butter dish lid measures 5" exactly. Those measurements are from outside edge to outside edge! If you find a lid that measures 5", do not try to fit it on a candy bottom — it will not work!

Custard cups or jello molds remain the most elusive piece in Florentine No. 2, although the bulbous 76 oz. pitcher evades many collectors.

The grill plate with the indent for the cream soup has yet to be found in yellow; not many have been seen in green or crystal. Since they were only recently found, it stands to reason they are not very plentiful. Green Florentine is more in demand than crystal, but the crystal is more rarely seen; thus pricing for both remains about the same.

That footed, cone shaped pitcher in the middle of the yellow photograph is the rarely found 6¼", 24 oz. The more commonly found footed pitcher stands 7½" tall.

Amber is the least found Florentine color; but to date, there is not enough available to collect a set. It was either experimental or a small, special order. Most sizes of flat tumblers have been found in amber, but still no pitcher has surfaced. You can see amber colored Florentine in previous editions.

Fired-on blue shakers in Florentine were shown in an earlier book. Now, **luncheon sets** of red and blue have been reported. The fired-on colors are sprayed over crystal. Once it has been fired-on, (baked, so to speak) the colors will not strip off even with paint removers as some collectors have learned. The fired-on colors are not common, but they also are not extremely collectible.

I predict that someday we will discover that the flat bottomed tumblers and flat bottomed straight sided pitchers were actually Florentine No.1. Why? The handles on the flat bottomed pitchers match the handles on the footed Florentine No. 1 pitcher. Cobalt tumblers seem to go with all the other pieces of cobalt No.1 including the rarely found pitcher. I also suspect that the ruffled comport is not a part of Florentine No. 2. Only a catalogue or a boxed set will help unravel this mystery! Somebody, please find one!

| | Crystal, Green | Pink | Yellow | Cobalt Blue | | Crystal, Green | Pink | Yellow | Cobalt Blue |
|---|---|---|---|---|---|---|---|---|---|
| Bowl, 4½" berry | 11.00 | 15.00 | 18.00 | | Plate, 10" dinner | 14.00 | 15.00 | 13.00 | |
| Bowl, 4¾" cream soup | 12.50 | 15.00 | 20.00 | | Plate, 10¼" grill | 11.00 | | 11.00 | |
| Bowl, 5½" | 30.00 | | 37.50 | | Plate, 10¼", grill | | | | |
| Bowl, 6" cereal | 26.00 | | 35.00 | | w/cream soup ring | 30.00 | | | |
| Bowl, 7½" shallow | | | 85.00 | | Platter, 11" oval | 15.00 | 15.00 | 18.00 | |
| Bowl, 8" large berry | 20.00 | 27.50 | 30.00 | | Platter, 11½" for | | | | |
| Bowl, 9" oval vegetable | | | | | gravy boat | | | 40.00 | |
| and cover | 47.50 | | 60.00 | | Relish dish, 10", 3 part | | | | |
| Bowl, 9" flat | 24.00 | | | | or plain | 19.00 | 24.00 | 28.00 | |
| Butter dish and cover | 95.00 | | 140.00 | | **Salt and pepper, pr. | 42.50 | | 48.00 | |
| Butter dish bottom | 22.50 | | 67.50 | | Saucer (amber 15.00) | 4.00 | | 5.00 | |
| Butter dish top | 72.50 | | 72.50 | | Sherbet, ftd. | | | | |
| Candlesticks, 2¾" pr. | 42.50 | | 57.50 | | (amber 40.00) | 10.00 | | 11.00 | |
| Candy dish and cover | 98.00 | 115.00 | 140.00 | | Sugar | 8.50 | | 11.00 | |
| Coaster, 3¼" | 12.00 | 15.00 | 20.00 | | Sugar cover | 14.00 | | 22.00 | |
| Coaster/ash tray, 3¾" | 17.50 | | 22.50 | | Tray, condiment for | | | | |
| Coaster/ash tray, 5½" | 17.50 | | 34.00 | | shakers, creamer and | | | | |
| Comport, 3½", ruffled | 22.00 | 12.00 | | 55.00 | sugar (round) | | | 60.00 | |
| Creamer | 8.00 | | 10.00 | | Tumbler, 3⅜", 5 oz. juice | 11.00 | 11.00 | 20.00 | |
| Cup (amber 50.00) | 7.50 | | 9.50 | | Tumbler, 3 9/16", 6 oz. blown | 16.00 | | | |
| Custard cup or jello | 55.00 | | 75.00 | | ***Tumbler, 4", | | | | |
| Gravy boat | | | 50.00 | | 9 oz. water | 12.00 | 15.00 | 20.00 | 65.00 |
| Pitcher, 6¼", 24 oz. | | | | | Tumbler, 5", 12 oz., blown | 17.50 | | | |
| cone-ftd. | | | 130.00 | | ****Tumbler, 5", 12 oz. | | | | |
| * Pitcher, 7½", 28 oz. | | | | | iced tea | 32.00 | | 42.00 | |
| cone-ftd. | 30.00 | | 28.00 | | Tumbler, 3¼", 5 oz. | | | | |
| Pitcher, 7½", 48 oz. | 65.00 | 110.00 | 165.00 | | ftd. | 14.00 | 15.00 | | |
| Pitcher, 8¼", 76 oz. | 85.00 | 200.00 | 375.00 | | Tumbler, 4", 5 oz. ftd. | 14.00 | | 16.00 | |
| Plate, 6" sherbet | 4.00 | | 6.00 | | Tumbler, 4½", 9 oz. | | | | |
| Plate, 6¼" with indent | 16.00 | | 26.00 | | ftd. | 25.00 | | 32.00 | |
| Plate, 8½" salad | 8.50 | 8.50 | 9.00 | | Vase or parfait, 6" | 29.00 | | 57.50 | |

* Ice Blue - $500.00
** Fired-On Red, Orange or Blue, Pr. - $42.50
*** Amber - $75.00
**** Amber - $75.00

**Please refer to Foreword for pricing information**

# FLOWER GARDEN WITH BUTTERFLIES, "BUTTERFLIES AND ROSES"
## U.S. GLASS COMPANY, Late 1920's

Colors: Pink, green, blue-green, canary yellow, crystal, amber and black.

Our collection of Flower Garden with Butterflies is making several other collectors happy now. Everything runs in cycles including collecting. The photographs of blue on page 91 represent what we were able to find in eighteen years of collecting. We never found the bulb for that atomizer shown.

New carpet throughout our house in Kentucky was an instigator for selling several of our accumulations. After six days of packing glass to make carpet laying easier, Cathy announced that some of this has to go, and Flower Garden was one of the casualties. We had great pleasure in finding it, and those collectors who showed up at the Peach State Depression Glass show last July were more than happy to take some of our collection home with them. One lady asked, "How can you sell your own collection?" It's not easy; but you price it and set it on the table waiting for another collector to come along and treasure it - just as we did!

Flower Garden has three different powder jars; that may be why the oval and rectangular trays are so plentiful. The trays and 8" plates are the only commonly found pieces (if there are pieces that could be considered common). Evidently, more powder jars than trays were broken over the years. There are two different footed powders. The smaller, shown in the top photograph on page 91, stands 6¼" tall; the taller, shown below, stands 7½" high. Lids to the footed powders are interchangeable. The flat powder jar, also shown in green atop page 93, has a 3½" diameter. (We never found a blue flat powder.)

Prices have dipped for the ash trays, as they have in almost all patterns. These are still difficult to find in Flower Garden. This is the only pattern in Depression glass that has a cigarette box holder, match pack holder and butt snuffer all on the same piece.

In the last book, I talked about the "Shari" perfume or cologne set, but I'm still getting letters about it. It's a semi-circular, footed dresser box that holds five wedge (pie) shaped bottles. It is often confused with Flower Garden. I spotted one at a show recently that still had the original labels intact on the bottles. They touted the New York/Paris affiliation of "Charme Volupte" but no where was the word "Shari" mentioned on the labels. One bottle had contained cold cream, another vanishing cream and three others once held parfumes (sic). There are dancing girls at either end of the box, and flowers abound on the semi-circle. This is not Flower Garden, however; neither are the 7" and 10" trivets made by U.S. Glass with flowers all over them. They were mixing bowl covers and they do not have butterflies.

| Item | Amber Crystal | Pink Green Blue-Green | Blue Canary Yellow |
|---|---|---|---|
| Ash tray, match-pack holders | 175.00 | 85.00 | 195.00 |
| Candlesticks, 4" pr. | 42.50 | 55.00 | 95.00 |
| Candlesticks, 8" pr. | 77.50 | 135.00 | 130.00 |
| Candy w/cover, 6", flat | 130.00 | 155.00 | |
| Candy w/cover, 7½" cone-shaped | 80.00 | 130.00 | 165.00 |
| Candy w/cover, heart-shaped | | 1,200.00 | 1,250.00 |
| * Cologne bottle w/stopper, 7½" | | 175.00 | 250.00 |
| Comport, 2⅞" h. | | 23.00 | 28.00 |
| Comport, 3" h. fits 10" plate | 20.00 | 23.00 | 28.00 |
| Comport, 4¼" h. x 4¾" w. | | | 50.00 |
| Comport, 4¾" h. x 10¼" w. | 48.00 | 65.00 | 85.00 |
| Comport, 5⅞" h. x 11" w. | 55.00 | | 95.00 |
| Comport, 7¼" h. x 8¼" w. | 60.00 | 80.00 | |
| Creamer | | 70.00 | |
| Cup | | 60.00 | |

| Item | Amber Crystal | Pink Green Blue-Green | Blue Canary Yellow |
|---|---|---|---|
| Mayonnaise, ftd. 4¾" h. x 6¼" w., w/7" plate & spoon | 67.50 | 80.00 | 125.00 |
| Plate, 7" | 16.00 | 21.00 | 30.00 |
| Plate, 8", two styles | 15.00 | 17.50 | 25.00 |
| Plate, 10" | | 42.50 | 48.00 |
| Plate, 10", indent for 3" comport | 32.00 | 40.00 | 45.00 |
| Powder jar, 3½", flat | | 75.00 | |
| Powder jar, ftd., 6¼"h. | 75.00 | 120.00 | 160.00 |
| Powder jar, ftd., 7½"h. | 80.00 | 125.00 | 185.00 |
| Sandwich server, center handle | 50.00 | 65.00 | 95.00 |
| Saucer | | 26.00 | |
| Sugar | | 65.00 | |
| Tray, 5½" x 10", oval | 50.00 | 55.00 | |
| Tray, 11¾" x 7¾", rectangular | 50.00 | 65.00 | 85.00 |
| Tumbler, 7½" oz. | 175.00 | | |
| Vase, 6¼" | 70.00 | 125.00 | 130.00 |
| Vase, 10½" | | 125.00 | 190.00 |

*Stopper, if not broken off, ½ price of bottle

**Please refer to Foreword for pricing information**

PRICE LIST FOR BLACK ITEMS ONLY

| | |
|---|---|
| Bon bon w/cover, 6⅝" diameter | 250.00 |
| Bowl, 7¼", w/cover, "flying saucer" | 375.00 |
| Bowl, 8½", console, w/base | 150.00 |
| Bowl, 9" rolled edge, w/base | 200.00 |
| Bowl, 11" ftd. orange | 225.00 |
| Bowl, 12" rolled edge console w/base | 200.00 |
| Candlestick 6" w/6½" candle, pr. | 350.00 |
| Candlestick, 8", pr. | 275.00 |
| Cheese and cracker, ftd., 5⅜" h. x 10" w. | 325.00 |
| Comport and cover, 2¾" h. (fits 10" indented plate) | 200.00 |
| Cigarette box & cover, 4⅜" long | 150.00 |
| Comport, tureen, 4¼" h. x 10" w. | 225.00 |
| Comport, ftd., 5⅝" h. x 10" w. | 225.00 |
| Comport, ftd., 7" h. | 175.00 |
| Plate, 10", indented | 100.00 |
| Sandwich server, center-handled | 125.00 |
| Vase, 6¼", Dahlia, cupped | 135.00 |
| Vase, 8", Dahlia, cupped | 200.00 |
| Vase, 9", wall hanging | 325.00 |
| Vase, 10", 2-handled | 225.00 |
| Vase, 10½", Dahlia, cupped | 250.00 |

**Please refer to Foreword for pricing information**

# FORTUNE HOCKING GLASS COMPANY, 1937-1938

Colors: Pink and crystal.

I reported that a crystal Fortune candy dish with a Royal Ruby lid had been found; however, I still have not been able to confirm its existence with a photograph. If you have one, please send me a picture. This would be an exciting find for candy dish collectors since that **is** the best selling piece in this pattern. More candy dish collectors purchase these than do Fortune collectors.

With an investment of a lot of time and little money compared to other patterns, a small pink set can be collected. Tumblers, cups, saucers and the luncheon plates are not plentiful. Luncheon plates are getting expensive and you generally find them one at a time.

You will not be able to rush out to a Depression glass show and purchase a set. Many dealers who stock Fortune do not carry it to shows. A cup and saucer in Fortune takes up the same amount of space as does a cup and saucer in any other pattern. A dealer can carry a popular pattern cup and saucer that many collectors are searching for at $25.00 or he can carry a Fortune set for a lot less money that few people are looking to buy. Which would you do? If you want to collect Fortune, leave your name with several dealers who are willing to help you find it. That way the dealer has a ready made sale when he finds the glass!

Both tumblers listed below are shown on page 95. A few pitchers are surfacing that are similar to this pattern, and many collectors are buying them for use with their sets. So far, no actual Fortune pitcher has turned up; but there is always hope!

|  | Pink, Crystal |  | Pink, Crystal |
|---|---|---|---|
| Bowl, 4" berry | 3.50 | Cup | 4.00 |
| Bowl, 4½" dessert | 4.50 | Plate, 6" sherbet | 3.00 |
| Bowl, 4½" handled | 4.50 | Plate, 8" luncheon | 15.00 |
| Bowl, 5¼" rolled edge | 6.00 | Saucer | 3.00 |
| Bowl, 7¾" salad or large berry | 12.50 | Tumbler, 3½", 5 oz. juice | 7.00 |
| Candy dish and cover, flat | 22.50 | Tumbler, 4", 9 oz. water | 9.00 |

---

# FRUITS HAZEL ATLAS AND OTHER GLASS COMPANIES, 1931-1935

Colors: Pink, green, some crystal and iridized.

Fruits collectors have all been trying to find the 5", 12 oz. tumbler. I have never seen one in pink, yet a few have been reported over the years. The 3½" juice tumbler is not common either, but I have not had as many folks ask for it as the iced tea. Most collectors seek green tumblers, since there has never been a pitcher discovered in pink.

Fruits pattern water tumblers (4") in all colors are the pieces generally found. There are a multitude of iridized "Pears" tumblers. These iridescent tumblers were probably made by Federal Glass Company while they were making iridescent Normandie and a few pieces in Madrid. Tumblers with cherries or other fruits are commonly found in pink, but finding **any** green tumblers is more of a dilemma.

Fruits pitchers in crystal sell for about half the price of green. Fruits pitchers only have cherries in the pattern. Notice that the handle is shaped like that of the flat Florentine pitchers (Hazel Atlas Company) and not like Cherry Blossom (Jeannette Glass Company) flat pitchers. This will keep you from confusing Cherry pitchers with Fruits. Crystal pieces are rarely collected, but tumblers are available if you would like an inexpensive beverage set.

Fruits berry bowl sets are among the hardest to obtain in Depression glass. Since this is not one of the major patterns and does not have the hord of collectors that some other patterns do, the true dearth of these berry bowls is just beginning to be recognized.

|  | Green | Pink |  | Green | Pink |
|---|---|---|---|---|---|
| Bowl, 5" berry | 22.50 | 20.00 | Sherbet | 8.00 | 6.50 |
| Bowl, 8" berry | 52.50 | 37.00 | Tumbler, 3½" juice | 22.50 | 17.50 |
| Cup | 8.00 | 7.00 | * Tumbler, 4" (1 fruit) | 17.50 | 15.00 |
| Pitcher, 7" flat bottom | 80.00 |  | Tumbler, 4" (combination of fruits) | 25.00 | 20.00 |
| Plate, 8" luncheon | 6.50 | 6.50 | Tumbler, 5", 12 oz. | 95.00 | 90.00 |
| Saucer | 5.50 | 4.00 |  |  |  |

* Iridized $7.50

**Please refer to Foreword for pricing information**

# GEORGIAN, "LOVEBIRDS" FEDERAL GLASS COMPANY, 1931-1936

Colors: Green and crystal.

Georgian has little "lovebirds" sitting side by side on most pieces except for some dinner plates, tumblers and hot plates. Tumblers have only the basket design on each side. Baskets usually alternate with birds on other pieces. Sometimes you can find a bargain priced tumbler if the seller does not see birds on it. The hot plate and some dinner plates carry only the center motif.

Georgian tumblers are hard to find. The iced teas have almost doubled the price of water tumblers. I have owned a dozen waters for every tea to give you an idea of how difficult teas are to find. No pitcher has ever been found, but it took years for someone to uncover Parrot pitchers (our other "bird" pattern that is sometimes confused with Georgian) and 37 of those were found all at once. So, there's still hope!

Few of the lazy susan or cold cuts servers have been found. Finally, you can see one pictured on the next page. One turned up in Ohio with an original label that read "Kalter Aufschain Cold Cuts Server Schirmer Cincy." That may be why so many have been found in Kentucky and southern Ohio. These lazy susans are made of walnut and are 18½" across with seven 5" openings for holding the hot plates. Maybe someone misnamed these 5" hot plates since they are being found on a cold cuts server!

Dinner plates come in two styles. The harder to find style (shown behind the larger creamer in the photo) is the least desired. This style has no "lovebirds," but only the center design motif. The more collectible plate (with lovebirds) is pictured to the left of the other plate. This is a case where a less plentiful piece of glass is cheaper because of lack of demand. **Demand** and not rarity alone affects prices. Even a rare piece can be hard to sell if no one wants it!

Those 6" deep berry bowls were heavily utilized; so watch out for pieces that are scratched and worn from usage. You pay a premium for condition! Remember that prices listed in this book are for **mint condition** pieces. Damaged or scratched and worn pieces should fetch less depending upon the extent of damage and wear. If you are collecting the glass to use, it may not make as much difference as collecting for eventual resale. Mint condition glass will sell more readily and for a much better price if you ever decide to part with your collection.

A few Georgian pieces are commonly found. Berry bowls, cups, saucers, sherbets, sherbet plates and luncheon plates can be seen with regularity. There are not as many collectors searching for this pattern, today, as there were in the mid-1970's when a set was donated to the Smithsonian by the Peach State Depression Glass Club in the name of President Jimmy Carter. You may have to search a while for other pieces.

There is no true mug in Georgian. Someone found a creamer without a spout and called it a mug. There are many patterns that have creamers or pitchers without a spout; and one Federal pattern, Sharon, has at least one two-spouted creamer known! Spouts were applied by hand at most glass factories using a wooden tool. That some escaped without the spout or that some worker had fun by adding an extra one is not surprising!

|  | Green |
| --- | --- |
| Bowl, 4½" berry | 8.00 |
| Bowl, 5¾" cereal | 22.50 |
| Bowl, 6½" deep | 62.50 |
| Bowl, 7½" large berry | 60.00 |
| Bowl, 9" oval vegetable | 60.00 |
| Butter dish and cover | 70.00 |
| Butter dish bottom | 40.00 |
| Butter dish top | 30.00 |
| Cold cuts server, 18½" wood with seven 5" openings for 5" coasters | 800.00 |
| Creamer, 3", ftd. | 11.00 |
| Creamer, 4", ftd. | 14.00 |
| Cup | 9.00 |
| * Hot Plate, 5" center design | 45.00 |
| Plate, 6" sherbet | 6.00 |
| Plate, 8" luncheon | 9.00 |
| Plate, 9¼" dinner | 25.00 |
| Plate, 9¼" center design only | 20.00 |
| Platter, 11½" closed-handled | 60.00 |
| Saucer | 4.00 |
| Sherbet | 12.00 |
| Sugar, 3", ftd. | 9.50 |
| Sugar, 4", ftd. | 11.00 |
| Sugar cover for 3" | 35.00 |
| Sugar cover for 4" | 100.00 |
| Tumbler, 4", 9 oz. flat | 50.00 |
| Tumbler, 5¼", 12 oz. flat | 97.50 |

*Crystal-$20.00                    **Please refer to Foreword for pricing information**

# HEX OPTIC, "HONEYCOMB" JEANNETTE GLASS COMPANY, 1928-1932

Colors: Pink, green, ultramarine and iridescent in 1950's.

Do you notice anything you have not seen before? A new piece of Hex Optic has been discovered and is pictured here. All right, it is the pitcher - not the footed one which is seldom seen, but the flat bottomed one beside it. This pitcher is 8" tall and holds 96 ozs. Maybe there is a green one lurking out there, just awaiting you to find it. **New items** are being found after all these years; so keep your eyes open!

Kitchenware buyers are more aware of Hex Optic than most of the other patterns of Depression glass. The sugar shaker, bucket reamer and butter dish are enthusiastically sought in both green and pink. Refrigerator dishes, stacking sets and mixing bowls are also obtainable, but are not as much in demand as other kitchen pieces. In fact, were it not for Kitchenware collectors getting hooked on this pattern, Hex Optic might still be ignored.

Green is less available, but also more desirable than pink. This color preference affects Depression glass collectors more than Kitchenware collectors who seek both colors.

Iridized tumblers, oil lamps and pitchers were all made during Jeannette's iridized craze of the 1950's. I have never been able to verify when the company made the ultramarine tumblers. A guess would be in the late 1930's when the company was making Doric and Pansy, but that is only a guess.

| | Pink, Green | | Pink, Green |
|---|---|---|---|
| Bowl, 4¼" ruffled berry | 5.50 | Plate, 8" luncheon | 5.50 |
| Bowl, 7½" large berry | 7.50 | Platter, 11" round | 12.50 |
| Bowl, 7¼" mixing | 12.00 | Refrigerator dish, 4" x 4" | 10.00 |
| Bowl, 8¼" mixing | 17.50 | Refrigerator stack set, 3 pc. | 47.50 |
| Bowl, 9" mixing | 18.00 | Salt and pepper, pr. | 26.00 |
| Bowl, 10" mixing | 22.00 | Saucer | 2.50 |
| Bucket reamer | 55.00 | Sugar, 2 styles of handles | 5.50 |
| Butter dish and cover, rectangular 1 lb. size | 70.00 | Sugar shaker | 135.00 |
| Creamer, 2 style handles | 5.50 | Sherbet, 5 oz. ftd. | 4.50 |
| Cup, 2 style handles | 4.50 | Tumbler, 3¾", 9 oz. | 4.50 |
| Ice bucket, metal handle | 18.00 | Tumbler, 5", 12 oz. | 7.00 |
| Pitcher, 5", 32 oz. sunflower motif in bottom | 22.00 | Tumbler, 4¾", 7 oz. ftd. | 7.50 |
| Pitcher, 9", 48 oz. ftd. | 40.00 | Tumbler, 5¾" ftd. | 10.00 |
| Pitcher, 8", 96 oz. flat | 195.00 | Tumbler, 7" ftd. | 12.00 |
| Plate, 6" sherbet | 2.50 | Whiskey, 2", 1 oz. | 8.00 |

# HOBNAIL HOCKING GLASS COMPANY, 1934-1936

Colors: Crystal, crystal w/red trim and pink.

Hobnail patterns were made by dozens of other glass companies, but Hocking's Hobnail is more easily recognized because of the shapes of its many pieces. Most Hobnail pieces made by Hocking have shapes similar to those found in Moonstone or even in Miss America. After all, the 1940's pattern Moonstone is nothing more than Hobnail with an added white highlight to the hobs. Hobnail serving pieces are difficult to find, but there is no lack of beverage sets!

Red trimmed crystal Hobnail (see photo) has caught the fancy of a few collectors; but this is found mostly on the West coast. I have had several collectors trying to buy the red trimmed pieces I have pictured.

That footed juice tumbler was sold along with the decanter as a wine set; so, it was also a wine glass. (Terminology in glassware catalogues drives me to distraction. I have to decide whether to list what the factory said in catalogues or to list items in today's jargon. I have tried to consolidate both where practicable without creating a problem for new collectors. There is a glossary of terms listed in the back of my *Pocket Guide to Depression Glass* for those who have need to refer to it. I try to include what I can throughout this book, but that means you have to read the whole book to find them!)

For collectors who wish to purchase an inexpensively priced set, Hobnail is the candidate. A major problem in collecting this is finding dealers who stock it. There are many ways collectors can overcome this handicap. I suggest you make out a want list and give it to dealers and have them call you collect when they find pieces on your list.

Only four pieces in pink were made by Hocking, five, if you count the sherbet plate and saucer as two pieces. You can pick another pink Hobnail pattern, such as one made by MacBeth-Evans, to go along with Hocking's; that way, you add a pitcher and tumbler set, something unavailable in this Hocking ware. Most Hobnail patterns are compatible with Hocking's.

| | Pink | Crystal | | Pink | Crystal |
|---|---|---|---|---|---|
| Bowl, 5½" cereal | | 4.00 | Plate, 8½" luncheon | 3.50 | 3.50 |
| Bowl, 7" salad | | 4.50 | Saucer/sherbet plate | 2.00 | 2.00 |
| Cup | 4.50 | 4.50 | Sherbet | 3.50 | 3.00 |
| Creamer, ftd. | | 3.50 | Sugar, ftd. | | 4.00 |
| Decanter and stopper, 32 oz. | | 26.00 | Tumbler, 5 oz. juice | | 4.00 |
| Goblet, 10 oz. water | | 6.50 | Tumbler, 9 oz., 10 oz. water | | 5.50 |
| Goblet, 13 oz. iced tea | | 7.50 | Tumbler, 15 oz. iced tea | | 7.00 |
| Pitcher, 18 oz. milk | | 18.00 | Tumbler, 3 oz. ftd. wine/juice | | 6.00 |
| Pitcher, 67 oz. | | 25.00 | Tumbler, 5 oz. ftd. cordial | | 5.50 |
| Plate, 6" sherbet | 2.00 | 2.00 | Whiskey, 1½ oz. | | 6.00 |

# HOMESPUN, "FINE RIB" JEANNETTE GLASS COMPANY, 1939-1949

Colors: Pink and crystal.

Children's sets of Homespun are still in demand. Not only do Depression glass collectors buy these, but doll collectors and miniature collectors do, too. There is no children's tea pot in crystal and there are no sugar and creamers in this tea set. The tea pot looks like a creamer with a sugar lid; so don't be fooled as I once was when I first saw this set. (You can see said teapot in the center of the photograph.)

Homespun tumblers are a nemesis to collectors of this pattern. The commonly found 5 oz. juice is readily available and pictured between the two flat tumblers. These were sold in sets of six on the platter as a cocktail or beverage set. They must have sold well! Other tumblers range from hard to nearly impossible to find. Another problem is that all tumblers are found in two different styles. The tumbler to the left of this juice is a 6 oz., flat juice measuring 3⅞". This has been incorrectly listed as 9 oz. in the past. There are two styles of 9 oz. tumblers. The one shown with a plain band at the top stands 4¼" while the other has ribs to the top, is slightly flared and only 4" tall. There are also two styles of 15 oz. footed tumblers. One tumbler (6¼") is fatter at the bottom and has practically no stem at all; the other (6⅜") has a pronounced stem. Both of these have been listed at 6¼", but there is ⅛" difference!

Homespun is a challenging set to complete; and if you choose to buy only one style of tumbler, then it is even more frustrating finding that one style. I suggest you buy every water and tea tumbler you find regardless of style! Someday, you will be glad that you listened to me. You will not go broke; there are not that many.

There is no sugar lid! The lid sometimes found on the Homespun sugar is actually a fine rib pattern powder jar top. It does fit, so many have been added to the sugars over the years. Yet, fitting the sugar does not make it Homespun.

| | Pink, Crystal | | Pink, Crystal |
|---|---|---|---|
| Bowl, 4½", closed handles | 10.00 | Saucer | 4.00 |
| Bowl, 5" cereal | 18.00 | Sherbet, low flat | 16.00 |
| Bowl, 8¼" large berry | 17.50 | Sugar, ftd. | 9.50 |
| Butter dish and cover | 55.00 | Tumbler, 3⅞", 6 oz. straight | 20.00 |
| Coaster/ash tray | 6.50 | Tumbler, 4", 9 oz. water, flared top | 16.00 |
| Creamer, ftd. | 10.00 | Tumbler, 4¼", 9 oz. band at top | 16.00 |
| Cup | 10.00 | Tumbler, 5¼", 13 oz. iced tea | 27.50 |
| Plate, 6" sherbet | 6.00 | Tumbler, 4", 5 oz. ftd. | 7.00 |
| Plate, 9¼" dinner | 15.00 | Tumbler, 6¼", 15 oz. ftd. | 24.00 |
| Platter, 13", closed handles | 15.00 | Tumbler, 6⅜", 15 oz. ftd. | 24.00 |

## HOMESPUN CHILD'S TEA SET

| | Pink | Crystal | | Pink | Crystal |
|---|---|---|---|---|---|
| Cup | 30.00 | 20.00 | Tea pot cover | 75.00 | |
| Saucer | 10.00 | 8.00 | Set: 14-pieces | 325.00 | |
| Plate | 12.50 | 9.00 | Set: 12-pieces | | 148.00 |
| Tea pot | 45.00 | | | | |

---

# INDIANA CUSTARD, "FLOWER AND LEAF BAND" INDIANA GLASS COMPANY 1930's; 1950's

Colors: Ivory or custard, early 1930's; white, 1950's.

Indiana Custard continues to attract few collectors, and that is an unexpected benefit for those who do collect it. There is not enough of this pattern to support massive numbers of customers.

Indiana Custard is the only pattern in Depression glass where both cups and sherbets are the most difficult pieces to find. Some collectors think the sherbet is overpriced; but others who have searched for years without attaining one, would not agree! Cups have been more difficult for me to find than the sherbets, but I seem to find the sherbets in groups of six or eight and the cups one at a time. Both sell quickly; so there is a demand even at the high prices. More Indiana Custard collectors are in the central Indiana area than any place. Of course, it is more plentiful there, making it easier to get hooked on it!

I wonder if there is a full set of yellow floral decorated pieces. There is a set of Indiana Custard decorated like the saucer standing up behind the oval vegetable. A major problem to this set is that the decorations flake off easily. If you can find a set with the colors intact, you will fall in love with it. Finding it a piece or two at a time would be quite a chore! But, then, some people like a challenge! I had one collector tell me that he purposely chose a hard to get pattern because it doubled his pleasure when he found a piece!

| | French Ivory | | French Ivory |
|---|---|---|---|
| Bowl, 5½" berry | 8.00 | Plate, 7½" salad | 15.00 |
| Bowl, 6½" cereal | 19.00 | Plate, 8⅞" luncheon | 15.00 |
| Bowl, 7½" flat soup | 29.00 | Plate, 9¾" dinner | 25.00 |
| Bowl, 9", 1¾" deep, large berry | 27.50 | Platter, 11½" oval | 30.00 |
| Bowl, 9½" oval vegetable | 26.00 | Saucer | 8.00 |
| Butter dish and cover | 60.00 | Sherbet | 85.00 |
| Cup | 37.50 | Sugar | 11.00 |
| Creamer | 16.00 | Sugar cover | 19.00 |
| Plate, 5¾" bread and butter | 6.50 | | |

# IRIS, "IRIS AND HERRINGBONE" JEANNETTE GLASS COMPANY, 1928-1932; 1950's; 1970's

Colors: Crystal, iridescent; some pink and green; recently bi-colored red/yellow and blue/green combinations and white.

Iris was one of the more difficult patterns to place in the division of this book and the *Collectible Glassware from the 40's, 50's, 60's...* since it fit both time periods. Actually, crystal production goes back to 1928 for its start. However, some crystal was made in the late 1940's, 1950's and some candy bottoms and vases, as late as the early 1970's. Iridescent belongs entirely within the time frame of my *Collectible Glassware from the 40's, 50's, 60's....* I had said I would not continue to put iridescent prices in this book; but I received enough letters to persuade me to carry prices for both colors here.

I am utterly amazed at what collectors are paying for some pieces of Iris. Had you bought a twelve place setting three years ago, you could almost double your investment now. Iris **was** a plentiful pattern, but, right now, there is so much in collector's hands that it is no longer plentiful. There was already a short supply of several pieces because of the heavy demand from the South, Tennessee in particular, where Iris is the state flower. No dealer can have enough inventory of this pattern; and demand has far surpassed the supply lately. I notice that some collectors have decided that prices being asked are more than they are willing to pay. (Collectors always have the option of influencing prices by refusing to buy.)

Demitasse **cups** are available; saucers are scarce. Many of these cups were originally sold on copper saucers instead of glass, Iris patterned saucers.

Realize those candy bottoms in iridescent are a product of the 1970's when Jeannette made crystal bottoms and flashed them with two-tone colors such as red/yellow or blue/green. Many of these were sold as vases; and, over time, the colors have washed or peeled off making them, again, crystal candy bottoms. These later made ones can be distinguished by the lack of rays on the foot of the dish. Similarly, white vases were made and sprayed on the outside in green, red and blue. White vases sell in the $10.00–12.50 range. Yes, the color can be removed producing a white milk glass vase that should sell in the same price range. These are not rare!

I recently found a nut dish using the 9½" salad bowl instead of the 11½" as its base. It is the first one I have seen; be on the lookout for another.

The decorated red and gold Iris that keeps turning up was called "Corsage" and "styled by Century" in 1946. This information was on a card attached to a 1946 wedding gift of this ware.

Price escalation of iridescent pieces has been affected by the persons in Pennsylvania and New York who have discovered a way to remove the iridescence from Iris and thus change iridescent soup bowls ($50.00 to $55.00) back to crystal selling at three times the iridescent price. However, these changed items seem to have a very cloudy look to the Iris flowers on the pieces. It is quite a resourceful project because, years ago, I had been told by former glass factory workers that iridescence could not be removed!

A word about pink vases is in order. Good pink color will bring the price below, but weakly colored pink will not. Find a exceptionally vivid pink vase, and it will fetch even more! That red candlestick in the top photograph is flashed red and not truly red glass!

"The bowls advertising 'Badcock Furniture will treat you right' seem to be coming from the southern part of the country. Does anyone know where this store was or still is?" That question was posed in the last book and did I get letters! When I asked that I had only been living in Florida a short while and was not familiar with this large chain of furniture stores. Cathy has said I never notice furniture. I guess this proves her right! In any case, thanks for all the calls, letters, explanations at shows, mailing envelopes from the stores and even a recent advertising mug from Badcock Furniture whose motto is still the same after all these years! Thanks, too, for really reading the book!

| | Crystal | Iridescent | Green/Pink | | Crystal | Iridescent | Green/Pink |
|---|---|---|---|---|---|---|---|
| Bowl, 4½", berry, beaded edge | 38.00 | 9.00 | | Goblet, 4½", 4 oz., cocktail | 24.00 | | |
| Bowl, 5", ruffled, sauce | 9.00 | 24.00 | | Goblet, 4½", 3 oz., wine | 16.00 | | |
| Bowl, 5", cereal | 100.00 | | | Goblet, 5½", 4 oz. | 24.00 | | |
| Bowl, 7½", soup | 145.00 | 55.00 | | Goblet, 5½", 8 oz. | 24.00 | 150.00 | |
| Bowl, 8", berry, beaded edge | 75.00 | 20.00 | | **Lamp shade, 11½" | 85.00 | | |
| Bowl, 9½", ruffled, salad | 12.50 | 13.00 | 95.00 | Pitcher, 9½", ftd. | 37.50 | 40.00 | |
| Bowl, 11½", ruffled, fruit | 15.00 | 14.00 | | Plate, 5½", sherbet | 14.00 | 13.00 | |
| Bowl, 11", fruit, straight edge | 50.00 | | | Plate, 8", luncheon | 95.00 | | |
| Butter dish and cover | 47.50 | 40.00 | | Plate, 9", dinner | 50.00 | 37.50 | |
| Butter dish bottom | 13.50 | 12.00 | | Plate, 11¾", sandwich | 30.00 | 30.00 | |
| Butter dish top | 34.00 | 28.50 | | Saucer | 12.00 | 11.00 | |
| Candlesticks, pr. | 40.00 | 42.50 | | Sherbet, 2½", ftd. | 24.00 | 14.00 | |
| Candy jar and cover | 125.00 | | | Sherbet, 4", ftd. | 20.00 | | |
| Coaster | 90.00 | | | Sugar | 11.00 | 11.00 | 100.00 |
| Creamer, ftd. | 11.00 | 12.00 | 100.00 | Sugar cover | 12.00 | 12.00 | |
| Cup | 15.00 | 14.00 | | Tumbler, 4", flat | 120.00 | | |
| * Demitasse cup | 35.00 | 115.00 | | Tumbler, 6", ftd. | 18.00 | 16.00 | |
| * Demitasse saucer | 130.00 | 150.00 | | Tumbler, 6½", ftd. | 32.00 | | |
| Fruit or nut set | 60.00 | | | Vase, 9" | 27.50 | 24.00 | 125.00 |
| Goblet, 4", wine | | 30.00 | | | | | |

*Ruby, Blue, Amethyst priced as Iridescent
**Colors, $65.00

# JUBILEE LANCASTER GLASS COMPANY, Early 1930's

Colors: Yellow and pink.

Trying to keep up with all the new discoveries in Jubilee is exciting! The major problem is weeding the many "look-alike" items that continue to deceive collectors who do not study this pattern closely. Some Jubilee collectors irritate dealers to death with their preciseness as to what constitutes Jubilee while others are happily accepting many similar flower cuttings on Lancaster blanks.

Newly found pieces that I can now confirm include an 11½", three-footed, scalloped, flat bowl to go with the curved up 11½" bowl that is similar to a rose bowl in other elegant patterns. Also found is the 3", 8 oz., non stemmed sherbet that has eleven petals as does the three-footed covered candy that will be discussed later. Additional stemware being found includes a 3 oz. wine standing 4⅞" tall and a 7½" water goblet (listed under stems below) that holds 11 oz. Add to those a 13" three-footed bowl and a 14" three-footed plate (both shown in the photographs) and you have quite a list of newly found Jubilee! Yet these are not all the new unveilings! There have also been four of the 12" vases found! The top of this vase is 4" in diameter while the base is only 3½" in diameter. The bulbous middle is 6".

Having only eleven petals on the candy and sherbet came about from cutting problems experienced when using a standard six inch cutting wheel. The foot of the sherbet and the knob on the candy get in the way when a petal of the design is cut directly up and down. The glass cutter had to move over to cut a petal. This makes only an eleven petal flower possible. I hope that is clear, but those two eleven petal pieces **are** Jubilee!

An interesting auction occurred near Columbus, Ohio, last summer. The widow of a glass cutter for Lancaster sold sets of Jubilee. Several of the newly listed pieces came from that auction; but the real story is that a glass dealer who bought some of the basic yellow pieces at high prices, left all the pink and crystal sets of Jubilee without bidding on them! Somewhere in Ohio there are crystal Jubilee items which had never previously been reported. Where you there?

Luncheon sets consisting of cups, saucers, creamer, sugar and luncheon plates are readily found. After those pieces, you have a problem getting anything else. I have found more in Florida recently than any place other than Ohio. (Of course, Florida is where I have been searching for glass; so that may account for finding more of it here.)

According to the catalog number, the liner plate to the mayonnaise is the same piece as the 8¾" plate. There is no plate shown in the catalogues with an indent for the mayonnaise. However, you can see an indented plate under the mayonnaise in the top photograph. However, this mayonnaise has sixteen petals! As I have mentioned before, TRUE Jubilee should have twelve petals and an open-centered flower, but there are exceptions! There are other Lancaster "look-alike" patterns that have sixteen petals or twelve petals with a smaller petal in between the larger ones. Many collectors are willing to settle for these at a lesser price; however, purist collectors will accept nothing but the twelve petal, open center pieces. Most of my customers enjoy buying "look-alike" pieces for less than prices paid for "the real thing."

I have eliminated the terminology of goblets and have properly listed footed tumblers and stemware.

| | Pink | Yellow |
|---|---|---|
| Bowl, 8", 3-ftd., 5⅛" high | 250.00 | 200.00 |
| Bowl, 9" handled fruit | | 110.00 |
| Bowl, 11½", flat fruit | 195.00 | 160.00 |
| Bowl, 11½", 3-ftd. | 250.00 | 250.00 |
| Bowl, 11½", 3-ftd., curved in | | 225.00 |
| Bowl, 13", 3-ftd. | 250.00 | 225.00 |
| Candlestick, pr. | 185.00 | 175.00 |
| Candy jar, w/lid, 3-ftd. | | 300.00 |
| Cheese & cracker set | 255.00 | 250.00 |
| Creamer | 35.00 | 22.00 |
| Cup | 40.00 | 16.00 |
| Mayonnaise & plate | 280.00 | 250.00 |
| w/original ladle | 310.00 | 265.00 |
| Plate, 7" salad | 22.50 | 14.00 |
| Plate, 8¾" luncheon | 27.50 | 16.00 |
| Plate, 13½" sandwich | 85.00 | 50.00 |
| Plate, 14", 3- ftd. | | 200.00 |
| Saucer, two styles | 12.00 | 8.00 |
| Sherbet, 3", 8 oz. | | 65.00 |
| Stem, 4", 1 oz., cordial | | 225.00 |
| Stem, 4⅞", 3 oz. | | 135.00 |
| Stem, 5½", 7 oz., sherbet/champagne | | 75.00 |
| Stem, 7½", 11 oz. | | 135.00 |
| Sugar | 35.00 | 21.00 |
| Tray, 11", 2-handled cake | 65.00 | 45.00 |
| Tumbler, 5", 6 oz., ftd. juice | | 85.00 |
| Tumbler, 6⅛", 12½", iced tea | | 125.00 |
| Tumbler, 6", 10 oz., water | 75.00 | 40.00 |

| | Pink | Yellow |
|---|---|---|
| Tray, 11", center-handled sandwich | 195.00 | 200.00 |
| Vase, 12" | | 350.00 |

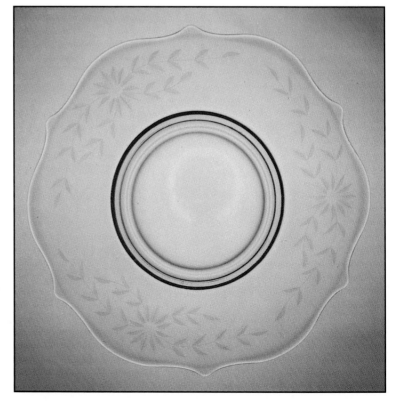

# "LACE EDGE," "OPEN LACE" OLD COLONY HOCKING GLASS COMPANY, 1935-1938

Colors: Pink and some crystal.

My re-discovery of the true name of **Old Colony** (instead of Lace Edge) has taken some time to get used to, but more and more collectors are converting. In the next edition, I will move Old Colony to its proper alphabetical placement in the book. I have received more letters and comments on the store window photographs in this pattern than anything else besides the Iris/Badcock Furniture comment! One reader went so far as to say that I should never remove it from my book as it is the best feature in it!

To repeat how this discovery was made. In December of 1990 I spent a day at Anchor Hocking going through files and catalogues. I got excited when I spotted these old store display photographs. After studying them for a few seconds I really could not believe what I was seeing. Both displays named the glass **Old Colony**. There it was in color tinted pink! Finally, the **real** name of this pattern! Originally, this trip was for my *Collectible Glassware from the 40's, 50's, 60's...* book; this one discovery made the whole trip worthwhile! The information attained for that other book was just not as electrifying.

Previously, I said to notice that the saucers in the photo were also sold as sherbet plates. At least, I assumed that they were saucers and not sherbet plates. One reader, who does scale drawings in his business, said that he had calculated that the plates under the sherbets were salad plates. He said to look at the horizontal photograph that has saucers and the sherbet underliner nearly side by side. I believe I have been scientifically corrected!

The true 9" comport in Old Colony has a **rayed base**. See page 108 to identify it. There is a similar comport that measures 9" also. This "pretender" has a plain foot and was probably made by Standard or Lancaster Glass. Hocking may have gotten the idea for Old Colony from one of these other companies that they bought. Both Lancaster and Standard had very similar designs, but their glass is better quality and "rings" when **gently** flipped on the edge with your finger. Hocking's Old Colony makes a "clunk" sound. The pink color of other companies' glass is usually a brighter shade of pink. If the piece is not shown in my listing or is in any color other than pink or crystal, the likelihood of your having an Old Colony piece is slim at best.

A major problem to collecting Old Colony (besides finding it) concerns the damaged lace on the outside of the pieces. It chipped and cracked very easily and still does. Plates and bowls have to be stacked cautiously because of that. Candlesticks, console bowls and vases are other pieces hard to find in mint condition.

Ribs on the footed tumbler extend approximately half way up the side as they do on the cup. This tumbler is often confused with the Coronation tumbler which has a similar shape and design. To compare, refer to the Coronation photograph. Notice the fine ribbed effect from the middle up on the Coronation tumbler. This is missing on the Old Colony tumbler. The flat bottomed juice is rarely seen while the flat water is fairly common. Maybe you will find the flat juices priced and marked as Queen Mary. A reader in California did, but was worried that she may have made a mistake since she had never seen them before! The only mistake was made by the seller!

The butter bottom is also a 7¾" salad bowl according to catalogues, but many collectors think the true salad bowl is ribbed. Ribbing does make a big difference in pricing on this bowl! The 9½" large salad is also found ribbed or plain, but there is no price difference on them.

Satinized or frosted pieces, such as the vase shown here, sell for only a fraction of their unfrosted counter parts. Lack of demand is the main reason. Although a few collectors think frosted Old Colony is beautiful, most apparently do not!

| | | *Pink | | *Pink |
|---|---|---|---|---|
| ** | Bowl, 6⅜" cereal | 17.50 | Plate, 8¼" salad | 20.00 |
| | Bowl, 7¾" ribbed salad | 42.50 | Plate, 8¾" luncheon | 17.50 |
| | Bowl, 8¼" (crystal) | 11.00 | Plate, 10½" dinner | 25.00 |
| | Bowl, 9½" plain or ribbed | 18.00 | Plate, 10½" grill | 18.00 |
| *** | Bowl, 10½", 3 legs, (frosted, $30.00) | 180.00 | Plate, 10½", 3-part relish | 22.50 |
| | Butter dish or bon bon with cover | 60.00 | Plate, 13", solid lace | 27.50 |
| | Butter dish bottom, 7¾" | 22.50 | Plate, 13", 4-part solid lace | 28.00 |
| | Butter dish top | 37.50 | Platter, 12¾" | 26.00 |
| *** | Candlesticks, pr. (frosted $40.00) | 180.00 | Platter, 12¾", 5-part | 25.00 |
| | Candy jar and cover, ribbed | 45.00 | Relish dish, 7½", 3-part deep | 55.00 |
| | Comport, 7" | 22.50 | Saucer | 11.00 |
| | Comport, 7" and cover, ftd. | 45.00 | *** Sherbet, ftd. | 77.50 |
| | Comport, 9" | 700.00 | Sugar | 21.00 |
| | Cookie jar and cover | 55.00 | Tumbler, 3½", 5 oz. flat | 30.00 |
| | Creamer | 21.00 | Tumbler, 4½", 9 oz. flat | 16.00 |
| | Cup | 21.00 | Tumbler, 5", 10½ oz. ftd. | 60.00 |
| | Fish bowl, 1 gal. 8 oz. (crystal only) | 26.00 | Vase, 7", (frosted $50.00) | 300.00 |
| | Flower bowl, crystal frog | 21.00 | | |

  * Satin or frosted items 50% lower in price or less
  ** Officially listed as cereal or cream soup
  *** Price is for absolute mint condition

# LACED EDGE, "KATY BLUE" IMPERIAL GLASS COMPANY, Early 1930's

Colors: Blue w/opalescent edge and green w/opalescent edge.

Laced Edge, as this pattern was christened by Imperial, is sometimes called "Katy Blue" by vintage collectors. Unfortunately, not all pieces are blue; displays labeled that way when green opalescent is shown can give you a chuckle. I suggest "Katy Green" would be more apropos or use the real name. I have shown the green this time!

Having bought and sold over one hundred and eighty pieces of blue for the shop earlier this year, I can make several observations from dealing with collectors from coast to coast. Few of these collectors have oval vegetables or platters. Most do not accept the 12" luncheon plate or the 9" vegetable bowl as Laced Edge because the edges are different from that of the other items. I will be able to show you an advertisement next time that shows these two pieces with all the rest of the pattern listed. The ad shows the cost in coupons for each piece. I am researching the product to see if I can find out the time it existed!

The large accumulation I bought came from the family of a butter and eggs salesman who stopped that occupation in 1941; pieces I purchased were left over premiums he was to give out to his customers. There were five creamers and only one sugar. Each creamer had a different style lip. Cereal bowls varied from 4⅞" to 5⅝"; soup bowls varied from 6⅞" to 7¼" and berry bowls from 4⅜" to 4¾". Size differences were due to the turning out of the edge of the bowl. There were major differences in the edge coloration. Some white barely covered the edge and other pieces had a bold white opalescent edge up to ½" down the side. To get all your pieces to match exactly in coloration would be a major task!

The white edging technique was called "Sea Foam" by Imperial and was put on many other Imperial colors and on other patterns besides Laced Edge.

Prices for the blue continue to escalate; but prices for green follow along since it is much rarer than the blue. Presently, there are fewer collectors looking for green which helps hold the price–else it might surpass the blue!

You will find pieces in this design without the white edging technique. Blue and green pieces without the white sell for about half of the prices listed if you can find a buyer. Crystal pieces do not seem to be selling at any price. I have never seen crystal pieces with white edging in this pattern; if you have a piece, I would appreciate knowing what you have.

I am removing the vase from the listing as it does not seem to be Laced Edge!

| | Opalescent | | Opalescent |
|---|---|---|---|
| Bowl, 4⅜"-4¾" fruit | 27.00 | Mayonnaise, 3-piece | 130.00 |
| Bowl, 5" | 35.00 | Plate, 6½" bread & butter | 18.00 |
| Bowl, 5½" | 35.00 | Plate, 8" salad | 32.00 |
| Bowl, 5⅞"" | 35.00 | Plate, 10" dinner | 80.00 |
| Bowl, 7" soup | 75.00 | Plate, 12" luncheon (per catalogue description) | 70.00 |
| Bowl, 9" vegetable | 85.00 | Platter, 13" | 145.00 |
| Bowl, 11" divided oval | 110.00 | Saucer | 15.00 |
| Bowl, 11" oval | 135.00 | Sugar | 38.00 |
| Cup | 33.00 | Tidbit, 2-tiered, 8" & 10" plates | 95.00 |
| Creamer | 38.00 | Tumbler, 9 oz. | 58.00 |

# LAKE COMO HOCKING GLASS COMPANY, 1934-1937

Color: White with blue scene.

Lake Como is rarely seen in my travels and when it is, it is usually very worn. Occasionally, I see shakers, sugars and creamers at shows but rarely anything else. When displayed, Lake Como sells very quickly if in top condition. The prices below are for mint condition glass with little wear on the design. Evidently, this pattern was used heavily. You should be able to buy worn Lake Como at 50 % to 80% of the prices listed depending upon the amount of wear. Part of all collections I have purchased have been worn. One collector told me that he had "settled" on buying less than mint glass in order to have more pieces.

Notice the flat soup in the middle. The floral decoration on the edge is embossed instead of painted in blue. I have only seen a few of these. Recently a lady brought one into a glass show to make sure she had found this rare soup. She had - and more than one! I believe she said that they were found for a $1.00 each. There are still bargains to be found!

Platters and vegetable bowls are hard to find, as are both styles of cups.

| | White | | White |
|---|---|---|---|
| Bowl, 6" cereal | 22.00 | Plate, 9¼" dinner | 27.50 |
| Bowl, 9¾" vegetable | 55.00 | Platter, 11" | 55.00 |
| Bowl, flat soup | 90.00 | Salt & pepper, pr. | 40.00 |
| Creamer, ftd. | 27.50 | Saucer | 11.00 |
| Cup, regular | 27.50 | Saucer, St. Denis | 12.00 |
| Cup, St. Denis | 25.00 | Sugar, ftd. | 27.50 |
| Plate, 7¼" salad | 17.50 | | |

# LAUREL McKEE GLASS COMPANY, 1930's

Colors: French Ivory, Jade Green, White Opal and Poudre Blue.

"Poudre Blue" Laurel is still the color most in demand, but it is also the hardest color to acquire. Add to that fact that many items were not made in blue and you get a double whammy. Therefore, many collectors are turning to Jade Green for variety. French Ivory attracts few new collectors; so prices have remained rather steady. Serving bowls in all colors have always been scarce. I will mention here that more and more collectors of Depression Glass patterns are sending me photos showing how they have successfully blended many colors of a pattern into a satisfying serving arrangement. Scarcity of pieces in a single color is giving birth to some wonderful creativity!

Children's Laurel tea sets with the Scotty Dog decoration have become the most sought after children's sets in Depression Glass! Jade Green is hardly seen, but the French Ivory is coveted as well. When have you seen a set for sale? For that matter, when have you seen a solitary piece for sale?

Collectors of Scotty dog items have also discovered these sets. The same thing happened to the Akro Agate Scotty dog powder jars a few years ago. (Those collectors would even buy the bottoms to the powder jars that Depression Glass dealers had not been able to give away.) Other children's sets in Laurel continue to be eagerly collected, but there are a few more of these available than the Scotty sets. Red, green or orange trimmed children's sets are found in a limited supply with orange being the most difficult color to find. Watch for wear on these trims; it appears many children played with these dishes if wear is any indication of use.

Several people are beginning to buy the trimmed ivory. The red trimmed is the most plentiful, but a set can also be gathered with green trim. As with the children's pieces, wear on the trim is a detriment. Both of these trims are shown in the top photograph.

The shakers are hard to find with strong patterns. Many of the designs are weak or obscure. Absolutely, it's better to own a patterned pair than a pair that has only the right shape! Doric and Pansy shakers are the only other Depression pattern where this is  problem!

| | White Opal, Jade Green | French Ivory | Poudre Blue | | White Opal, Jade Green | French Ivory | Poudre Blue |
|---|---|---|---|---|---|---|---|
| Bowl, 5" berry | 6.50 | 7.50 | 13.00 | Cup | 7.50 | 7.00 | 20.0 |
| Bowl, 6" cereal | 7.50 | 9.00 | 20.00 | Creamer, tall | 12.00 | 12.00 | 30.00 |
| Bowl, 6", three legs | 12.50 | 14.00 | | Cup | 7.50 | 7.00 | 20.00 |
| Bowl, 7⅞" soup | 30.00 | 30.00 | | Plate, 7½" salad | 10.00 | 9.00 | 14.00 |
| Bowl, 9" large berry | 16.50 | 20.00 | 37.50 | Plate, 9⅛" dinner | 12.00 | 11.00 | 20.00 |
| Bowl, 9¾" oval vegetable | 17.00 | 17.00 | 37.50 | Plate, 9⅛" grill | 11.00 | 11.00 | |
| Bowl, 10½", three legs | 28.00 | 33.00 | 55.00 | Platter, 10¾" oval | 20.00 | 25.00 | 35.00 |
| Bowl, 11" | 27.00 | 35.00 | 55.00 | Salt and pepper | 55.00 | 40.00 | |
| Candlestick, 4" pr. | 30.00 | 27.50 | | Saucer | 3.50 | 3.00 | 7.50 |
| Cheese dish and cover | 52.50 | 55.00 | | Sherbet | 10.00 | 11.00 | |
| Creamer, short | 10.00 | 10.00 | | Sherbet/champagne, 5" | 35.00 | 30.00 | |
| Creamer, tall | 12.00 | 12.00 | 30.00 | Sugar, short | 8.50 | 9.00 | |
| Cup | 7.50 | 7.00 | 20.00 | Sugar, tall | 11.00 | 11.00 | 30.00 |
| Plate, 6" sherbet | 5.00 | 5.00 | 10.00 | Tumbler, 4½", 9 oz. flat | 40.00 | 27.50 | |
| Creamer, tall | 12.00 | 12.00 | 30.00 | Tumbler, 5", 12 oz. flat | | 40.00 | |

## CHILDREN'S LAUREL TEA SET

| | Plain | Green or Decorated Rims | Scotty Dog Green | Scotty Dog Ivory |
|---|---|---|---|---|
| Creamer | 25.00 | 40.00 | 110.00 | 85.00 |
| Cup | 20.00 | 30.00 | 60.00 | 40.00 |
| Plate | 10.00 | 16.00 | 55.00 | 35.00 |
| Saucer | 8.00 | 10.00 | 55.00 | 25.00 |
| Sugar | 25.00 | 40.00 | 110.00 | 85.00 |
| 14-piece set | 202.00 | 305.00 | 900.00 | 575.00 |

**Please refer to Foreword for pricing information**

# LINCOLN INN   FENTON GLASS COMPANY, Late 1920's

Colors: Red, cobalt, light blue, amethyst, black, green, green opalescent, pink, crystal, amber and jade (opaque).

Lincoln Inn, once again, has a newly discovered piece! An 11" center handled server has been found in both red and cobalt blue. The multitude of colors found in Lincoln Inn gives collectors a wide range for collecting, but red and the different shades of blue remain the most amassed colors. Red and cobalt blue are the easiest colors to find in Lincoln Inn. The good news is that those are the colors that are also the most desired by collectors!

Sherbet/champagnes remain abundant in all colors. If you ever have a desire to collect high sherbets, then this is a pattern that will add quite a few to your set. You can find a high sherbet in any color made in this pattern. Were these the "cat's meow" cocktail glasses around Prohibition? You can find other tumblers and stems, but attaining serving pieces in **any** color is not easily done.

Pitchers are rarely found; but keep in mind that Fenton remade an iridized, dark carnival colored pitcher several years ago! All the light blue pitchers have been found in Florida; so watch for them there!

Lincoln Inn plates can also be found with a fruit design in the center according to a 1930's catalogue; I can finally show you one. I recently spotted a crystal bowl with fruit designs in the bottom. It was at an Antique Mall here in Florida, but the owner of said piece evidently thought it was Lalique or gold! It is still in the mall although it would have made another great addition for the picture!

Shakers continue to be difficult to find in all colors. We recently sold a red one to a collector in Chicago who seemed extremely glad to find it! There are some collectors who only search for shakers. Although these are not the highest priced shakers in Depression glass, they are among the toughest to find. Red and black shakers are the most desired colors; but don't pass by **any** color in your travels. I found a red pair sitting with Royal Ruby in a corner of a shop a few years ago! Sometimes you have to look in some not so obvious places when you visit shops.

Many red pieces are amberina in color. Amberina is a red that has a yellow cast to it. Red glass is made by reheating glass that comes out of the furnace yellow. Uneven reheating causes some of this to remain yellow. Some dealers have told collectors this is a rare color in order to sell it. Actually, it was a mistake; and the amounts of yellow on each piece make it difficult to match pieces.

Beware of deals that sound too good to be true! They usually are!

| | Cobalt Blue, Red | All Other Colors |
|---|---|---|
| Ash tray | 17.50 | 12.00 |
| Bon bon, handled square | 15.00 | 12.00 |
| Bon bon, handled oval | 16.00 | 12.00 |
| Bowl, 5" fruit | 11.50 | 8.50 |
| Bowl, 6" cereal | 13.00 | 9.00 |
| Bowl, 6" crimped | 13.00 | 8.50 |
| Bowl, handled olive | 15.00 | 9.50 |
| Bowl, finger | 18.00 | 12.50 |
| Bowl, 9", shallow | | 23.00 |
| Bowl, 9¼" ftd. | 33.00 | 19.00 |
| Bowl, 10½" ftd. | 43.00 | 29.00 |
| Candy dish, ftd. oval | 22.50 | 13.00 |
| Comport | 25.00 | 14.50 |
| Creamer | 22.50 | 14.50 |
| Cup | 16.50 | 9.00 |
| Goblet, water | 24.00 | 15.50 |
| Goblet, wine | 27.00 | 16.50 |
| Nut dish, ftd. | 17.50 | 12.00 |
| Pitcher, 7¼", 46 oz. | 780.00 | 680.00 |
| Plate, 6" | 7.50 | 4.50 |
| Plate, 8" | 12.50 | 7.50 |
| Plate, 9¼" | 26.00 | 11.50 |
| Plate, 12" | 32.00 | 15.50 |
| * Salt/pepper, pr. | 235.00 | 135.00 |
| Sandwich server, center hdld. | 75.00 | 65.00 |
| Saucer | 4.50 | 3.50 |
| Sherbet, 4½", cone shape | 17.00 | 11.50 |
| Sherbet, 4¾" | 19.00 | 12.50 |

*Black $275.00

| | Cobalt Blue, Red | All Other Colors |
|---|---|---|
| Sugar | 20.00 | 14.00 |
| Tumbler, 4 oz. flat juice | 26.00 | 9.50 |
| Tumbler, 9 oz. flat water | | 19.50 |
| Tumbler, 5 oz. ftd. | 25.00 | 11.00 |
| Tumbler, 9 oz. ftd. | 26.00 | 14.00 |
| Tumbler, 12 oz. ftd. | 40.00 | 19.00 |
| Vase, 12" ftd. | 135.00 | 87.50 |

**Please refer to Foreword for pricing information**

# LORAIN, "BASKET," No. 615 INDIANA GLASS COMPANY, 1929-1932

Colors: Green, yellow and some crystal.

After buying several collections of Lorain, and from talking and corresponding with collectors who have searched for Lorain for years, I have learned that cereal bowls are the hardest to find item and the inner rims are usually rough. The 8" deep berry in yellow is the next hardest piece to locate. Green dinner plates are almost as scarce as green cereals. Lorain suffers from that persistent problem of mould roughness; if you are a fanatic about mint condition glassware, then you had better turn your attention to some other pattern. Indiana seemed to have had mould roughness problems with many of its popular patterns!

Oval vegetable bowls have become scarce in both colors. Saucers are harder to locate than cups because of mould roughness and wear and tear on them over the years. It is amazing how collecting has changed. Dealers used to refuse to buy saucers unless you also had the cup. Today, many of these once scorned saucers are eagerly bought and the cup be hanged!

New collectors, please note that the white and green avocado colored sherbets (which have an open edge border) are a 1950's and later issue and should be treated as such. They were used heavily by florists and many are found with a tacky, clay-like substance in the bottom used to hold flowers. They have always been assumed to be an Indiana product; but several have been found with Anchor Hocking stickers. I have not been able to verify this, but Hocking did attach sticker labels in the late 1950's and early 1960's. If any one out there has more information on these, please offer some assistance.

Prices for the harder to find pieces continue to rise. However, there have been more new collectors starting to collect green Lorain than yellow. Cost and availability have much to do with this. Green is less expensive and more readily found. There are so few pieces found in crystal, I would not suggest you try to complete a set. It would be extremely difficult.

Lorain collectors have written to ask what I was talking about when I said snack tray. A yellow trimmed snack tray is shown in the bottom photograph with the yellow. These are found in crystal (with colored borders of red, yellow, green and blue) and have an off center indent for the cup. The crystal cups that go with these trays are sometimes decorated in the same colored borders, but many times they are only crystal.

| | Crystal, Green | Yellow |
|---|---|---|
| Bowl, 6" cereal | 35.00 | 55.00 |
| Bowl, 7¼" salad | 37.00 | 55.00 |
| Bowl, 8" deep berry | 77.50 | 130.00 |
| Bowl, 9¾" oval vegetable | 37.50 | 47.50 |
| Creamer, ftd. | 16.00 | 21.00 |
| Cup | 11.00 | 15.00 |
| Plate, 5½" sherbet | 7.50 | 11.00 |
| Plate, 7¾" salad | 10.00 | 15.00 |
| Plate, 8⅜" luncheon | 16.00 | 26.00 |
| Plate, 10¼" dinner | 36.00 | 50.00 |
| Platter, 11½" | 24.00 | 40.00 |
| Relish, 8", 4-part | 16.50 | 33.00 |
| Saucer | 4.50 | 6.00 |
| Sherbet, ftd. | 18.00 | 29.00 |
| Snack tray, crystal/trim | 21.00 | |
| Sugar, ftd. | 15.00 | 22.00 |
| Tumbler, 4¾", 9 oz. ftd. | 18.00 | 27.00 |

**Please refer to Foreword for pricing information**

# MADRID FEDERAL GLASS COMPANY, 1932-1939; INDIANA GLASS COMPANY, 1980's

Colors: Green, pink, amber, crystal and "Madonna" blue. (*See Reproduction Section*)

Madrid has been an authentic headache for collectors since 1976 when Federal reissued this pattern for the Bicentennial under the name "Recollection" glassware. Fine, it was dated 1976; but it WAS issued in the original color of amber instead of some additional color. Collectors were apprised and many assumed it would someday be collectible and squirreled away some sets. However, Indiana Glass bought the moulds for Madrid when Federal went bankrupt and there have been problems for collectors ever since. First Indiana removed the 1976 and made crystal. The old crystal butter was selling for several hundred dollars and the new one sold for $2.99. Prices plummeted!

Shortly afterwards, Indiana made pink, and even though it was a lighter pink than the original, prices nose-dived on the old. Then Indiana made blue; and although it is a brighter, harsher blue than the original, it has decimated the prices of the 1930's blue. You can see the new pink in the Reproduction Section in the back. All pieces made in pink have now been made in blue. The latest color, teal, is a very greenish blue and is the first color made that was not previously made in the 1930's.

Only the items listed below were originally made in blue. Some of the old items have been remade; so, buyer, know your dealer if collecting Madrid! If a piece is found in blue that is not priced below, rest assured it is new!

Madrid gravy boats and platters have most always been found in Iowa. Someday someone will remember how these were attained. I am betting it was a premium for some item used by rural folks! One is shown in the foreground of the top photograph. Mint condition sugar lids in any color are finds! Footed tumblers are harder to find than the flat ones. Collectors of green Madrid have turned out to be almost as scarce as the pattern!

A group of fourteen amber ash trays found at an auction in Illinois have now been absorbed by collectors. Sometimes a find of rarely seen items will drop the price, but it did not in this case!

The wooden lazy susans are still being found in eastern Kentucky and southern Ohio. A label found on one of these says "Kalter Aufschain Cold Cuts Server Schirmer Cincy." You can see one of these pictured in *Very Rare Glassware of the Depression Years, Second Series.*

| | Amber | Pink | Green | Blue | | Amber | Pink | Green | Blue |
|---|---|---|---|---|---|---|---|---|---|
| Ash tray, 6" square | 185.00 | | 135.00 | | ** Pitcher, 8", 60 oz. | | | | |
| Bowl, 4¾" cream | | | | | square | 45.00 | 35.00 | 135.00 | 150.00 |
| soup | 15.00 | | | | Pitcher, 8½", 80 oz. | 60.00 | | 200.00 | |
| Bowl, 5" sauce | 6.00 | 6.50 | 6.50 | | Pitcher, 8½", | | | | |
| Bowl, 7" soup | 15.00 | | 16.00 | 30.00 | 80 oz. ice lip | 60.00 | | 225.00 | |
| Bowl, 8" salad | 14.00 | | 17.50 | | Plate, 6" sherbet | 4.00 | 3.50 | 4.00 | 8.00 |
| Bowl, 9⅜" large | | | | | Plate, 7½" salad | 11.00 | 9.00 | 9.00 | 20.00 |
| berry | 18.50 | 19.00 | | | Plate, 8⅞" luncheon | 8.00 | 7.00 | 9.00 | 18.00 |
| Bowl, 9½" deep | | | | | Plate, 10½" dinner | 35.00 | | 30.00 | 65.00 |
| salad | 30.00 | | | | Plate, 10½" grill | 9.50 | | 15.00 | |
| Bowl, 10" oval | | | | | Plate, 10¼" relish | 15.00 | 12.50 | 16.00 | |
| vegetable | 15.00 | 15.00 | 17.00 | 38.00 | Plate, 11¼" round | | | | |
| * Bowl, 11" low | | | | | cake | 14.00 | 10.00 | | |
| console | 15.00 | 11.00 | | | Platter, 11½" oval | 15.00 | 14.00 | 16.00 | 24.00 |
| Butter dish and | | | | | Salt/pepper, 3½" | | | | |
| cover | 67.00 | | 80.00 | | ftd., pr. | 65.00 | | 80.00 | 130.00 |
| Butter dish bottom | 27.50 | | 37.50 | | Salt/pepper, 3½" | | | | |
| Butter dish top | 37.50 | | 42.50 | | flat, pr. | 45.00 | | 64.00 | |
| * Candlesticks, | | | | | Saucer | 4.00 | 5.00 | 5.00 | 10.00 |
| 2¼" pr. | 22.00 | 20.00 | | | Sherbet, two styles | 7.50 | | 11.00 | 15.00 |
| Cookie jar and | | | | | Sugar | 7.50 | | 8.50 | 15.00 |
| cover | 45.00 | 30.00 | | | Sugar cover | 35.00 | | 40.00 | 155.00 |
| Creamer, ftd. | 8.50 | | 11.00 | 20.00 | Tumbler, 3⅞", | | | | |
| Cup | 6.50 | 7.50 | 8.50 | 16.00 | 5 oz. | 14.00 | | 32.00 | 38.00 |
| Gravy boat and | | | | | Tumbler, 4¼", 9 oz. | 15.00 | 15.00 | 20.00 | 25.00 |
| platter | 1,075.00 | | | | Tumbler, 5½", | | | | |
| Hot dish coaster | 40.00 | | 37.50 | | 12 oz. 2 styles | 20.00 | | 30.00 | 38.00 |
| Hot dish coaster | | | | | Tumbler, 4", 5 oz. | | | | |
| w/indent | 37.50 | | 37.50 | | ftd. | 24.00 | | 37.50 | |
| Jam dish, 7" | 21.00 | | 18.50 | 35.00 | Tumbler, 5½", | | | | |
| Jello mold, 2⅛" | | | | | 10 oz. ftd. | 24.00 | | 38.00 | |
| high | 13.00 | | | | Wooden lazy susan, | | | | |
| Pitcher, 5½" | | | | | cold cuts coasters | 675.00 | | | |
| 36 oz. juice | 40.00 | | | | | | | | |

* Iridescent priced slightly higher
** Crystal - $150.00

**Please refer to Foreword for pricing information**

119

# MANHATTAN, "HORIZONTAL RIBBED" ANCHOR HOCKING GLASS COMPANY, 1938-1943

Colors: Crystal, pink; some green, ruby and iridized.

I have received a few letters about discoveries of new pieces in Manhattan; however these have all turned out to be Anchor Hocking's newer line PARK AVENUE, so I will repeat what I said for those who do not update your books regularly.

PARK AVENUE was a new pattern line introduced by Anchor Hocking in 1987 to "re-create the Glamour Era of 1938 when Anchor Hocking first introduced a classic" according to the Inspiration '87 catalogue issued by the company. Anchor Hocking went to the trouble to preserve the integrity of their older glassware, however! None of the pieces in this line are exactly like the old Manhattan! They are only similar and Manhattan was never made in blue as this line has been. Many collectors of Manhattan have bought this new pattern to use as everyday dishes. Thus, everyone remains happy, company and collector alike. Manhattan's collectability has not been affected by the making of PARK AVENUE; however, it has caused some confusion with the older Manhattan cereal bowls. These 5¼" cereals are rarely seen, especially in mint condition; you need to be aware of the differences in these pieces. PARK AVENUE lists a small bowl at 6". All the original Manhattan bowls measure 1 15/16" in height. If the bowl you have measures more than this, then you have a piece of Park Avenue! Be very suspicious if the bowl is mint! I hope this clears up the measuring problems that people ordering through the mail have had in buying the cereal bowls. You can see an original on the right in front of the creamer (top photograph).

All with metal accessories were made outside the factory. Anchor Hocking sold their wares to other companies who made these accoutrements with tongs or spoons hanging or otherwise attached to them.

Manhattan comports are being sold as Margarita glasses! Not being a drinker, I can only observe from the people I know who do drink - these would not hold enough salt for them, let alone drink.

Pink Manhattan cups, saucers and dinner plates are rarely seen. You can view a cup in the bottom photograph, but I have never seen a saucer to go with it. The saucer/sherbet plates of Manhattan are like many of Hocking's saucers; they have no cup ring. There was a pink dinner plate displayed at the Houston show for at least two years. The price was high, but I guess someone must have finally bought it, since I have not seen it there the last few years. There is also a Manhattan Royal Ruby juice pitcher in the Texas area, found in Washington Court House, Ohio, a long time ago.

The handled berry measures 5⅜". These closed handled bowls are not the cereal! I mention the measurements because there is a vast price difference. In fact, the reason the 5⅜" handled berry has increased in price so much has come from dealers selling these as cereals!

Manhattan is one pattern that collectors do not seem to mind adding pieces that look similar. In fact, many collectors use Hazel Atlas shakers with Manhattan since they are round and look better to them than the original squared ones that Hocking made. I have specifically left out all the Manhattan "look-alike" pieces in the photo this time. Too many new collectors are being confused by pieces that are not Manhattan.

The sherbet in Manhattan has a beaded bottom, but the center insert to the relish tray does not have these beads. Relish tray inserts can be found in crystal, pink and Royal Ruby. The center insert is always crystal on the relish trays although I see a pink sherbet was placed in the center of the pink relish in the bottom picture by some helpful gremlin.

| | Crystal | Pink |
|---|---|---|
| * Ashtray, 4" round | 11.00 | |
| Ashtray, 4½" square | 18.00 | |
| Bowl, 4½" sauce, handles | 9.00 | |
| Bowl, 5⅜" berry w/handles | 17.50 | 17.50 |
| Bowl, 5¼" cereal, no handles | 27.50 | |
| Bowl, 7½" large berry | 14.00 | 14.00 |
| Bowl, 8", closed handles | 20.00 | 22.00 |
| Bowl, 9" salad | 19.00 | 20.00 |
| Bowl, 9½" fruit open handle | 35.00 | 32.00 |
| Candlesticks, 4½" (square) pr. | 15.00 | |
| Candy dish, 3 legs | | 11.00 |
| ** Candy dish and cover | 37.50 | |
| Coaster, 3½" | 15.00 | |
| Comport, 5¾" | 30.00 | 30.00 |
| Creamer, oval | 10.00 | 10.00 |
| Cup | 17.50 | 140.00 |
| Relish tray, 14", 4-part | 18.00 | |
| Relish tray, 14" with inserts | 50.00 | 50.00 |
| *** Relish tray insert | 5.50 | 6.00 |
| Pitcher, 24 oz. | 30.00 | |
| Pitcher, 80 oz. tilted | 40.00 | 55.00 |
| Plate, 6" sherbet or saucer | 6.50 | 50.00 |
| Plate, 8½ salad | 14.00 | |
| Plate, 10¼" dinner | 18.00 | 110.00 |
| Plate, 14" sandwich | 21.00 | |
| Salt & pepper, 2" pr. (square) | 27.50 | 45.00 |
| Saucer/sherbet plate | 6.50 | 50.00 |
| Sherbet | 8.50 | 14.00 |
| Sugar, oval | 10.00 | 10.00 |
| **** Tumbler, 10 oz. ftd. | 16.00 | 16.00 |
| Vase, 8" | 17.50 | |
| ** Wine, 3½" | 5.50 | |

* Ad for Hocking $15.00; ad for others $12.50
** "Look-Alike"
*** Ruby-$3.50
**** Green or iridized-$15.00

**Please refer to Foreword for pricing information**

# MAYFAIR FEDERAL GLASS COMPANY, 1934

Colors: Crystal, amber and green.

Hocking patented the name "Mayfair" first which caused Federal to redesign their own "Mayfair" glass moulds into what finally became known as the "Rosemary" pattern. The green pieces pictured in the bottom photograph represent a "transitional period" of glassware made between the old Federal "Mayfair" pattern and what was to become "Rosemary." Notice these transitional pieces have arching in the bottom of each piece rather than the waffle design, and there is no waffling between the top arches. If you turn to the Rosemary (174-175) for reference, you will see that the glass under the arches is perfectly plain. Most collectors consider these transitional pieces a part of Federal Mayfair rather than Rosemary, which was eventually the final design after working on Mayfair at least twice. I suspect that after examining the reworking of the moulds, someone decided that the changes made were not different enough and they were again redesigned. That's speculation today, but it seems logical.

After several years of buying Federal's Mayfair, I conclude that Mayfair was a very limited production possibly because of pattern name difficulties. Amber and crystal are the colors that can be collected (in the true pattern form), but not all pieces occur in amber. Amber cream soups can only be found in the transitional pattern. That may mean that cream soups were only designed for the transitional pattern and never for Mayfair itself. There may be no cream soup in crystal since no crystal transitional pieces have been seen. Crystal Mayfair can be collected as a set. Green can only be purchased in transitional form and amber is found in both. Now that I am out on this limb, feel free to prove me wrong!

I still prefer the scalloped lines of the Mayfair to that of Rosemary, but that is only my perspective. This is a challenging set to collect. Once you accumulate it, you will not be sorry. Mix the transitional with the regular pattern in amber. They go well together and only an experienced collector will notice the difference. Did you notice the tumblers in the top photograph? Both styles are shown there. The green is the transitional style.

There are no sherbets. The Mayfair sugar, like Rosemary, looks like a large sherbet since it does not have handles. Both the Mayfair and the transitional pattern differences can be seen in the amber sugar.

You will often find several pieces of Mayfair together, rather than a piece here and there. That way you can get off to a flying start!

| | Amber | Crystal | Green | | Amber | Crystal | Green |
|---|---|---|---|---|---|---|---|
| Bowl, 5" sauce | 8.50 | 6.50 | 12.00 | Plate, 9½" dinner | 12.50 | 9.00 | 12.50 |
| Bowl, 5" cream soup | 18.00 | 11.00 | 18.00 | Plate, 9½" grill | 13.50 | 8.50 | 13.50 |
| Bowl, 6" cereal | 17.50 | 9.50 | 20.00 | Platter, 12" oval | 25.00 | 17.00 | 29.00 |
| Bowl, 10" oval vegetable | 27.50 | 16.00 | 27.50 | Saucer | 4.50 | 2.50 | 4.50 |
| Creamer, ftd. | 13.00 | 10.50 | 16.00 | Sugar, ftd. | 13.00 | 11.00 | 13.00 |
| Cup | 8.50 | 5.00 | 8.50 | Tumbler, 4½", 9 oz. | 25.00 | 13.00 | 27.00 |
| Plate, 6¾" salad | 7.00 | 4.50 | 9.00 | | | | |

# MAYFAIR, "OPEN ROSE" HOCKING GLASS COMPANY, 1931-1937

Colors: Ice blue, pink; some green, yellow and crystal. *(See Reproduction Section)*

Mayfair may be the most collected pattern of Depression glass. I spend more time answering questions and calls about pieces in Mayfair than for any other pattern. Reproductions and rare pieces are the major concerns. I have updated the *Reproduction Section* in the back to take care of the odd colors of cookie jars and shakers now being found.

Two collectors in Texas who were buying all the rarely found pieces of Mayfair have both dissolved their collections. This means that numerous rare pieces that have not been on the open market for years are now being offered! You may see some prices advertised or displayed at shows for more than my listed prices. It is difficult to list vastly higher prices for unsold items that there are so few of in the first place.

For instance, recently a three legged Mayfair console was advertised at $6850.00; another sold at an auction last month for $3600.00. My newly listed price of $5000.00 may still be too conservative for some and too high for others! Notice the covered, three-footed Mayfair console bowl in the top picture. At least two of the known pink footed bowls were found this way. The lid is the same one that fits the 10" vegetable bowl.

Many of the unusual pink stems in Mayfair were also in these aforementioned collections, and they are beginning to find their way into new collections at increased prices. Remember the year that a man from Pennsylvania set up at the Washington Court House, Ohio, flea market with nine Mayfair cordials for only $300.00 each? The catch was that you had to buy all nine. At that time, most of us would not have bought one at that ridiculous price, let alone **nine**. Now, we would gladly pay that price! I often wonder where they went. I have only owned three of these, and the one in my cordial collection is damaged. You, the collector, ultimately decide what a piece is "worth."

I used to have time to get out and find rare glass. After twelve weeks of self-imposed prison at my computer, believe me, I would prefer to be out among all the flea markets and shows! (I have been able to squeeze in a few hours fishing early in the mornings when the cold fronts, rain and wind will let me.) I wish you luck in finding rare and unusual glassware! It is generally found by those who work at it!

Yellow and green Mayfair **can be collected,** but it takes both time and money to do so! Of course, that holds true for pink or blue! Even a setting for four with all the pieces in easily found colors is expensive! However, if you try not to buy **everything** made, you can put a small set together for about the same money as most other patterns.

Pink Mayfair collectors have a dilemma when picking out the tumbler size and stems to collect. Most collectors buy flat waters, footed teas and water goblets to start. After they finish these, additional stems can be added.

There are some secondary details about this pattern that need to be pointed out. Some Mayfair stems have a plain foot while others are rayed. All stems and tumblers shown in yellow and green are rayed, but the footed water in pink has a plain foot. Footed iced teas vary in height. Some teas have a short stem above the foot and others have practically none. This stem causes the heights to vary to some extent. It is just a mould variation, but may account for capacity differences. Note under measurements on page 4 the listings of tumblers that I have taken from old Hocking catalogues. In two catalogues from 1935 these were listed as 13 oz., but in 1936 both catalogues listed the tumbler as 15 oz. All I have ever measured have held 15 oz. Does yours?

Crystal Mayfair occurs in only a few pieces. Most commonly found are the pitcher, shakers and the divided platter. A reader writes that the divided platter was given as a premium with the purchase of coffee or spices in late 1930's. I have a report of a sugar and lid in crystal. I believe putting a set of crystal together would be impossible since few pieces were made. It would be enough problem finding a creamer to go with the sugar!

The 10" celery measures 11¼" handle to handle and the 9" one measures 10¼" handle to handle. The measurements in this book normally do not include handles!

| | *Pink | Blue | Green | Yellow | | *Pink | Blue | Green | Yellow |
|---|---|---|---|---|---|---|---|---|---|
| Bowl, 5" cream soup | 40.00 | | | | Butter dish and cover or 7" covered vegetable | 60.00 | 275.00 | 1,200.00 | 1,200.00 |
| Bowl, 5½" cereal | 22.00 | 45.00 | 70.00 | 70.00 | Butter bottom with indent | | | | 265.00 |
| Bowl, 7" vegetable | 23.00 | 45.00 | 120.00 | 120.00 | Butter dish top | 37.00 | 185.00 | 1,000.00 | 1,000.00 |
| Bowl, 9", 3⅛ high, 3 leg console | 5,000.00 | | 5,000.00 | | Cake plate, 10" ftd. | 26.00 | 65.00 | 95.00 | |
| Bowl, 9½" oval vegetable | 26.00 | 65.00 | 110.00 | 115.00 | Candy dish and cover | 50.00 | 275.00 | 550.00 | 450.00 |
| Bowl, 10" vegetable | 24.00 | 65.00 | | 115.00 | Celery dish, 9" divided | | | 150.00 | 150.00 |
| Bowl, 10" same covered | 110.00 | 115.00 | | 900.00 | Celery dish, 10" | 37.50 | 55.00 | 105.00 | 105.00 |
| Bowl, 11¾" low flat | 50.00 | 65.00 | 35.00 | 185.00 | Celery dish, 10" divided | 180.00 | 55.00 | | |
| Bowl, 12" deep scalloped fruit | 50.00 | 85.00 | 35.00 | 215.00 | | | | | |

**Please refer to Foreword for pricing information**

*Frosted or satin finish items slightly lower

125

# MAYFAIR, "OPEN ROSE" (Cont.)

|  |  | *Pink | Blue | Green | Yellow |
|---|---|---|---|---|---|
|  | Cookie jar and lid | 47.50 | 275.00 | 550.00 | 800.00 |
|  | Creamer, ftd. | 25.00 | 75.00 | 195.00 | 185.00 |
|  | Cup | 17.00 | 50.00 | 145.00 | 145.00 |
|  | Cup, round | 300.00 |  |  |  |
|  | Decanter and stopper, 32 oz. | 150.00 |  |  |  |
|  | Goblet, 3¾", 1 oz. cordial | 1,000.00 |  | 800.00 |  |
|  | Goblet, 4⅛", 2½ oz. | 800.00 |  | 800.00 |  |
|  | Goblet, 4", 3 oz. cocktail | 70.00 |  | 350.00 |  |
|  | Goblet, 4½", 3 oz. wine | 70.00 |  | 400.00 |  |
|  | Goblet, 5¼", 4½ oz. claret | 800.00 |  | 800.00 |  |
|  | Goblet, 5¾", 9 oz. water | 55.00 |  | 400.00 |  |
|  | Goblet, 7¼", 9 oz. thin | 200.00 | 165.00 |  |  |
| ** | Pitcher, 6", 37 oz. | 50.00 | 145.00 | 500.00 | 475.00 |
|  | Pitcher, 8", 60 oz. | 50.00 | 160.00 | 450.00 | 400.00 |
|  | Pitcher, 8½", 80 oz. | 95.00 | 180.00 | 500.00 | 500.00 |
|  | Plate, 5¾" (often substituted as saucer) | 12.00 | 24.00 | 85.00 | 85.00 |
|  | Plate, 6½" round sherbet | 12.50 |  |  |  |
|  | Plate, 6½" round, off-center indent | 24.00 | 26.00 | 110.00 |  |
|  | Plate, 8½" luncheon | 24.00 | 50.00 | 75.00 | 75.00 |
|  | Plate, 9½" dinner | 47.50 | 75.00 | 130.00 | 130.00 |
|  | Plate, 9½" grill | 38.00 | 50.00 | 75.00 | 75.00 |
|  | Plate, 11½" handled grill |  |  |  | 85.00 |
|  | Plate, 12" cake w/handles | 38.00 | 65.00 | 35.00 |  |
| *** | Platter, 12" oval, open handles | 25.00 | 65.00 | 150.00 | 150.00 |
|  | Platter, 12½" oval, 8" wide, closed handles |  |  | 210.00 | 210.00 |
|  | Relish, 8⅜", 4-part | 28.00 | 60.00 | 150.00 | 150.00 |
|  | Relish, 8⅜" non-partitioned | 195.00 |  | 250.00 | 250.00 |
| **** | Salt and pepper, flat pr. | 57.50 | 275.00 | 1,000.00 | 750.00 |
|  | Salt and pepper, ftd. | 7,500.00 |  |  |  |
|  | Sandwich server, center handle | 42.50 | 75.00 | 35.00 | 115.00 |
|  | Saucer (cup ring) | 30.00 |  |  | 135.00 |
|  | Saucer (see 5¾" plate) |  |  |  |  |
|  | Sherbet, 2¼" flat | 155.00 | 110.00 |  |  |
|  | Sherbet, 3" ftd. | 16.00 |  |  |  |
|  | Sherbet, 4¾" ftd. | 77.50 | 75.00 | 145.00 | 145.00 |
|  | Sugar, ftd. | 27.50 | 80.00 | 180.00 | 180.00 |
|  | Sugar lid | 1,450.00 |  | 1,000.00 | 1,000.00 |
|  | Tumbler, 3½", 5 oz. juice | 40.00 | 110.00 |  |  |
|  | Tumbler, 4¼", 9 oz. water | 26.00 | 95.00 |  |  |
|  | Tumbler, 4¾", 11 oz. water | 165.00 | 120.00 | 180.00 | 185.00 |
|  | Tumbler, 5¼", 13½ oz. iced tea | 43.00 | 195.00 |  |  |
|  | Tumbler, 3¼", 3 oz. ftd. juice | 75.00 |  |  |  |
|  | Tumbler, 5¼", 10 oz. ftd. | 34.00 | 120.00 |  | 180.00 |
|  | Tumbler, 6½", 15 oz. ftd. iced tea | 34.00 | 180.00 | 210.00 |  |
|  | Vase (sweet pea) | 130.00 | 105.00 | 275.00 |  |
|  | Whiskey, 2¼", 1½ oz. | 62.50 |  |  |  |

\* Frosted or satin finish items slightly lower
\** Crystal-$15.00
\*** Divided Crystal-$12.50
\**** Crystal-$17.50 pr. – Beware reproductions.

**Please refer to Foreword for pricing information**

# MISS AMERICA (DIAMOND PATTERN) HOCKING GLASS COMPANY, 1935-1938

Colors: Crystal, pink; some green, ice blue, Jad-ite and Royal Ruby. *(See Reproduction Section)*

Royal Ruby Miss America has never before been shown in such quantity! Enjoy! Twenty years ago there were four water goblets, and a sugar and creamer for sale as a lot. I already had a sugar and creamer, so I waited for another dealer to buy these pieces hoping I could get one goblet for my book. At the time I was a school teacher and $200.00 for six pieces of glass was a lot of money when I only needed one of the pieces. It took over six months of shows for someone to purchase them, but I did, finally, obtain a goblet that way. It was shown on the cover of the second edition. The sugar, creamer, and a wine were shown on the cover of the first edition. By the way, those first edition books are selling for more than $200.00 in excellent condition! I should have kept them instead of the glass!

In any case, I bought a set of fifty pieces last year from the grandson of a factory worker who had retired from Anchor Hocking in 1962. What made this so interesting for me was that I discovered that there were two styles of water goblets, footed juices and sherbets! Notice how one of the water goblets and one of the footed juices flare out at the top. The sherbets do the same; but, unfortunately, I packed two of the same style for the photography session. This set contained the first cups, sherbets, footed and flat juices I had seen. It was a basic set for eight with cups, saucers and luncheon plates, but it had only a few other items. A collector in Arkansas is happily displaying this set now. I hope you enjoy seeing it here!

Reproductions have been the problem for Miss America since the early 1970's. Please refer to page 220 for a complete run down on this problem. I will point out that there are many reports of cobalt creamers and sugars coming in; so be aware that this pattern was **not made in cobalt** originally. That also means that other colors are sure to follow.

One of the toughest problems has concerned the reproduction shakers. There are few green shakers available that are old. In fact, I haven't seen an older pair since the early 1970's. Rarely, have I had as many questions about Miss America shakers as in the last few years because there have been reproductions of the reproductions and even those have now been copied by another importer. There are at least four or five generations of reproduction shakers; so it depends upon which one you find as to what to look for on them. Interestingly enough, there originally were two different moulds used for old shakers. The shakers that stay fat toward the base are the best ones to buy, since they have not been reproduced. The shakers that get thin (as shown in the photograph) are the style that has been reproduced. Both styles were made originally, but only the thin style has been copied. Buy shakers from a **reputable dealer**.

Any time a pattern was made for several years, it will be possible to find pieces that vary in design. There was more than one mould made for each piece; so items can vary as often as each mould was changed.

A pink divided relish was sold at the Peach State Depression Show several years ago! Few of these have surfaced recently.

There are a few odd-colored or flashed pieces of Miss America that surface occasionally. Flashed-on red, green or amethyst make interesting conversation pieces, but are not plentiful enough to collect a set. A Jad-ite 8" bowl has now been found to go with the luncheon plate shown in an earlier edition!

| | Crystal | Pink | Green | Royal Ruby | | | Crystal | Pink | Green | Royal Ruby |
|---|---|---|---|---|---|---|---|---|---|---|
| Bowl, 4½" berry | | | 11.00 | | | Goblet, 5½", 10 oz. | | | | |
| * Bowl, 6¼" cereal | 9.50 | 20.00 | 16.00 | | | water | 21.00 | 40.00 | | 225.00 |
| Bowl, 8" curved in at | | | | | | Pitcher, 8", 65 oz. | 46.00 | 115.00 | | |
| top | 37.50 | 70.00 | | 400.00 | | Pitcher, 8½", 65 oz. | | | | |
| Bowl, 8¾" straight | | | | | | w/ice lip | 65.00 | 125.00 | | |
| deep fruit | 34.00 | 55.00 | | | *** | Plate, 5¾" sherbet | 6.00 | 9.50 | 7.00 | 40.00 |
| Bowl, 10" oval | | | | | | Plate, 6¾" | | 7.50 | | |
| vegetable | 15.00 | 26.00 | | | | Plate, 8½" salad | 7.50 | 21.00 | 9.50 | 125.00 |
| Bowl, 11", shallow | | | | 775.00 | **** | Plate, 10¼" dinner | 14.00 | 25.00 | | |
| ** Butter dish and | | | | | | Plate, 10¼" grill | 11.00 | 22.00 | | |
| cover | 210.00 | 525.00 | | | | Platter, 12¼" oval | 14.00 | 24.00 | | |
| Butter dish bottom | 9.50 | 20.00 | | | | Relish, 8¾", 4 part | 11.00 | 22.00 | | |
| Butter dish top | 200.50 | 505.00 | | | | Relish, 11¾" round | | | | |
| Cake plate, 12" ftd. | 26.00 | 42.00 | | | | divided | 25.00 | 950.00 | | |
| Candy jar and | | | | | | Salt and pepper, pr. | 29.00 | 55.00 | 290.00 | |
| cover, 11½" | 57.50 | 130.00 | | | | Saucer | 4.00 | 7.00 | | 50.00 |
| **** Celery dish, 10½" | | | | | *** | Sherbet | 800 | 14.00 | | 95.00 |
| oblong | 15.00 | 26.00 | | | | Sugar | 8.00 | 16.00 | | 160.00 |
| Coaster, 5¾" | 15.00 | 26.00 | | | **** | Tumbler, 4", 5 oz. | | | | |
| Comport, 5" | 14.00 | 24.00 | | | | juice | 16.50 | 43.00 | | 150.00 |
| Creamer, ftd. | 9.50 | 17.50 | | 165.00 | | Tumbler, 4½", | | | | |
| Cup | 10.00 | 21.00 | 11.00 | 200.00 | | 10 oz. water | 15.00 | 28.00 | 18.00 | |
| Goblet, 3¾", 3 oz. | | | | | | Tumbler, 5¾", 14 oz. | | | | |
| wine | 20.00 | 65.00 | | 235.00 | | iced tea | 25.00 | 70.00 | | |
| Goblet, 4¾", 5 oz. | | | | | | | | | | |
| juice | 25.00 | 77.50 | | 235.00 | | | | | | |

*Also has appeared in Cobalt Blue $125.00    **Absolute mint price    ***Also in Ice Blue $40.00    ****Also in Ice Blue $100.00

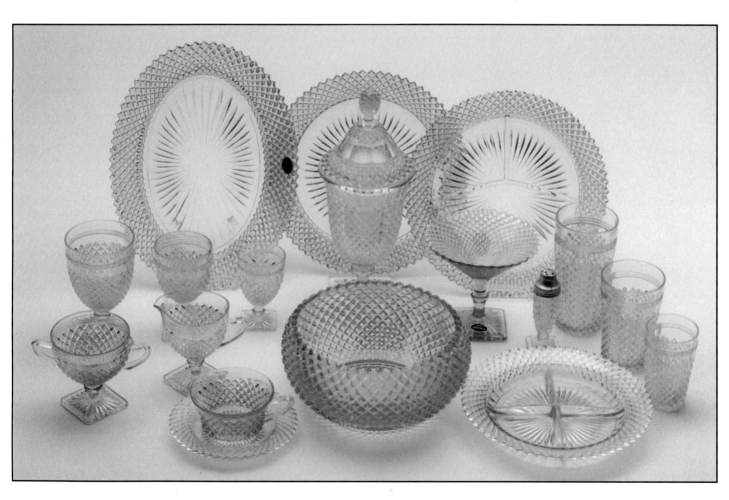

# MODERNTONE HAZEL ATLAS GLASS COMPANY, 1934-1942; Late 1940's-Early 1950's

Colors: Amethyst, cobalt blue; some crystal, pink and Platonite fired-on colors.

Since it better fits the time of that book, platonite Moderntone has been moved into my book *Collectible Glassware from the 40's, 50's, 60's...* The cobalt and amethyst Moderntone will remain here.

Anything cobalt blue sells; so this makes Moderntone doubly desirable. Many people in Florida, including non collectors, put cobalt colored glassware in their windows. The sun really makes it show up!

I am always asked just which lid is the "real" lid for the butter or sugar. There is no true sugar or butter lid. Evidently the butter bottom and sugar were sold to some other company who made the tops. Who knows whether the lids are supposed to have black, red or blue knobs? I certainly do not, but I have had reports of all those colored knobs! Red seems to be the predominate color found.

Mustards have been made from the handle-less custard and lid as well as the roly poly and lid. I placed the roly poly and lid in the last picture to see if it would spark any letters. It did not, unless there is one in the box full of mail that has arrived since I started writing books eleven weeks ago. Actually, it is merely cobalt blue, not Moderntone. There is also a punch set being found that is being called Moderntone with these same roly polys found on the Royal Lace toddy set. This was assembled by someone else but some collectors accept it to go with Moderntone. It is merely a blue punch set. A similar set uses a Hazel Atlas cobalt blue mixing bowl in a metal holder with Moderntone custard cups sitting on the metal rim, that **is** being accepted as a Moderntone punch set by many collectors.

The boxed set with the crystal "shot glasses" in the metal holder came with a Colonial Block creamer. The box was marked "Little Deb" Lemonade Server Set. I paid $20.00 for it. You can see the set in the bottom photograph. It's a shame the shot glasses and pitcher were not cobalt! That pitcher has turned up in cobalt and several have turned up with Shirley Temple's picture!

Iced tea and juice tumblers are still the tumblers to find in both cobalt and amethyst. I will mention again that there are no true Moderntone tumblers listed in catalogues. The tumblers being collected were advertised alongside the Moderntone in store and newspaper ads. For lack of a true tumbler, the ones shown here have been "adopted" as tumblers for this set. Green, pink or crystal tumblers are also found, but there is little marketability for these except the shot or whiskey glass that is sought by other collectors as well as Depression glass enthusiasts. Where have all the ruffled cream soups and sandwich plates gone? Sandwich plates can be found, but many are heavily scratched causing collectors to avoid them. The cheese dish lid has been moved to the side to show the wooden cheese plate that fits inside the metal lid. There have been some big prices paid for these recently. This cheese dish is a salad plate with a metal cover and wooden cutting board.

Both green and pink ash trays are found occasionally, but there is little demand for them now. Blue ash trays still command a hefty price for an ash tray. Crystal Moderntone is found occasionally; and there are a few collectors for it. Price it about half the lowest price listed and hope one of the few collectors stops by to see you. Finding bowls without inner rim roughness is a problem for collectors. Prices below are for mint condition pieces. That is why bowls are so highly priced. Mint condition bowls are rare; but used, nicked, battered bowls are not!

| | Cobalt | Amethyst | | Cobalt | Amethyst |
|---|---|---|---|---|---|
| * Ash tray, 7¾", match holder in center | 150.00 | | Plate, 7¾" luncheon | 12.50 | 9.00 |
| Bowl, 4¾" cream soup | 20.00 | 17.00 | Plate, 8⅞" dinner | 17.50 | 12.00 |
| Bowl, 5" berry | 22.50 | 22.50 | Plate, 10½" sandwich | 50.00 | 35.00 |
| Bowl, 5" cream soup, ruffled | 45.00 | 25.00 | Platter, 11" oval | 40.00 | 30.00 |
| Bowl, 6½" cereal | 67.50 | 67.50 | Platter, 12" oval | 60.00 | 40.00 |
| Bowl, 7½" soup | 100.00 | 85.00 | Salt and pepper, pr. | 40.00 | 35.00 |
| Bowl, 8¾" large berry | 50.00 | 40.00 | Saucer | 5.00 | 4.00 |
| Butter dish with metal cover | 98.00 | | Sherbet | 13.00 | 12.00 |
| Cheese dish, 7" with metal lid | 425.00 | | Sugar | 11.00 | 10.00 |
| Creamer | 11.00 | 10.00 | Sugar lid in metal | 37.50 | |
| Cup | 11.00 | 11.00 | Tumbler, 5 oz. | 35.00 | 25.00 |
| Cup (handle-less) or custard | 18.00 | 14.00 | Tumbler, 9 oz. | 32.00 | 25.00 |
| Plate, 5⅞" sherbet | 6.50 | 5.00 | Tumbler, 12 oz. | 90.00 | 75.00 |
| Plate, 6¾" salad | 11.00 | 9.00 | ** Whiskey, 1½ oz. | 35.00 | |

\* Pink $75.00; green $95.00
\*\* Pink or green $17.50

# MOONDROPS NEW MARTINSVILLE GLASS COMPANY, 1932-1940

Colors: Amber, pink, green, cobalt, ice blue, red, amethyst, crystal, dark green, light green, jadite, smoke and black.

Moondrops collectors are relentless in their pursuit of red and cobalt blue! In my shop, I have a waiting list of people to call whenever a piece surfaces. Yet, there are other colors available. Amber is the least desired color; if you like that color, you could probably find a bargain or two awaiting you. A lady at a show recently told me she absolutely adores amber colored glassware. In Moondrops there is a variety of pieces that are not found in many of the other patterns in this book! Perfume bottles, powder jars, mugs, gravy boats, triple candlesticks are indications that this glassware is more "elegant" than most of its contemporaries. Bud vases, decanters and stems with the "rocket" style add to a wide range of unusual pieces from which to choose.

The butter has to have a glass top to obtain the price listed below. The metal top with a bird finial found on butter bottoms is better than none; that top only sells for about $25.00 on a good day. However, the metal top **with the fan finial** brings about $55.00!

| | Blue, Red | Other Colors | | Blue, Red | Other Colors |
|---|---|---|---|---|---|
| Ash tray | 32.00 | 17.00 | Goblet, 5⅛", 3 oz. metal stem wine | 16.00 | 11.00 |
| Bowl, 5¼" berry | 12.50 | 6.50 | Goblet, 5½", 4 oz. metal stem wine | 20.00 | 11.00 |
| Bowl, 6¾" soup | 73.00 | | Goblet, 6¼", 9 oz. metal stem water | 23.00 | 16.00 |
| Bowl, 7½" pickle | 22.00 | 14.00 | Gravy boat | 120.00 | 90.00 |
| Bowl, 8⅜" ftd., concave top | 35.00 | 22.00 | Mayonnaise, 5¼" | 55.00 | 32.00 |
| Bowl, 8½" 3-ftd. divided relish | 29.00 | 18.00 | Mug, 5⅛", 12 oz. | 40.00 | 23.00 |
| Bowl, 9½" 3-legged ruffled | 45.00 | | Perfume bottle, "rocket" | 210.00 | 150.00 |
| Bowl, 9¾" oval vegetable | 33.00 | 23.00 | Pitcher, 6⅞", 22 oz. small | 165.00 | 90.00 |
| Bowl, 9¾" covered casserole | 140.00 | 97.50 | Pitcher, 8⅛", 32 oz. medium | 185.00 | 115.00 |
| Bowl, 9¾" handled oval | 52.50 | 36.00 | Pitcher, 8", 50 oz. large, with lip | 195.00 | 115.00 |
| Bowl, 11" boat-shaped celery | 32.00 | 23.00 | Pitcher, 8⅛", 53 oz. large, no lip | 185.00 | 125.00 |
| Bowl, 12" round 3-ftd. console | 85.00 | 32.00 | Plate, 5⅞" | 11.00 | 8.00 |
| Bowl, 13" console with "wings" | 120.00 | 42.00 | Plate, 6⅛" sherbet | 8.00 | 5.00 |
| Butter dish and cover | 430.00 | 255.00 | Plate, 6" round, off-center sherbet indent | 12.00 | 9.00 |
| Butter dish bottom | 62.50 | 47.50 | Plate, 7⅛" salad | 14.00 | 10.00 |
| Butter dish top (glass) | 367.50 | 207.50 | Plate, 8½" luncheon | 15.00 | 12.00 |
| Candles, 2" ruffled pr. | 40.00 | 24.00 | Plate, 9½" dinner | 25.00 | 16.00 |
| Candles, 4½" sherbet style pr. | 27.00 | 20.00 | Plate, 14" round sandwich | 38.00 | 18.00 |
| Candlesticks, 5" ruffled, pr. | 35.00 | 21.00 | Plate, 14" 2-handled sandwich | 43.00 | 23.00 |
| Candlesticks, 5" "wings" pr. | 88.00 | 46.00 | Platter, 12" oval | 35.00 | 22.00 |
| Candlesticks, 5¼" triple light pr. | 95.00 | 50.00 | Powder jar, 3 ftd. | 140.00 | 96.00 |
| Candlesticks, 8½" metal stem pr. | 40.00 | 30.00 | Saucer | 6.00 | 5.00 |
| Candy dish, 8" ruffled | 37.50 | 20.00 | Sherbet, 2⅝" | 16.00 | 11.00 |
| Cocktail shaker with or without hdl., | | | Sherbet, 4½" | 26.00 | 16.00 |
| metal top | 60.00 | 35.00 | Sugar, 2¾" | 15.00 | 10.00 |
| Comport, 4" | 23.00 | 16.00 | Sugar, 3½" | 16.00 | 11.00 |
| Comport, 11½" | 58.00 | 32.00 | Tumbler, 2¾", 2 oz. shot | 16.00 | 10.00 |
| Creamer, 2¾" miniature | 18.00 | 11.00 | Tumbler, 2¾", 2 oz. handled shot | 16.00 | 11.00 |
| Creamer, 3¾" regular | 16.00 | 10.00 | Tumbler, 3¼", 3 oz. ftd. juice | 16.00 | 11.00 |
| Cup | 16.00 | 10.00 | Tumbler, 3⅝", 5 oz. | 15.00 | 10.00 |
| Decanter, 7¾" small | 67.50 | 38.00 | Tumbler, 4⅜", 7 oz. | 16.00 | 10.00 |
| Decanter, 8½" medium | 70.00 | 42.00 | Tumbler, 4⅜", 8 oz. | 16.00 | 11.00 |
| Decanter, 11¼" large | 98.00 | 50.00 | Tumbler, 4⅞", 9 oz. handled | 28.00 | 16.00 |
| Decanter, 10¼" "rocket" | 410.00 | 360.00 | Tumbler, 4⅞", 9 oz. | 19.00 | 15.00 |
| Goblet, 2⅞", ¾ oz. cordial | 38.00 | 26.00 | Tumbler, 5⅛", 12 oz. | 28.00 | 14.00 |
| Goblet, 4", 4 oz. wine | 22.00 | 13.00 | Tray, 7½", for mini sugar/creamer | 37.50 | 19.00 |
| Goblet, 4¾", "rocket" wine | 60.00 | 30.00 | Vase, 7¾" flat, ruffled top | 60.00 | 57.00 |
| Goblet, 4¾", 5 oz. | 24.00 | 15.00 | Vase, 8½" "rocket" bud | 230.00 | 155.00 |
| Goblet, 5¾" 8 oz. | 33.00 | 19.00 | Vase, 9¼" "rocket" style | 225.00 | 120.00 |

**Please refer to Foreword for pricing information**

# MT. PLEASANT, "DOUBLE SHIELD" L. E. SMITH GLASS COMPANY, 1920's-1934

Colors: Black amethyst, amethyst, cobalt blue, crystal, pink, green, white.

Mt. Pleasant has no new additions to add although I keep getting letters from people who say they have an unlisted piece which they never photograph or enumerate. Keep looking! A correction has been made in the size of the square 4" footed fruit. Somehow the ⅞" part was left off the 4", and since that is closer to 5", a couple of readers noticed. Thank you for notifying me of our mistakes. With all these prices, listings, and retyping, there may always be some mistakes getting by us. The larger leaf that measures 11¼" is being found infrequently. Maybe that is why I never knew it existed until a few years ago.

I have been saving the two white pieces with black decorations for a few years hoping to find more, but I have not seen any others. These were a gift from Keys Glass Cottage of Hazel, Kentucky, for the book. The striped decoration on crystal would make a striking set if you could find enough of it. Decaled and enameled pieces are not often found, but they do embellish the photographs!

Collectors of cobalt blue and black glass are frequent buyers of Mt. Pleasant. Many times at shows someone has brought a piece of this pattern in for me to identify and were excited to know that it was even in a book! Demand for blue is strongly evidenced at shows as dealers have trouble keeping enough cobalt Mt. Pleasant. Black is often found, but there are more collectors for the blue. I have had sporadic reports of some pieces being found in pink or green.

More cobalt blue is being found in Kansas, Nebraska and western New York than any place. Mt. Pleasant was promoted heavily at hardware stores in those areas; black predominates in most other areas of the country. Many pieces are found with a platinum (silver) band around them. This band wears with use; thus pieces are found with only partial evidence of this decoration. The trim doesn't inflate the price.

| | Pink, Green | Amethyst, Black, Cobalt | | Pink, Green | Amethyst, Black, Cobalt |
|---|---|---|---|---|---|
| Bonbon, 7", rolled-up, handled | 16.00 | 23.00 | Leaf, 11¼" | | 28.00 |
| Bowl, 4" opening, rose | 18.00 | 26.00 | Mayonnaise, 5½", 3-ftd. | 18.00 | 28.00 |
| Bowl, 4⅞", square ftd. fruit | 13.00 | 18.00 | Mint, 6", center handle | 16.00 | 22.00 |
| Bowl, 6", 2-handled, square | 13.00 | 16.00 | Plate, 7", 2-handled, scalloped | 9.00 | 15.00 |
| Bowl, 7", 3 ftd., rolled out edge | 16.00 | 22.00 | Plate, 8", scalloped or square | 10.00 | 15.00 |
| Bowl, 8", scalloped, 2-handled | 19.00 | 27.50 | Plate, 8", 2-handled | 11.00 | 18.00 |
| Bowl, 8", square, 2-handled | 19.00 | 30.00 | Plate 8¼, square w/indent for cup | | 16.00 |
| Bowl, 9", scalloped, 1¾" deep, ftd. | | 28.00 | Plate, 9" grill | | 11.00 |
| Bowl, 9¼", square ftd. fruit | 19.00 | 30.00 | Plate, 10½", cake, 2-handled | 16.00 | 28.00 |
| Bowl, 10", scalloped fruit | | 38.00 | Plate, 10½", 1¼" high, cake | | 37.50 |
| Bowl, 10", 2-handled, turned-up edge | | 30.00 | Plate, 12", 2-handled | 20.00 | 33.00 |
| Cake plate, 10½", ftd., 1¼" high | | 36.00 | Salt and pepper, 2 styles | 24.00 | 40.00 |
| Candlestick, single, pr. | 20.00 | 28.00 | Sandwich server, center-handled | | 38.00 |
| Candlestick, double, pr. | 26.00 | 45.00 | Saucer | 2.50 | 5.00 |
| Creamer | 18.00 | 19.00 | Sherbet | 10.00 | 16.00 |
| Cup (waffle-like crystal) | 4..50 | | Sugar | 18.00 | 18.00 |
| Cup | 9.50 | 12.00 | Tumbler, ftd. | | 20.00 |
| Leaf, 8" | | 16.00 | Vase, 7¼" | | 30.00 |

# NEW CENTURY, and incorrectly, "LYDIA RAY" HAZEL ATLAS GLASS COMPANY, 1930-1935

Colors: Green; some crystal, pink, amethyst and cobalt.

New Century is one of those smaller patterns that a few collectors just love. The green is gathered more than any other color; in fact, sets can only be acquired in crystal and green. Few attempt to put a set together in crystal which is so scarce that prices are on the same level as green. So far, pink, cobalt blue and amethyst have only been found in water sets and an occasional cup or saucer.

I haven't shown a decanter or cocktail for several editions; I finally acquired these to display again. The wine goblet has eluded me.

Years ago, I ran into several crystal powder jars. They were made with a sugar lid on the top of a sherbet. The knob of the sherbet had glass marbles or beads attached by a wire. I have not seen these for a while. You can make a footed powder jar in many patterns by putting a sugar lid on a sherbet. It will not work for all patterns, but it will for many. There are seven different tumblers if you count the whiskey, but only the nine and ten ounce are found regularly. As with Adam, the casserole bottom is harder to find than the top.

New Century is the **official** name for this pattern made by Hazel Atlas. "Lydia Ray" was the name used by collectors until an **official** name was found. I mention this for new collectors since the name "New Century" was also used (incorrectly) by another author to identify the **Ovide**. This has caused confusion in the past; so I want you to be aware of this minor problem.

| | Green, Crystal | Pink, Cobalt Amethyst | | Green, Crystal | Pink, Cobalt Amethyst |
|---|---|---|---|---|---|
| Ash tray/coaster, 5⅜" | 28.00 | | Plate, 8½" salad | 8.50 | |
| Bowl, 4½" berry | 12.00 | | Plate, 10" dinner | 16.00 | |
| Bowl, 4¾" cream soup | 17.50 | | Plate, 10" grill | 10.00 | |
| Bowl, 8" large berry | 17.50 | | Platter, 11" oval | 15.00 | |
| Bowl, 9" covered casserole | 55.00 | | Salt and pepper, pr. | 35.00 | |
| Butter dish and cover | 55.00 | | Saucer | 3.00 | 7.50 |
| Cup | 6.50 | 19.00 | Sherbet, 3" | 9.00 | |
| Creamer | 8.50 | | Sugar | 8.00 | |
| Decanter and stopper | 50.00 | | Sugar cover | 15.00 | |
| Goblet, 2½ oz. wine | 23.00 | | Tumbler, 3½", 5 oz. | 11.00 | 12.00 |
| Goblet, 3¼ oz. cocktail | 20.50 | | Tumbler, 4¼", 9 oz. | 15.00 | 14.00 |
| Pitcher, 7¾", 60 oz. with or | | | Tumbler, 5", 10 oz. | 15.00 | 16.00 |
|    without ice lip | 35.00 | 35.00 | Tumbler, 5¼", 12 oz. | 22.00 | 23.00 |
| Pitcher, 8", 80 oz. with or | | | Tumbler, 4", 5 oz. ftd. | 16.00 | |
|    without ice lip | 40.00 | 42.00 | Tumbler, 4⅞", 9 oz. ftd. | 19.00 | |
| Plate, 6" sherbet | 3.50 | | Whiskey, 2½", 1½ oz. | 15.00 | |
| Plate, 7⅛" breakfast | 7.50 | | | | |

# NEWPORT, "HAIRPIN" HAZEL ATLAS GLASS COMPANY, 1936-1940

Colors: Cobalt blue, amethyst; some pink, "Platonite" white and fired-on colors.

Newport collectors search more for cobalt blue than for amethyst and I have always showed more of the blue. This time I decided to show the color not as often collected. Amethyst Newport makes a great table setting! I personally like the shapes of this pattern more than Moderntone which is about the only other choice you have in accumulating a set of amethyst glassware from this era. Moroccan Amethyst came much later!

I have recently been informed by several avid collectors there is a **dinner plate** as well as a luncheon plate although there is no official listing of two sizes. The dinner plate measures 8¹³⁄₁₆" while the luncheon plate measures 8½". The only official listing I have catalogues plates of 6", 8½" and 11½". However, after obtaining these plates, I found actual measurements quite different as you can see by the size listings in the price guide. Also there is a new size correction for the larger plate, 11¾". One of the problems with catalogue measurements is that they are not always accurate and sometimes not very close!

Sets of pink Newport were given away as premiums for buying seeds from a catalogue in the 1930's. A few of these sets are entering the market but are not presently selling very well. It is cobalt blue and amethyst that draw collectors' attention. Cereal bowls and tumblers can not be found in any quantity. I am having trouble replacing the large berry bowls in both colors that got "crunched" before our photography session for the last book. It is bad enough to lose pieces of glass, but losing them before they are pictured upsets me even more. Worse, they were so "crunched" (hundreds and hundreds of pieces) that they could not be salvaged with glue for future use. My borrowed help does not always wrap and pack as securely as does Cathy.

Platonite Newport can now be found in my book *Collectible Glassware from the 40's, 50's, 60's....*

| | Cobalt | Amethyst | | Cobalt | Amethyst |
|---|---|---|---|---|---|
| Bowl, 4¾" berry | 16.00 | 13.00 | Plate, 8¹³⁄₁₆", dinner | 27.50 | 27.50 |
| Bowl, 4¾" cream soup | 17.50 | 16.00 | Plate, 11¾" sandwich | 37.50 | 30.00 |
| Bowl, 5¼" cereal | 32.00 | 25.00 | Platter, 11¾" oval | 40.00 | 32.00 |
| Bowl, 8¼" large berry | 37.50 | 30.00 | Salt and pepper | 47.50 | 40.00 |
| Cup | 11.00 | 10.00 | Saucer | 5.00 | 5.00 |
| Creamer | 16.00 | 13.00 | Sherbet | 15.00 | 13.00 |
| Plate, 5⅞" sherbet | 7.00 | 6.00 | Sugar | 16.00 | 14.00 |
| Plate, 8½" luncheon | 12.50 | 11.00 | Tumbler, 4½", 9 oz. | 33.00 | 30.00 |

---

# "NORA BIRD" PADEN CITY GLASS COMPANY, LINE #300, 1929-1930's

Colors: Pink, green, crystal.

"Nora Bird" is a name given to this Paden City pattern by collectors. It was a numbered etching on the popular #300 line blank. This blank is seen in several additional colors; yet pink, green and crystal are the only colors on which this "Nora Bird" etching has so far been found.

Note the octagonal lid on the flat candy dish. This is not a part of the #300 line as was the green, open handled, flat candy shown in the tenth edition. I have not seen the 5¼" footed candy dish, but I know it is shaped like the Cupid candy. This should make finding a candy in "Nora Bird" somewhat easier with three from which to choose. Yet finding even one is not easily accomplished. Some of these candy dishes are in the hands of candy dish collectors rather than "Nora Bird" collectors.

There are two different styles of sugars in the picture. These same two styles are also found in Cupid. There may be more pieces in this pattern than I have listed; please let me know if you find something else. A pitcher would be delightful to go with the three different tumblers found. The bird on each piece can be found in flight or getting ready to fly. Some collectors have suggested this bird is a pheasant which is probably true since several pheasant patterns made by other glass companies were available during this time.

| | Pink, Green | | Pink, Green |
|---|---|---|---|
| Candlestick, pr. | 70.00 | Plate, 8" | 22.50 |
| Candy dish w/cover, 6½", 3 part | 90.00 | Saucer | 14.00 |
| Candy with lid, ftd., 5¼" high | 67.50 | Sugar, 4½", round handle | 40.00 |
| Creamer, 4½", round handle | 42.50 | Sugar, 5", pointed handle | 40.00 |
| Creamer, 5", pointed handle | 42.50 | Tumbler, 3" | 37.50 |
| Cup | 48.00 | Tumbler, 4" | 47.50 |
| Ice tub, 6" | 98.00 | Tumbler, 4¾", ftd. | 55.00 |
| Mayonnaise and liner | 77.50 | | |

# NORMANDIE, "BOUQUET AND LATTICE" FEDERAL GLASS COMPANY 1933-1940

Colors: Iridescent, amber, pink, crystal.

Normandie in pink has been elusive for sometime for those collectors searching for it. Amber has been available in most items, but tumblers, sugar lids and dinner plates have recently become scarce in this color. Those same items mentioned above have never been easily found in pink, even in the "good old days" of collecting!

Some iridescent Normandie is again being seen at Depression Glass shows. That usually means that collectors are asking for it, and dealers are listening to their requests. For years this color was wanted by no one at **any** price. I put some iridescent in my booth at an Antique Mall for half my book price and cleaning the dust off it was a chore each year! Recently, however, a rumor circulated that it was getting hard to find and suddenly there were numerous collectors buying this iridescent color of Normandie. There were enough buyers to raise all the prices a little; and the prices of the larger serving pieces have risen even more. Iridescent is still reasonably priced in comparison to the pink and amber. When have you seen an iridescent Normandie salad plate?

Amber colored Depression glassware seems to be the least alluring color collected in all patterns – not just Normandie. However, I have noticed there have been some fashion color shifts recently. Yellows and oranges are appearing again. If some women's magazine, such as *Country Living*, would feature it on the cover as a fashion statement, then we would have a run on amber like has never been seen before. Have you noticed the price of cobalt blue "Ships" glasses recently? They were shown on the cover a few years ago and prices almost doubled overnight. If you are one of those who do like amber colored glassware, then this would be a good pattern to start. It has most basic items, and it is inexpensive enough that you will not have to take out an equity loan to collect a setting for six or eight. Find and buy those hard to find items first! That is really good advice for collecting any pattern. The rarer and harder to find items increase in price much faster than any of the commonly found items. One collector came by to shake my hand at the Georgia show last year. He had taken that money saving advice and was so pleased he stopped by to tell me about it!

The console bowl and candlesticks sometimes found with iridized Normandie are Madrid. These were sold about the same time. Several collectors have reported finding this console set with Normandie sets. That does not make it Normandie; it is still Madrid! The pattern on the glass determines what it is, not the color.

|  | Amber | Pink | Iridescent |
|---|---|---|---|
| Bowl, 5" berry | 5.50 | 6.50 | 5.00 |
| * Bowl, 6½" cereal | 14.00 | 18.50 | 8.50 |
| Bowl, 8½" large berry | 15.00 | 20.00 | 12.00 |
| Bowl, 10" oval veg. | 15.00 | 30.00 | 15.00 |
| Creamer, ftd. | 8.50 | 11.00 | 8.00 |
| Cup | 7.50 | 8.50 | 6.00 |
| Pitcher, 8", 80 oz. | 70.00 | 115.00 | |
| Plate, 6" sherbet | 4.50 | 4.00 | 3.00 |
| Plate, 7¾" salad | 8.50 | 11.00 | 52.50 |
| Plate, 9¼ luncheon | 8.50 | 13.00 | 15.00 |
| Plate, 11" dinner | 28.00 | 93.00 | 11.50 |
| Plate, 11" grill | 14.00 | 17.00 | 9.00 |
| Platter, 11¾" | 16.00 | 23.00 | 12.00 |
| Salt and pepper, pr. | 47.50 | 70.00 | |
| Saucer | 4.00 | 4.00 | 3.00 |
| Sherbet | 6.50 | 8.50 | 7.00 |
| Sugar | 8.00 | 9.00 | 6.00 |
| Sugar lid | 84.00 | 155.00 | |
| Tumbler, 4", 5 oz. juice | 25.00 | 42.00 | |
| Tumbler, 4¼", 9 oz. water | 15.00 | 36.00 | |
| Tumbler, 5", 12 oz. iced tea | 30.00 | 65.00 | |

*Mistaken by many as butter bottom.

# No. 610, "PYRAMID" INDIANA GLASS COMPANY, 1926-1932

Colors: Green, pink, yellow, white, crystal, blue or black in 1974-1975 by Tiara.

"Pyramid" is a collectors' name for this pattern. The official name of the pattern was No. 610. Indiana gave most patterns a number and not a name. Collectors do not seem to be fond of calling patterns by numbers however; so most of Indiana's patterns are known by an unofficial name.

An enthusiastic collector wrote to say that the 8 oz. tumblers come in two styles. One style has a 2¼" square foot while the other has a 2½" square foot. That is a variance that most people would not notice unless these two tumblers were placed side by side.

Blue or black pieces of "Pyramid" were made by Indiana during the 1970's for Tiara. Normally, you see two sizes of black tumblers or the 4-part center handled relish in either color. If you like these colors, it is all right to buy them if you realize that they are **not** old, and you do not pay an **old** price for them. Berry bowls were also made. These colors are recent and not Depression glass! That handled 4-part relish is sometimes mistaken for Tea Room, but it is not.

This art deco style pattern has gotten very popular in circles outside of Depression Glass and prices have risen dramatically with the increased competition for this glassware in the last few years.

The pattern was and still is easily damaged. Be sure to check all the ridged panels and all the corners on each piece. You will be amazed how easy it is to miss a chipped or crack piece of "Pyramid."

Crystal pitchers and tumblers in "Pyramid" are harder to find than colored counterparts, although there are fewer collectors searching for them. Prices on crystal pitchers are higher than all but the yellow. The yellow pitchers are found frequently; but there are so many collectors of yellow No. 610 that the price continues an upward trend! Ice **buckets** are readily found, even in yellow. It is the yellow **lid** that is nearly impossible to find! When you have both pieces, you have a rare piece of glass!

Oval bowls and pickle dishes are both 9½". The oval bowl has pointed edges as can be seen in bowls of white, green and yellow. The pickle dish is shown only on the left side in pink in the top photograph. The edges of that pickle dish are rounded instead of pointed.

| | Crystal | Pink | Green | Yellow |
|---|---|---|---|---|
| Bowl, 4¾" berry | 11.00 | 17.50 | 19.00 | 32.00 |
| Bowl, 8½" master berry | 16.00 | 28.00 | 29.00 | 55.00 |
| Bowl, 9½" oval | 27.00 | 28.00 | 26.00 | 50.00 |
| Bowl, 9½" pickle, 5¾" wide | 19.00 | 30.00 | 28.00 | 53.00 |
| Creamer | 16.00 | 23.00 | 23.00 | 32.00 |
| Ice tub | 52.50 | 75.00 | 84.00 | 190.00 |
| Ice tub lid | | | | 600.00 |
| Pitcher | 310.00 | 215.00 | 200.00 | 430.00 |
| Relish tray, 4-part handled | 23.00 | 40.00 | 45.00 | 60.00 |
| Sugar | 16.00 | 24.00 | 24.00 | 32.00 |
| Tray for creamer and sugar | 15.00 | 22.00 | 25.00 | 50.00 |
| Tumbler, 8 oz. ftd., 2 styles | 33.00 | 30.00 | 32.00 | 50.00 |
| Tumbler, 11 oz. ftd. | 57.50 | 42.50 | 52.50 | 70.00 |

**Please refer to Foreword for pricing information**

# No. 612, "HORSESHOE" INDIANA GLASS COMPANY, 1930-1933

Colors: Green, yellow, pink, crystal.

The official name for this Indiana pattern is No. 612, but collectors dubbed it "Horseshoe." Butter dishes are rarely seen at any price and it has been several editions since I had one pictured. It took seven years to put this top and bottom together. Want a chuckle? A butter dish collector I knew was searching for a top to the No. 612 butter base he had bought. He gathered three additional bottoms while he was searching for a top. His reasoning was that he did not want three other collectors searching for a top until he had his own! I now know what he went through.

This butter dish has always been highly priced. If you can find a first edition of my book, the butter dish was $90.00 back in 1972. That was an expensive butter then!

Many new collectors have ignored "Horseshoe" for years since it has so many highly priced pieces. That is changing; and several new collectors have begun to spur prices upward with their constant searching for all the hard to find pieces. Prices are rising for the first time in several years.

Be aware that there are two styles of plates and platters. Many plates and platters are plain in the center, while others have a pattern. See the difference on the standing plates at the rear of the photo.

Candy dishes only have the pattern on the top. The bottom is plain.  No yellow butter dish, candy dish or flat tumblers have ever been found! If you discover the first of these, consider yourself lucky - and please let me know about it!

| | Green | Yellow | | Green | Yellow |
|---|---|---|---|---|---|
| Bowl, 4½" berry | 20.00 | 19.00 | Plate, 6" sherbet | 6.00 | 7.00 |
| Bowl, 6½" cereal | 22.00 | 22.00 | Plate, 8⅜" salad | 9.00 | 10.00 |
| Bowl, 7½" salad | 18.00 | 21.00 | Plate, 9⅜" luncheon | 12.50 | 13.50 |
| Bowl, 8½" vegetable | 21.00 | 27.50 | Plate, 10⅜" grill | 55.00 | |
| Bowl, 9½" large berry | 30.00 | 32.00 | Plate, 11½" sandwich | 15.00 | 16.00 |
| Bowl, 10½" oval vegetable | 20.00 | 24.00 | Platter, 10¾" oval | 22.00 | 22.00 |
| Butter dish and cover | 675.00 | | Relish, 3 part ftd. | 20.00 | 37.50 |
| Butter dish bottom | 175.00 | | Saucer | 5.00 | 5.00 |
| Butter dish top | 500.00 | | Sherbet | 14.00 | 15.00 |
| Candy in metal holder motif | | | Sugar, open | 14.50 | 15.00 |
|    on lid | 135.00 | | Tumbler, 4¼", 9 oz. | 150.00 | |
|    also, pink | 150.00 | | Tumbler, 4¾", 12 oz. | 150.00 | |
| Creamer, ftd. | 15.00 | 16.00 | Tumbler, 9 oz. ftd. | 20.00 | 18.00 |
| Cup | 10.00 | 11.00 | Tumbler, 12 oz. ftd. | 130.00 | 130.00 |
| Pitcher, 8½", 64 oz. | 225.00 | 275.00 | | | |

---

# No. 616, "VERNON" INDIANA GLASS COMPANY, 1930-1932

Colors: Green, crystal, yellow.

Another of Indiana's numbered lines, No. 616, is not easily found. It was given the name "Vernon" by another author, but No. 616 is the actual name. Cathy and I used crystal No. 616 as "every day" dishes for a while in the early 1970's. After a few months, Cathy decided that she finally had felt enough of the sharp protruding mould lines on the tumblers. Those rough lines are hard on the lips when you try to drink from them! As I mentioned earlier, mould roughness on Indiana patterns is something you will have to learn to live with or pick some other pattern. Many crystal pieces are found trimmed in platinum (silver). Few of the trimmed pieces have worn rims. Evidently, Indiana's process for applying this trim was better than many of the other glass companies! Those 11½" sandwich plates make great dinner plates to my way of thinking. If you use this pattern, it is either that or the 8" luncheon. No choice!

Showing the pattern is our biggest problem in photographing No. 616. The pattern is very delicate and light passes through without picking up the design well.

Yellow and green colors are both difficult to accumulate in sets, but there is even less green than yellow available. Green tumblers are especially hard to locate. Notice its perceivable absence in the photograph!

| | Green | Crystal | Yellow | | Green | Crystal | Yellow |
|---|---|---|---|---|---|---|---|
| Creamer, ftd. | 24.00 | 12.00 | 23.00 | Saucer | 5.50 | 3.50 | 5.50 |
| Cup | 15.00 | 8.00 | 15.00 | Sugar, ftd. | 23.50 | 11.00 | 23.50 |
| Plate, 8" luncheon | 9.50 | 6.00 | 9.50 | Tumbler, 5" ftd. | 32.00 | 14.00 | 32.00 |
| Plate, 11½" sandwich | 25.00 | 12.00 | 25.00 | | | | |

# No. 618, "PINEAPPLE & FLORAL" INDIANA GLASS COMPANY, 1932-1937

Colors: Crystal, amber; some fired-on red, green; late 1960's, avocado; 1980's pink, cobalt blue, etc.

Indiana has re-made No. 618 diamond shaped comports and 7" salad bowls in all kinds of colors. Many of these have sprayed-on colors, although the light pink is a excellent transparent color. The price of these two older crystal pieces has diminished because of these remakes. Amber and fired-on red are safe colors to collect to avoid reproductions. In crystal, you just have to be careful of those two items.

Crystal makes a challenging set to collect. Although it is not easily put together, it is not impossible either. You will find that tumblers, cream soups and sherbets are the most challenging pieces to find. As with many of Indiana's patterns, mould roughness around the seams is a detriment to many collectors. This is true on all sizes of tumblers! If this roughness does not turn you off, then start searching for the harder to find pieces as soon as you can!

Amber No. 618 is not collected as much as the crystal, simply because there is much less of it available.

The same fired-on red pitcher that has been found with sets of "Pineapple and Floral" has also been found with a set of fired-on red Daisy. The pitcher is of poor quality, as is most of the red in this color. There is a cross hatching design on the base similar to that of No. 618, but that is where the similarity to Pineapple and Floral ends.

|  | Crystal | Amber, Red |  | Crystal | Amber, Red |
|---|---|---|---|---|---|
| Ash tray, 4½" | 17.50 | 19.00 | Plate, 11½" w/indentation | 24.00 | |
| Bowl, 4¾" berry | 23.00 | 16.00 | Plate, 11½" sandwich | 15.00 | 16.00 |
| Bowl, 6" cereal | 24.00 | 20.00 | Platter, 11" closed handles | 15.00 | 18.00 |
| * Bowl, 7" salad | 2.00 | 10.00 | Platter, relish, 11½" divided | 19.00 | |
| Bowl, 10" oval vegetable | 24.00 | 20.00 | Saucer | 5.00 | 5.00 |
| * Comport, diamond-shaped | 1.00 | 8.00 | Sherbet, ftd. | 18.00 | 18.00 |
| Creamer, diamond-shaped | 7.50 | 10.00 | Sugar, diamond-shaped | 7.50 | 10.00 |
| Cream soup | 19.00 | 19.00 | Tumbler, 4¼", 8 oz. | 33.00 | 22.00 |
| Cup | 10.00 | 9.00 | Tumbler, 5", 12 oz. | 40.00 | |
| Plate, 6" sherbet | 5.00 | 6.00 | Vase, cone-shaped | 40.00 | |
| Plate, 8⅜ salad | 8.50 | 8.50 | Vase holder (17.50) | | |
| ** Plate, 9⅜" dinner | 16.00 | 15.00 | | | |

* Reproduced in several colors
** Green $35.00

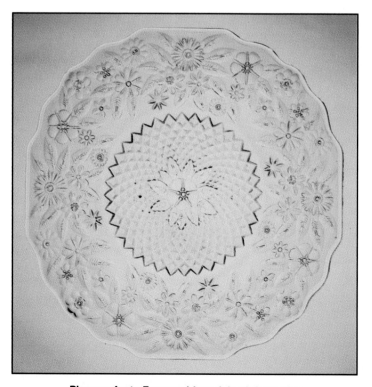

**Please refer to Foreword for pricing information**

# OLD CAFE HOCKING GLASS COMPANY, 1936-1940

Colors: Pink, crystal and Royal Ruby.

Both Old Cafe pitchers are displayed this time which should show that they do exist. These pitchers are rarely found; but since there are few collectors of Old Cafe, the prices have remained reasonable for pieces so difficult to find. Those "go-with" pitchers (with evenly spaced panels and not alternating large with two small panels) that many collectors are using with this set can even be found in green, a color never found in Old Cafe. The pitcher is a good "go-with" piece and it was made by Hocking. Several collectors have told me they are happy with it for their sets even if it is not the **real** thing.

The juice pitcher seems to be Old Cafe even though it is not shown in Hocking's catalogues, (neither was the larger one).

Dinner plates continue to be the hardest pieces of Old Cafe to find except pitchers. All other items are available with searching. This is another pattern that you will have to ask dealers to bring to shows. Bowls have been confusing. The 5" bowl has an open handle while the 4½" bowl has two closed handles as does the 3¾" berry. The sherbet is footed, but also measures 3¾". It is pictured to the left of the cup and saucer.

That Royal Ruby "Old Cafe" cup is found on crystal saucers just as in Coronation pattern. No Royal Ruby saucers have been found. Few lamps have been seen. Lamps were made by drilling a vase, turning it upside down and wiring it.

The low candy is 8⅜" including the handles and 6½" without. It was not considered to be a plate. You can see pink and crystal ones in the photograph.

There is a Hocking cookie jar (a numbered line) which is also a excellent "go-with" piece. It is ribbed up the sides similar to Old Cafe but has a cross-hatched lid that is not even close to this pattern. Only the bottom is similar to Old Cafe.

| | Crystal, Pink | Royal Ruby | | Crystal, Pink | Royal Ruby |
|---|---|---|---|---|---|
| Bowl, 3¾" berry | 3.00 | 5.50 | Pitcher, 6", 36 oz. | 65.00 | |
| Bowl, 4½", tab handle | | | Pitcher, 80 oz. | 85.00 | |
| Bowl, 5" | 5.00 | | Plate, 6" sherbet | 2.50 | |
| Bowl, 5½" cereal | 6.50 | 10.00 | Plate, 10" dinner | 30.00 | |
| Bowl, 9", closed handles | 10.00 | 14.00 | Saucer | 3.00 | |
| Candy dish, 8" low | 11.00 | 11.00 | Sherbet, ¾" low ftd. | 6.00 | 10.00 |
| Cup | 5.00 | 8.00 | Tumbler, 3" juice | 11.00 | 8.00 |
| Lamp | 17.50 | 25.00 | Tumbler, 4" water | 11.00 | 16.00 |
| Olive dish, 6" oblong | 5.00 | | Vase, 7¼" | 13.00 | 16.00 |

# OLD ENGLISH, "THREADING" INDIANA GLASS COMPANY

Colors: Green, amber, pink, crystal and forest green.

You should know that Old English is predominately found in green. I just decided to show you the other colors found this time. Amber Old English has a very strong color that some collectors find more alluring than the paler amber colors of most patterns. This Indiana pattern has **color** more reminiscent of Cambridge or New Martinsville. Unlike other Indiana patterns, mould roughness has never seemed to be a problem with Old English.

The center handled sandwich server is rarely seen. Green ones are the piece most often missing from collections of that color. The only one I ever owned was shipped to a collector in Georgia, but arrived with tire tracks down the middle of the box. Needless to say, the server did not stand up too well to such treatment!

Flat pieces continue to be harder to find than footed pieces (not the normal circumstance). Berry bowls in both sizes and the flat candy dish are difficult to find.

The pitcher lid has the same cloverleaf type knob as sugar and candy jars. The flat candy lid is similar in size to the pitcher lid which is notched on the bottom rim.

A set can be collected in green with all pieces being found in that color. A complete amber set may not be as attainable since some pieces have never been seen in amber. That doesn't mean that they were never made, but the possibility is looking bleak at best. Pink is the most elusive color with only the center handled server, cheese and cracker and sherbets being found.

| | Pink, Green, Amber | | Pink, Green, Amber |
|---|---|---|---|
| Bowl, 4" flat | 16.00 | Pitcher | 65.00 |
| Bowl, 9" ftd. fruit | 26.00 | Pitcher and cover | 115.00 |
| Bowl, 9½" flat | 30.00 | Plate, indent for compote | 19.00 |
| Candlesticks, 4" pr. | 32.50 | Sandwich server, center handle | 50.00 |
| Candy dish & cover, flat | 50.00 | Sherbet, 2 styles | 19.00 |
| Candy jar with lid | 50.00 | Sugar | 17.50 |
| Compote, 3½" tall, 6⅜" across, 2 handled | 21.00 | Sugar cover | 35.00 |
| Compote, 3½" tall, 7" across | 18.00 | Tumbler, 4½" ftd. | 21.00 |
| Compote, 3½" cheese for plate | 16.00 | Tumbler, 5½" ftd. | 32.00 |
| Creamer | 17.50 | Vase, 5⅜", fan type, 7" wide | 47.50 |
| Egg cup (crystal only) | 8.00 | Vase, 8" ftd., 4½" wide | 45.00 |
| Fruit stand, 11" ftd. | 38.00 | Vase, 8¼" ftd., 4¼" wide | 45.00 |
| Goblet, 5¾", 8 oz. | 30.00 | Vase, 12" ftd. | 55.00 |

# "ORCHID" PADEN CITY GLASS COMPANY, EARLY 1930's

Colors: Yellow, cobalt blue, green, amber, pink, red and black.

Orchid etched pieces seem to turn up only on the Crow's Foot blanks made by Paden City. I have always found it on the #412 Line which is the squared Crow's Foot blank and not the rounded style which is #890 Line. If you find any pieces on some other blank of Paden City, be sure to let me know. There are two and maybe even three different orchid varieties being found on Paden City blanks. The quantity of any of them is so scarce that collectors do not mind mixing unlike Orchid designs together.

Availability of any Paden City patterns is limited at best. This causes prices to continue to rise. I suspect the small amount of glass made (in comparison to other companies) will always keep collectors driving up prices with each purchase. Orchid prices have not gone out of sight like those of Cupid, even though there are fewer pieces of Orchid being found.

Console bowls and candlesticks are the only pieces that crop up regularly. You have to realize that "regularly" for Orchid is like "hardly ever" for major collectible patterns. I have owned more Mayfair sugar lids (14) than I've seen Orchid consoles (3), for example (and I said the bowls were the most commonly found pieces)!

Although the abundance of collectors of **Heisey's** Orchid pattern is astounding, proportionately there are a small number searching for Paden City's Orchid. Orchid growers throughout the country collect Heisey's Orchid. Availability and the heavy national distribution for Heisey Orchid are key factors. Unfortunately, both of these factors were missing for Paden City's Orchid.

| | All Other Colors | Red Black Cobalt Blue | | All Other Colors | Red Black Cobalt Blue |
|---|---|---|---|---|---|
| Bowl, 4⅞" square | 16.00 | 32.00 | Comport, 3¼" tall, 6¼" wide | 18.00 | 38.00 |
| Bowl, 8½", 2-handled | 37.50 | 77.50 | Comport, 6⅝" tall, 7" wide | 26.00 | 55.00 |
| Bowl, 8¾" square | 32.00 | 62.50 | Ice bucket, 6" | 57.50 | 110.00 |
| Bowl, 10", ftd. | 46.00 | 95.00 | Mayonnaise, 3 piece | 55.00 | 98.00 |
| Bowl, 11", square | 37.50 | 70.00 | Plate, 8½", square | | 47.50 |
| Candlesticks, 5¾" pr. | 55.00 | 110.00 | Sandwich server, center handled | 37.50 | 67.50 |
| Candy with lid, 6½", square, three part | 48.00 | 98.00 | Sugar | 27.50 | 47.50 |
| Creamer | 27.50 | 47.50 | Vase, 10" | 50.00 | 110.00 |

# OVIDE, incorrectly dubbed "NEW CENTURY" HAZEL ATLAS GLASS COMPANY, 1930-1935

Colors: Green, black, white Platonite trimmed with fired-on colors in 1950's.

Ovide is another of Hazel Atlas' Platonite patterns that fit into both this and my *Collectible Glassware from the 40's, 50's, 60's....* book. I have chosen another of the many decorated sets of Ovide to enhance this book. Let's just call this one "Windmills" for lack of an actual name. Hazel Atlas tried a multitude of decorations on this popular ware of theirs. Evidently, the public found many of them acceptable judging from the multitude of pieces found today.

The "flying ducks" (geese) set belongs to the same collector who owns the Art Deco shown previously. Evidently, there was a strong distribution of decorated sets in the north central Ohio region. I have a letter telling of an egg cup being discovered in the "flying ducks" pattern!

The black flower decorated set crosses into Kitchenware with those stacking sets and mixing bowls. You can find a full line of that pattern from cups and saucers to two cup measuring pitchers.

Very little black, transparent green or yellow is being found. A luncheon set in black can be assembled if wanted, but it would be even easier to put together the same set in black Cloverleaf. Black Cloverleaf would cost three or four times as much. Depression glass dealers are inclined to bring the black Cloverleaf patterns to shows, but few handle black Ovide.

One collector conjectured that most Ovide pieces he saw were probably intended to be Cloverleaf but had lousy or weak patterns. It is a point well taken. Many Cloverleaf pieces are found with very weak patterns, weak enough that Cloverleaf collectors pass them.

| | Black | Green | Decorated White | Art Deco | | Black | Green | Decorated White | Art Deco |
|---|---|---|---|---|---|---|---|---|---|
| Bowl, 4¾" berry | | | 7.00 | | Plate, 8" luncheon | | 3.00 | 14.00 | 45.00 |
| Bowl, 5½" cereal | | | 13.00 | | Plate, 9" dinner | | | 20.00 | |
| Bowl, 8" large berry | | | 22.50 | | Platter, 11" | | | 22.50 | |
| Candy dish and cover | 42.00 | 22.00 | 35.00 | | Salt and pepper, pr. | 27.50 | 27.50 | 24.00 | |
| Cocktail, ftd. fruit | 5.00 | 4.00 | | | Saucer | 3.50 | 2.50 | 6.00 | 18.00 |
| Creamer | 6.50 | 4.50 | 17.50 | 80.00 | Sherbet | 6.50 | 3.00 | 14.00 | 45.00 |
| Cup | 6.50 | 3.50 | 12.50 | 50.00 | Sugar, open | 6.50 | 4.00 | 17.50 | 80.00 |
| Plate, 6" sherbet | | 2.50 | 6.00 | | Tumbler | | | 16.50 | 80.00 |

# OYSTER AND PEARL ANCHOR HOCKING GLASS CORPORATION, 1938-1940

Colors: Pink, crystal, Ruby Red, white with fired-on pink or green.

Royal Ruby Oyster and Pearl can be seen under the Royal Ruby pattern shown later in this book, but prices will also be included here. Many collectors buy Oyster and Pearl to use as accessory pieces for other patterns. Both the relish dish and candlesticks are hard for me to keep in my shop because they are so reasonably priced in comparison to other patterns. More often these pieces are purchased as gifts by non-collectors, because they are pretty pieces of pink glassware. Oft times this has produced a "new" collector who knew nothing about Depression glass until they received it as a gift. That relish dish is 11½" including the handles. I mention that because it is listed as 10¼". All measurements in this book are calculated without handles unless otherwise mentioned. Glass companies rarely measured the handles, so that tradition has continued in our collecting world. I have made a point to talk about measurements with handles in my commentary since I have been getting so many letters about measurements on pieces that I have already listed. There is no divided bowl in Oyster and Pearl; it was listed as a relish!

Red decorated crystal pieces are rarely found, but they sell faster than undecorated crystal. The 10½" fruit bowl is a great salad bowl and the 13½" plate makes a great server, but several collectors have told me they also make an ideal small punch bowl and liner. It wouldn't hold enough for our family gatherings!

The pink color fired-on over white was named "Dusty Rose"; the fired-on green was designated "Springtime Green" by Hocking. Collectors do not seem to have a middle ground on these fired-on colors. They either love them or hate them. There seem to be more of the fired-on colors available than the plain white.

The pink, 6½", deep, bowl with the metal attached to the handle was another of the marketing ploys of that time. With tongs it could serve as a small ice bowl or serving dish. It was another way to sell this bowl!

The spouted, 5¼" bowl is often referred to as heart shaped. It might serve as a gravy or sauce boat although most people use them for candy dishes. The same bowl is also found without the spout. Although pictured in "Dusty Rose" and "Springtime Green," this bowl has never been found without a spout in those colors.

| | Crystal, Pink | Royal Ruby | White and Fired-On Green Or Pink |
|---|---|---|---|
| Bowl, 5¼" heart-shaped, 1-handled | 7.00 | 12.00 | 8.00 |
| Bowl, 5½", 1-handled | 7.00 | 12.00 | |
| Bowl, 6½" deep-handled | 10.00 | 19.00 | |
| Bowl, 10½" deep fruit | 21.00 | 45.00 | 13.00 |
| Candle holder, 3½" pr. | 21.00 | 45.00 | 14.00 |
| Plate, 13½" sandwich | 16.00 | 40.00 | |
| Relish dish, 10¼" oblong | 9.00 | | |

# "PARROT," SYLVAN FEDERAL GLASS COMPANY, 1931-1932

Colors: Green, amber; some crystal and blue.

Lately prices of green Parrot have amazed even me! I do not amaze easily after twenty-two years of recording prices! After several years of pitcher's selling in the same price range, suddenly everyone wanted one and there were few to be found! The price has doubled since the tenth edition. Originally, there were thirty-seven pitchers found. Today, there are over thirty still in existence. Doubling in price in so short a time was the amazing part, since they were rather highly priced to begin with.

The hot plate has now been found in two styles! One is shaped like the Madrid hot plate with the pointed edges. The other is round, and more like Federal's other bird pattern, Georgian. These can be seen in the bottom photo. It seems the round hot plate may be the harder to find. Only three have been seen; but right now, **any** hot plate is hard to find! A newly found amber piece is a pointed edge hot plate. It stands to reason that Federal made these in amber as they did the Madrid. This one resides in a collection in Tennessee.

The round hot plate and the high sherbet have also made dramatic price explosions. Notice that I have had to separate the prices of hot plates because of the pricing differences that are occurring. Of course, there are less than a dozen of the sherbets known; and until now, I have never had one to show you in my books. The pricing reflects what has happened to these items. Remember, these are **selling prices** and not hoped for prices.

Hopefully, you will be able to see the birds on the pitcher and the sherbet. I had a new photographer for much of this book, and I broke him in with this "hard to photograph" pattern. There were many anxious moments in that week long photography session, but I believe we have finally found someone who can capture many of our elusive patterns.

Prices for amber Parrot have not increased very much, even though it is more rare. The amber butter dish, creamer and sugar lid are all harder to find than green. Since there are fewer collectors of amber, **scarcity** does not affect the price as **demand** does for the green!

People recognize the Madrid shapes on which we find Parrot. You will notice that most Parrot tumblers are found on these Madrid blanks except for the heavy footed tumbler. Evidently, the thin, moulded, footed tumbler did not accept the Parrot design very well and a new style tumbler was made. This thin, 10 oz. footed tumbler has only been found in amber. When you see one of these, you will understand what I mean when I say it does not accept the design well! The supply of heavy, footed tumblers and thin, flat iced teas in amber have more than met the demand of collectors. Prices for these two tumblers have remained steady.

There has been only one **mint** condition butter dish top found in amber. The butter bottom has an indented ledge for the top. The jam dish is the same as the butter bottom without the ledge, but it has never been found in green.

There are quantities of sugar and butter lids found. The major concern is finding MINT condition lids. The pointed edges and ridges on Parrot chipped **then** and **now**. You should carefully check these points when purchasing this pattern. Damaged or **repaired** glassware should not bring **mint** prices. I emphasize that here because many sugar and butter lids have been repaired. If it has been reworked, it should be sold as "repaired."

|  | Green | Amber |  |  | Green | Amber |
|---|---|---|---|---|---|---|
| Bowl, 5" berry | 22.00 | 16.00 | | Plate, 9" dinner | 48.00 | 35.00 |
| Bowl, 7" soup | 40.00 | 30.00 | | Plate, 10½" round grill | 30.00 | |
| Bowl, 8" large berry | 75.00 | 72.00 | | Plate, 10½" square grill | | 25.00 |
| Bowl, 10" oval vegetable | 52.50 | 60.00 | | Plate, 10¼" square (crystal only) | 26.00 | |
| Butter dish and cover | 325.00 | 1,100.00 | | Platter, 11¼" oblong | 50.00 | 65.00 |
| Butter dish bottom | 60.00 | 200.00 | | Salt and pepper, pr. | 225.00 | |
| Butter dish top | 265.00 | 900.00 | | Saucer | 15.00 | 15.00 |
| Creamer, ftd. | 45.00 | 50.00 | * | Sherbet, ftd. cone | 22.00 | 20.00 |
| Cup | 38.00 | 38.00 | | Sherbet, 4¼" high | 1,000.00 | |
| Hot Plate, 5", pointed | 795.00 | 850.00 | | Sugar | 35.00 | 40.00 |
| Hot plate, 5", round | 900.00 | | | Sugar cover | 130.00 | 400.00 |
| Jam dish, 7" | | 30.00 | | Tumbler, 4¼", 10 oz. | 135.00 | 100.00 |
| Pitcher, 8½", 80 oz. | 2,600.00 | | | Tumbler, 5½", 12 oz. | 150.00 | 110.00 |
| Plate, 5¾" sherbet | 35.00 | 20.00 | | Tumbler, 5¾" ftd. heavy | 120.00 | 100.00 |
| Plate, 7½" salad | 35.00 | | | Tumbler, 5½", 10 oz. ftd. (Madrid mould) | | 135.00 |

* Blue-$150.00

# PATRICIAN, "SPOKE" FEDERAL GLASS COMPANY, 1933-1937

Colors: Pink, green, crystal and amber ("Golden Glo").

Patrician is one amber pattern in Depression glass that is collected by large numbers of people. Amber is easily found and the large 10½" dinner plates are big enough for the heartiest of appetites. That may be why several collectors I have met comment on the attributes of Patrician for everyday use! I discovered that these plates were given away in twenty pound sacks of flour as "cake" plates. They saturated my area!

There are two styles of pitchers found. The one pictured has a moulded handle and is easier to find in amber than the one with an applied handle. In crystal, the applied handle pitcher is the easiest to find!

The only piece of amber that can truly be considered rare is that applied handled pitcher; but mint condition sugar lids, cookie or butter bottoms and footed tumblers are harder to find than other pieces. Check sugar lids for signs of repair. The cookie bottom is rare in green. There are several lids found for each bottom. Most people think that all tops are harder to find than bottoms. This does not hold true for butter dishes and cookie jars in Patrician. Saucers are also harder to find than cups. This phenomenon occurs in few patterns, but Patrician is one of them. Notice the price increases for green cookie jars and applied handle pitchers.

I had called this pattern hexagonal for years, but a reader pointed out that it is really pentagonal. I have to concede that since there are only five sides on the Patrician cookie jars, pitchers and tumblers! These oddly shaped pieces have always infatuated new collectors.

Green Patrician is more easily found and collected than pink or crystal. Green dinner plates are rather scarce; you will have to remember that if you start to collect it. After seeing so many in amber, you'd think other colors would also be plentiful. That is not the case! To complete a set in pink is difficult, but not yet impossible. It is in crystal. Not all pieces have been found in crystal; so you would have to settle for a smaller set – if you could find enough!

| | Amber, Crystal | Pink | Green | | Amber, Crystal | Pink | Green |
|---|---|---|---|---|---|---|---|
| Bowl, 4¾" cream soup | 15.00 | 16.50 | 18.00 | Plate, 6" sherbet | 10.00 | 8.00 | 8.00 |
| Bowl, 5" berry | 11.00 | 11.00 | 11.00 | Plate, 7½" salad | 15.00 | 15.00 | 14.00 |
| Bowl, 6" cereal | 22.00 | 22.00 | 24.00 | Plate, 9" luncheon | 12.00 | 10.00 | 11.00 |
| Bowl, 8½" large berry | 42.00 | 23.00 | 32.00 | Plate, 10½" dinner | 6.50 | 30.00 | 35.00 |
| Bowl, 10" oval vegetable | 30.00 | 12.00 | 30.00 | Plate, 10½" grill | 13.50 | 12.00 | 13.00 |
| Butter dish and cover | 85.00 | 200.00 | 100.00 | Platter, 11½" oval | 30.00 | 25.00 | 25.00 |
| Butter dish bottom | 57.50 | 159.50 | 52.50 | Salt and pepper, pr. | 55.00 | 80.00 | 60.00 |
| Butter dish top | 27.50 | 47.50 | 47.50 | Saucer | 9.50 | 9.50 | 9.50 |
| Cookie jar and cover | 84.00 | | 495.00 | Sherbet | 13.00 | 13.00 | 14.00 |
| Creamer, footed | 9.00 | 10.00 | 11.00 | Sugar | 9.00 | 9.00 | 9.00 |
| Cup | 8.00 | 9.00 | 10.00 | Sugar cover | 50.00 | 48.00 | 52.00 |
| Jam dish | 26.00 | 26.00 | 32.00 | Tumbler, 4", 5 oz. | 28.00 | 26.00 | 30.00 |
| Pitcher, 8", 75 oz. moulded | | | | Tumbler, 4¼", 9 oz. | 25.00 | 24.00 | 25.00 |
| handle | 100.00 | 110.00 | 125.00 | Tumbler, 5½", 14 oz. | 38.00 | 28.00 | 38.00 |
| Pitcher, 8¼", 75 oz., applied | | | | Tumbler, 5¼", 8 oz. ftd. | 45.00 | | 50.00 |
| handle | 130.00 | 135.00 | 150.00 | | | | |

# "PATRICK" LANCASTER GLASS COMPANY, EARLY 1930's

Colors: Yellow and pink.

Prices of pink Patrick were all confused in my last *Pocket Guide to Depression Glass*; I hope that the prices here will better reflect what pink is actually selling for in the market. Sugar or creamers are really selling for $75.00 each! There are a few pieces of pink Patrick, but this color appears to be in shorter supply than the yellow. The Patrick three-footed candy is shaped just like the one shown in Jubilee. I have never seen one except in a catalogue. As more Jubilee collectors turn their attention to collecting Patrick, the smaller supply of this pattern is diminishing rapidly and prices are rising! Although Jubilee was distributed heavily in the Northwest, I have not had any reported findings of Patrick there.

A letter from a man in Colorado explains why saucers may be harder to find than cups. His grandmother found a 1932 premium that offered four cups without saucers. If she bought two sets of four cups, eight saucers would be provided for an additional small cost. Since the cost was more than she could afford, she only bought four cups without the saucers. Maybe that was the plan in other areas. People could do without saucers better than they could without cups!

Jubilee and Patrick make great complimentary sets. There is not enough Patrick for everyone who wants a set; but by mixing it with Jubilee, you can stretch your collecting sphere. As in Jubilee, serving dishes are rare in Patrick. There are several additional floral patterns made by Lancaster with the same shapes of Patrick and Jubilee that can be blended into these sets if you get stymied in finding serving pieces.

| | Pink | Yellow | | Pink | Yellow |
|---|---|---|---|---|---|
| Bowl, 9", handled fruit | 125.00 | 50.00 | Mayonnaise, 3-piece | 195.00 | 130.00 |
| Bowl, 11", console | 125.00 | 80.00 | Plate, 7" sherbet | 20.00 | 12.00 |
| Candlesticks, pr. | 150.00 | 77.50 | Plate, 7½" salad | 25.00 | 20.00 |
| Candy dish, 3-ftd | 110.00 | 77.50 | Plate, 8" luncheon | 45.00 | 27.50 |
| Cheese & cracker set | 140.00 | 90.00 | Saucer | 20.00 | 12.00 |
| Creamer | 75.00 | 37.50 | Sherbet, 4¾" | 60.00 | 45.00 |
| Cup | 65.00 | 37.50 | Sugar | 75.00 | 37.50 |
| Goblet, 4" cocktail | 90.00 | 47.50 | Tray, 11", 2-handled | 75.00 | 60.00 |
| Goblet, 4¾", 6 oz. juice | 90.00 | 47.50 | Tray, 11", center-handled | 145.00 | 60.00 |
| Goblet, 6", 10 oz. water | 100.00 | 67.50 | | | |

# "PEACOCK REVERSE," LINE 412 PADEN CITY GLASS COMPANY, 1930's

Colors: Cobalt blue, red, amber, yellow, green, pink, black and crystal.

Additional pieces of Peacock Reverse continue to be found! However, one item is being removed from my listing and that is the 10" bud vase. Although very similar to this pattern, the ten inch vase has now been attributed to Morgantown. According to Jerry Gallagher's "Morgantown Newscaster," this is Morgantown's #305 vase style Luanna with etching name Cathay. (It is selling in the $135.00 range.) I have not seen the eight sided plate that I had reported to me previously; have you?

All colors are desirable, but crystal is the least wanted. Prices for Peacock Reverse are not determined by color as much as other patterns. Collectors accept any color they can acquire!

Paden City's Line #412 (commonly called "Crow's Foot" by collectors) and Line #991 (which is Penny Line) make up the blanks on which Peacock Reverse has been seen. Paden City lines were used for many different designs; so it is not unusual to spot a blank only to find that it does not have the pattern for which you are searching.

Almost any piece listed under Crow's Foot (squared), Orchid, or Cupid could be found with the Peacock Reverse design. Let me know what unlisted pieces or colors you happen to spot!

| | All Colors | | All Colors |
|---|---|---|---|
| Bowl, 4⅞" square | 32.00 | Plate, 8½" luncheon | 38.00 |
| Bowl, 8¾" square | 77.50 | Plate 10⅜", 2-handled | 47.50 |
| Bowl, 8¾" square with handles | 83.00 | Saucer | 17.50 |
| Bowl, 11¾" console | 77.50 | Sherbet, 4⅝" tall, 3⅜" diameter | 45.00 |
| Candlesticks, 5¾" square base, pr. | 115.00 | Sherbet, 4⅞" tall, 3⅝" diameter | 45.00 |
| Candy dish, 6½" square | 130.00 | Server, center-handled | 62.50 |
| Comport, 3¼" high, 6¼" wide | 50.00 | Sugar, 2¾" flat | 77.50 |
| Creamer, 2¾" flat | 77.50 | Tumbler, 4", 10 oz. flat | 60.00 |
| Cup | 67.50 | Vase, 10" | 90.00 |
| Plate, 5¾" sherbet | 22.50 | | |

---

# "PEACOCK & WILD ROSE" PADEN CITY GLASS COMPANY, LINE #1300, 1930's

Colors: Pink, green, amber, cobalt blue, black, crystal and red.

It's a shame that the abundant serving pieces in Paden City's Peacock and Wild Rose can not be transferred into Lancaster's patterns or other patterns that need serving pieces! Peacock and Rose appears to only have serving pieces and vases. No cups, saucers, creamers, sugars or luncheon plates have ever been reported.

The elliptical vase seems to be the most desired item in this pattern. Maybe that is because it has so recently surfaced! The bulbous base of the 12" vase shows signs of being faintly paneled. Vases are the most commonly found pieces in this Paden City line. There are two styles of 10" vases.

I still receive letters on the usage of the bowls and plates with handles in the middle. These were candy or pastry trays. They probably did not work well for mashed potatoes.

No more information has been forthcoming on the 5" pitcher reported to me earlier. Although there are several "bird" designs in Paden City patterns, there is more recognition for the peacock patterns than for any other.

| | All Colors | | All Colors |
|---|---|---|---|
| Bowl, 8½", flat | 55.00 | Candy dish w/cover, 7" | 130.00 |
| Bowl, 8½", fruit, oval, ftd. | 80.00 | Cheese and cracker set | 98.00 |
| Bowl, 8¾", ftd. | 70.00 | Comport, 3¼" tall, 6¼" wide | 47.50 |
| Bowl, 9½", center-handled | 65.00 | Ice bucket, 6" | 125.00 |
| Bowl, 9½", ftd. | 70.00 | Ice tub, 4¾" | 115.00 |
| Bowl, 10½", center-handled | 75.00 | Pitcher, 5" high | 115.00 |
| Bowl, 10½", ftd. | 85.00 | Plate, cake, low foot | 77.50 |
| Bowl, 10½", fruit | 85.00 | Relish, 3-part | 55.00 |
| Bowl, 11", console | 67.50 | Vase, 8¼" elliptical | 135.00 |
| Bowl, 14", console | 77.50 | Vase, 10", two styles | 87.50 |
| Candlestick, 5", pr. | 115.00 | Vase, 12" | 120.00 |

# PETALWARE MacBETH-EVANS GLASS COMPANY, 1930-1940

Colors: Monax, Cremax, pink, crystal, cobalt and fired-on red, blue, green and yellow.

Petalware with red trim has awakened collectors to the other decorated patterns of Petalware. While scouring the trail of this elusive red trimmed set, many have latched onto whatever decorated Petalware they can find. This means more collectors are now searching for Florette which is the pointed petal, red flower decoration sans red trim. All series of fruit and bird decorations are fair game. Some are even beginning to collect pastel decorated Cremax. I have been asked for it at three different shows recently. Since little of it is found, prices are creeping up on that also.

The red trimmed Petalware appeared on both the covers of my eighth edition book and my sixth edition *Pocket Guide to Depression Glass.* It was the first pattern ever to be featured on two covers! What can I say except my publisher loved it! The red trimmed Petalware also has three sizes of decorated tumblers to match it. I have priced the two sizes I have found and sold. You can find these tumblers both frosted (shown in photo on top page 159) or unfrosted. I sold some in the $20.00 range; but the last ones sold at the prices listed. Somebody send the measurements on the water tumbler, please! Prices for all red trimmed Petalware have gone "out of sight!"

This time, I have tried to show as wide a variety of decorated Monax Petalware as possible. Below and on the bottom of page 159 are plates from different series of fruits, birds and flowers. The fruit-decorated Petalware with the names of fruit printed on the plate is found in sets of eight. One such set consists of plates showing cherry, apple, orange, plum, strawberry, blueberry, pear and grape. I have seen a "wanted to buy" ad for these in a popular ladies magazine! You may find other sets with different fruits. Some sets have colored bands and others have 22K gold trim. My favorites (besides the Florence Cherry) are the Bluebird plates. Perhaps, it's that elusive "bluebird of happiness."

Monax and Cremax are names given the colors by MacBeth-Evans. Cremax refers to the opaque beige colored Petalware and Monax is the whiter color shown in all the pictures. Cremax will glow green under a black light, but Monax does not.

Pink Petalware sells very well in my shop. I suggested previously that pink was inexpensive and an excellent pattern for new collectors to start. That was the end of reasonable prices! Pink Petalware is still less expensive than most other pink patterns.

Lamp shades do not sell very well. If you want a cheap shade to go with this pattern, you should have little trouble finding one.

The cobalt mustard (foreground at the bottom of 159) has a metal lid and it is Petalware! A few additional pieces of cobalt blue Petalware turned up in the mid-1970's, but they all disappeared into collections and have not been seen since! The 9" berry bowl varies from 8¾" at times. You will find other quarter inch variances on many pieces in this pattern. It was made for a long time and replacing worn out moulds caused some size discrepancies.

# PETALWARE MacBETH-EVANS GLASS COMPANY, 1930-1940 (Cont.)

| | Crystal | Pink | Monax Plain | Cremax, Monax Florette, Fired-On Decorations | Red Trim Floral |
|---|---|---|---|---|---|
| Bowl, 4½" cream soup | 4.50 | 11.00 | 10.00 | 12.50 | |
| Bowl, 5¾" cereal | 4.00 | 8.50 | 6.00 | 12.50 | 30.00 |
| Bowl, 7" soup | | | 55.00 | | |
| * Bowl, 9" large berry | 8.50 | 15.00 | 18.00 | 30.00 | 110.00 |
| Cup | 3.00 | 6.50 | 5.00 | 10.00 | 25.00 |
| ** Creamer, ftd. | 3.00 | 7.50 | 6.00 | 12.50 | 30.00 |
| Lamp shade (many sizes) $8.00 to $15.00 | | | | | |
| Mustard with metal cover in cobalt blue only, $8.00 | | | | | |
| Pitcher, 80 oz. (crystal decorated bands) | 25.00 | | | | |
| Plate, 6" sherbet | 2.00 | 2.50 | 2.50 | 6.00 | 15.00 |
| Plate, 8" salad | 2.00 | 4.00 | 4.00 | 10.00 | 20.00 |
| Plate, 9" dinner | 4.00 | 10.00 | 6.50 | 14.00 | 27.50 |
| Plate, 11" salver | 4.50 | 10.00 | 8.50 | 16.00 | |
| Plate, 12" salver | | 9.00 | 18.00 | | 37.50 |
| Platter, 13" oval | 8.50 | 15.00 | 13.00 | 20.00 | |
| Saucer | 1.50 | 2.50 | 2.00 | 3.50 | 8.00 |
| Saucer, cream soup liner | | | 16.00 | | |
| Sherbet, 4" low ftd. | | | 26.00 | | |
| ** Sherbet, 4½" low ftd. | 3.50 | 7.00 | 7.00 | 12.00 | 32.00 |
| ** Sugar, ftd. | 3.00 | 6.50 | 6.00 | 10.00 | 30.00 |
| Tidbit servers or lazy susans, several styles 12.00 to 17.50 | | | | | |
| Tumbler, 3⅝", 6 oz. | 32.50 | | | | |
| Tumbler, 4⅝", 12 oz. | 35.00 | | | | |
| *** Tumblers (crystal decorated pastel bands) 7.50 to 10.00 | | | | | |

* Also in cobalt at $45.00
** Also in cobalt at $30.00
*** Several sizes

---

# PRIMO, "PANELLED ASTER" U.S. GLASS COMPANY, EARLY 1930's

Colors: Green and yellow.

Primo is another obscure pattern where little catalogue information is available. I continue to add new pieces to the listing as they are found. The report of a three-footed round console bowl in Primo turned out to be another U.S. Glass pattern known as "Thorn" which is found in pink, green and black. There have been no new reports of center handled servers, but it is possible these do exist!

Berry bowls and cake plates seem to be the hardest to find pieces. I still have not found a green berry bowl to photograph. Mould seam roughness is the norm for this pattern; so if you are turned off by that, look for some other pattern to collect.

The coaster/ash tray combinations do not have the pattern on them. Evidently, they were made by U.S. Glass to go with other patterns besides Primo, since no pieces of Primo have been found in the pink or black to go with those colored coasters (shown). Notice how exactly the tumbler fits the coaster! These coasters have been found in boxed Primo sets which were advertised as "Bridge Sets."

| | Yellow, Green | | Yellow, Green |
|---|---|---|---|
| Bowl, 4½" | 9.50 | Plate, 10" dinner | 16.00 |
| Bowl, 7¾" | 19.00 | Plate, 10" grill | 9.50 |
| Cake plate, 10", 3-footed | 19.00 | Saucer | 3.00 |
| Coaster/ash tray | 8.00 | Sherbet | 9.00 |
| Creamer | 10.00 | Sugar | 10.00 |
| Cup | 8.50 | Tumbler, 5¾", 9 oz. | 16.00 |
| Plate, 7½" | 7.50 | | |

161

# PRINCESS HOCKING GLASS COMPANY, 1931-1935

Colors: Green, Topaz yellow, apricot yellow, pink and blue.

Princess collectors all have trouble finding tumblers and bowls no matter which color they desire. Collectors of green Princess have to search long and hard for footed iced teas, cereal and berry bowls, undivided relishes and the elusive footed pitcher with tumblers to match. Collectors of pink Princess have problems finding the coasters, footed iced teas, berry and cereal bowls, and the footed pitcher with matching tumblers. The hardest to find yellow pieces include the butter dish, juice pitcher, footed iced tea, undivided relish, berry and cereal bowls, coasters and ash trays.

One of the problems in finding mint condition bowls is inner rim roughness. Some of this was caused by stacking the bowls together over the years, but a lot of damage was courted by the very sharply defined inner rim itself. The undivided relish is called a soup bowl by some dealers; so you need to be aware of that. It is so shallow, I wouldn't want to eat my soup out of it.

An unusual, three footed bowl has been found in Texas. It is 8¾" square and stands only 1½" high. What it was designed for is anyone's guess, but it is like the undivided relish in that it doesn't hold much!

Yellow Princess continues to give collectors headaches due to color variations. "Topaz" is the official color listed by Hocking, and it is an attractive shade of yellow. However, some yellow is almost amber and has been called "apricot" by collectors. Most prefer the "Topaz" which makes the darker, amber shade difficult to sell. The colors are so different that it is almost as if Hocking meant to have different colors.

The handled sandwich plate actually measures 10¼" (or 11¼" if measured including handles). These are rarely found in yellow and have been fetching high prices when they do occasionally turn up. This plate is just like the handled grill plate without the dividers. Notice its conspicuous absence from my picture! These are common in pink and green. The grill plate without handles and dinner plate have also been corrected to read 9½" instead of what old catalogues had listed.

Collectors seeking blue Princess are somewhat out of luck! There have been only a few pieces found in this color. Those that have been on the market are all marked with an asterisk in the listing below. Only the cookie jar and the cup and saucer are coveted by collectors of those items. From 1975 to date, almost all the blue reported has been found in the Southwest and Mexico. It must have been distributed or test marketed there! I have a photograph of a small blue luncheon set residing in Texas, but none of this set has ever been sold at any price. The pitcher found with this set is damaged; however, the pitcher is not Princess. It is blue Florentine like the one shown in my second book in 1975. That pitcher was found in a flea market in Mexico!

| | Green | Pink | Topaz, Apricot | | | Green | Pink | Topaz, Apricot |
|---|---|---|---|---|---|---|---|---|
| Ash tray, 4½" | 67.50 | 85.00 | 86.00 | ** | Plate, 9½" grill | 12.00 | 12.00 | 5.50 |
| Bowl, 4½" berry | 22.00 | 21.00 | 42.00 | | Plate, 10¼" handled sandwich | 12.00 | 20.00 | 150.00 |
| Bowl, 5" cereal or oatmeal | 27.00 | 22.00 | 28.00 | | Plate, 10½" grill, closed | | | |
| Bowl, 9" octagonal salad | 35.00 | 30.00 | 110.00 | |   handles | 9.50 | 11.00 | 5.50 |
| Bowl, 9½" hat-shaped | 40.00 | 30.00 | 110.00 | | Platter, 12" closed handles | 21.00 | 21.00 | 55.00 |
| Bowl, 10" oval vegetable | 25.00 | 20.00 | 55.00 | | Relish, 7½" divided | 24.00 | 26.00 | 98.00 |
| Butter dish and cover | 85.00 | 85.00 | 600.00 | | Relish, 7½" plain | 98.00 | 160.00 | 140.00 |
| Butter dish bottom | 27.50 | 27.50 | 200.00 | | Salt and pepper, 4½" pr. | 50.00 | 50.00 | 65.00 |
| Butter dish top | 57.50 | 57.50 | 400.00 | | Spice shakers, 5½" pr. | 40.00 | | |
| Cake stand, 10" | 21.00 | 26.00 | | *** | Saucer (same as sherbet | | | |
| Candy dish and cover | 55.00 | 55.00 | | |   plate) | 10.00 | 10.00 | 3.50 |
| Coaster | 32.50 | 62.50 | 85.00 | | Sherbet, ftd. | 20.00 | 20.00 | 35.00 |
| * Cookie jar and cover | 50.00 | 55.00 | | | Sugar | 10.00 | 12.00 | 8.50 |
| Creamer, oval | 14.00 | 15.00 | 14.00 | | Sugar cover | 20.00 | 20.00 | 16.00 |
| ** Cup | 12.00 | 12.00 | 8.00 | | Tumbler, 3", 5 oz. juice | 25.00 | 24.00 | 26.00 |
| Pitcher 6", 37 oz. | 48.00 | 50.00 | 500.00 | | Tumbler, 4", 9 oz. water | 25.00 | 24.00 | 22.00 |
| Pitcher, 7⅜", 24 oz. ftd. | 510.00 | 450.00 | | | Tumbler, 5¼", 13 oz. iced tea | 34.00 | 25.00 | 26.00 |
| Pitcher, 8", 60 oz. | 50.00 | 50.00 | 85.00 | | Tumbler, 4¾", 9 oz. sq. ftd | 60.00 | 55.00 | |
| *** Plate, 5½" sherbet | 10.00 | 10.00 | 4.00 | | Tumbler, 5¼", 10 oz. ftd. | 29.00 | 26.00 | 20.00 |
| Plate, 8" salad | 13.00 | 13.00 | 9.50 | | Tumbler, 6½", 12½ oz. ftd. | 80.00 | 75.00 | 130.00 |
| Plate, 9½" dinner | 24.00 | 22.00 | 14.50 | | Vase, 8" | 30.00 | 35.00 | |

\*Blue $800.00
\*\*Blue $100.00
\*\*\*Blue $55.00

**Please refer to Foreword for pricing information**

162

# QUEEN MARY (PRISMATIC LINE), "VERTICAL RIBBED"
## HOCKING GLASS COMPANY, 1936-1949

Colors: Pink, crystal and some Royal Ruby.

There are almost as many collectors of crystal Queen Mary as there are pink. It may be because the crystal dinner plates and tumblers **can be found**. I am hearing reports that those pieces in crystal are becoming less plentiful and prices are beginning to rise. Those prices will have a long way to go to catch up to the pink. A crystal set can still be garnered at reasonable prices if you start rounding it up before more people discover it.

Prices for pink Queen Mary dinner plates and footed tumblers just keep climbing - and not slowly either. This is a pattern that dealers now carry to shows!

Queen Mary collectors are asking about the pink footed creamer and sugar that I have shown previously. I still have not found any confirmation on them at Anchor Hocking, but I have seen these sets sell for $75.00. Considering the tumbler is up to $55.00, that may not be out of line. The collectors buying these sets were exhilarated and positive that they were, indeed, Queen Mary.

The 6" cereal bowl has the same shape as the butter bottom. Butter dishes were also called preserve dishes. There are two sizes of cups. The smaller cup sits on the saucer with cup ring. The larger cup rests on the combination saucer/sherbet plate.

Several pieces of Queen Mary were made in Royal Ruby including the candlesticks and large bowl. In the 1950's, the 3½" ash tray was made in Forest Green and Royal Ruby.

The 2" x 3¾" ash tray and 2" x 3¾" oval cigarette jar have been found together labeled "Ace Hi Bridge Smoking Set."

There were a pair of lamp shades found in this pattern. These had been made from frosted candy lids (with metal decorations), not the most beautiful pieces I have seen, but interesting!

|  | Pink | Crystal |  | Pink | Crystal |
|---|---|---|---|---|---|
| Ash tray, 2" x 3¾" oval | 5.00 | 3.00 | Creamer, ftd. | 37.50 |  |
| * Ash tray, 3½" round |  | 3.00 | Creamer, oval | 7.50 | 5.50 |
| Bowl, 4" one handle or none | 5.00 | 3.50 | Cup (2 sizes) | 7.00 | 5.50 |
| Bowl, 4½", berry | 6.00 | 4.00 | Plate, 6" and 6⅝" | 5.00 | 4.00 |
| Bowl, 5" berry | 10.00 | 6.00 | Plate, 8¾" salad |  | 5.50 |
| Bowl, 5½", two handles | 6.00 | 5.50 | Plate, 9¾" dinner | 45.00 | 13.00 |
| Bowl, 6" cereal | 23.00 | 6.50 | Plate, 12" sandwich | 14.00 | 9.00 |
| Bowl, 7" small | 12.00 | 7.00 | Plate, 14" serving tray | 20.00 | 12.00 |
| Bowl, 8¾" large berry | 16.00 | 10.00 | Relish tray, 12", 3-part | 14.00 | 9.00 |
| Butter dish or preserve and cover | 100.00 | 25.00 | Relish tray, 14", 4-part | 16.00 | 12.00 |
| Butter dish bottom | 27.50 | 6.50 | Salt and pepper, pr. |  | 19.00 |
| Butter dish top | 72.50 | 18.50 | Saucer | 3.00 | 2.50 |
| Candy dish and cover | 35.00 | 20.00 | Sherbet, ftd. | 6.50 | 4.00 |
| ** Candlesticks, 4½" double branch, pr. |  | 14.50 | Sugar, ftd. | 37.50 |  |
| Celery or pickle dish, 5" x 10" | 21.00 | 9.00 | Sugar, oval | 7.50 | 4.50 |
| Cigarette jar, 2" x 3" oval | 7.50 | 5.50 | Tumbler, 3½", 5 oz. juice | 9.00 | 4.00 |
| Coaster, 3½" | 4.00 | 2.50 | Tumbler, 4", 9 oz. water | 11.00 | 5.50 |
| Coaster/ash tray, 4¼" square | 6.00 | 5.00 | Tumbler, 5", 10 oz. ftd. | 55.00 | 25.00 |
| Comport, 5¾" | 12.50 | 6.50 |  |  |  |

*  Royal Ruby $5.00;     Forest Green $3.00;     **Royal Ruby $40.00

---

# RAINDROPS, "OPTIC DESIGN" FEDERAL GLASS COMPANY 1929-1933

Colors: Green and crystal.

Raindrops design has rounded bumps and not elongated ones as does Pear Optic or Thumbprint. Don't confuse the cups of these patterns as my photography helpers once did! Almost all Raindrops pieces are signed with Federal's trademark of an F in a shield.

Sugar bowl lids are still the most difficult piece to find; but since there are so few Raindrops collectors, the supply is adequate. To put these sugar lids into perspective, I have **owned** more Mayfair sugar lids and American Sweetheart sugar lids than I have **seen** Raindrops sugar lids. Raindrops makes a great little luncheon or bridge set. It even has a few accessory pieces that other smaller sets do not. You can find three sizes of serving bowls in Raindrops. The 7½" bowl will be the one you will see last. Few have surfaced!

Raindrops has two styles of cups. One is flat bottomed and the other has a slight foot. The flat bottomed is 2⁵⁄₁₆" high and the footed is 2¹¹⁄₁₆" (reported by a Raindrops collector). An additional tumbler has been added to the price list. It has a capacity of 14 oz. and is 5⅜" tall. My shaker still has not found a mate!

|  | Green |  | Green |
|---|---|---|---|
| Bowl, 4½" fruit | 5.00 | Sugar | 6.50 |
| Bowl, 6" cereal | 7.50 | Sugar cover | 38.00 |
| Bowl, 7½" berry | 36.00 | Tumbler, 3", 4 oz. | 4.50 |
| Cup | 5.50 | Tumbler, 2⅛", 2 oz. | 4.50 |
| Creamer | 7.50 | Tumbler, 3⅞", 5 oz. | 6.50 |
| Plate, 6" sherbet | 2.50 | Tumbler, 4⅛", 9½ oz. | 9.00 |
| Plate, 8" luncheon | 5.50 | Tumbler, 5", 10 oz. | 9.00 |
| Salt and pepper, pr. | 250.00 | Tumbler, 5⅜", 14 oz. | 12.00 |
| Saucer | 2.00 | Whiskey, 1⅞", 1 oz. | 7.00 |
| Sherbet | 6.50 |  |  |

# RADIANCE NEW MARTINSVILLE GLASS COMPANY, 1936-1939

Colors: Red, cobalt and ice blue, amber, crystal, pink and emerald green.

Colored punch bowls in Radiance remain elusive. You can see a red one below. The punch ladle is the coup de grace of this set. This ladle is a punch cup that has had a long handle attached. Evidently, many of these did not survive the test of time.

Crystal punch bowl sets being found on green and other colored plates may have been made by Viking after they bought out New Martinsville. You can see each style on the bottom of page 167. These flared crystal bowls are selling in the $35.00 range and cups are selling for $5.00 each. If anyone can shed some light on the crystal style punch bowls, I would appreciate hearing from you. A few collectors have suggested that Radiance is "too good" a glassware to be in this book, that it is better made glassware than those mass produced wares of the Depression era and belongs in my *Elegant Glassware of the Depression Era*. That argument could be made for many other patterns.

Red and the ice blue are the most collected colors. Few pieces were made in cobalt blue; yet you may include a recently found vase.

A few pieces are also being found in pink including creamer, sugar, tray, cup, saucer and shakers. These are selling in the same range as the red since they are scarce at this time.

Rarely found pieces in this pattern include the butter dish, pitcher, handled decanter and the five-piece condiment set. The vase has been found made into a lamp. I doubt this was a factory project, but it could have been.

There are several different gold and platinum decorated designs on crystal. The major problem with these decorated pieces is finding matching ones. Many collectors have shied away from buying decorated pieces; but, if not worn, they make an interesting addition to your collection.

Price crystal about fifty percent of amber. Only the crystal pieces that item collectors seek sell very well. These include pitchers, butter dishes, shakers, sugars, creamers and cordials.

| | Ice Blue, Red | Amber | | Ice Blue, Red | Amber |
|---|---|---|---|---|---|
| Bowl, 5", nut 2-handled | 16.00 | 8.50 | Condiment set, 4-piece w/tray | 255.00 | 135.00 |
| Bowl, 6", bonbon | 17.50 | 10.00 | Creamer | 22.00 | 14.00 |
| Bowl, 6", bonbon, footed | 18.00 | 11.00 | Cruet, indiv. | 55.00 | 36.00 |
| Bowl, 6", bonbon w/cover | 47.50 | 29.00 | Cup | 16.00 | 12.00 |
| Bowl, 7", relish, 2-part | 20.00 | 13.00 | Cup, punch | 13.00 | 7.00 |
| Bowl, 7", pickle | 19.00 | 12.00 | **Decanter w/stopper, handled | 145.00 | 85.00 |
| Bowl, 8", relish, 3-part | 27.50 | 18.00 | Goblet, 1 oz., cordial | 37.50 | 26.00 |
| Bowl, 10", celery | 23.00 | 14.00 | Ladle for punch bowl | 120.00 | 90.00 |
| Bowl, 10", crimped | 37.50 | 18.00 | Lamp, 12" | 98.00 | 56.00 |
| Bowl, 10", flared | 37.50 | 20.00 | Mayonnaise, 3 piece, set | 60.00 | 27.50 |
| Bowl, 12", crimped | 42.00 | 27.50 | ***Pitcher, 64 oz. | 210.00 | 140.00 |
| Bowl, 12", flared | 37.50 | 23.00 | Plate, 8", luncheon | 16.00 | 10.00 |
| *Bowl, punch | 175.00 | 95.00 | **** Plate, 14", punch bowl liner | 70.00 | 35.00 |
| Butter dish | 410.00 | 185.00 | Salt & pepper, pr. | 80.00 | 50.00 |
| Candlestick 6" ruffled pr. | 150.00 | 75.00 | Saucer | 8.50 | 5.50 |
| Candlestick 8" pr. | 65.00 | 40.00 | Sugar | 21.00 | 12.00 |
| Candlestick 2-lite, pr. | 90.00 | 60.00 | Tray, oval | 30.00 | 24.00 |
| Cheese/cracker, (11" plate) set | 47.50 | 26.00 | *****Tumbler, 9 oz. | 27.50 | 17.50 |
| Comport, 5" | 27.50 | 16.00 | ****** Vase, 10", flared | 55.00 | 40.00 |
| Comport, 6" | 30.00 | 20.00 | | | |

*Emerald Green $125.00
**Cobalt blue $185.00
***Cobalt blue $350.00
****Emerald green $25.00
*****Cobalt blue $28.00
******Cobalt blue $75.00

**Please refer to Foreword for pricing information**

## "RIBBON" HAZEL ATLAS GLASS COMPANY, Early 1930's

Colors: Green; some black, crystal and pink.

Maybe one of the reasons that Ribbon bowls are so elusive is that there were two designs made. The normally found smaller bowls have evenly spaced small panels on them while the panels on larger bowls expand in size as it approaches the top of the bowl. This makes the larger bowl flare at the top while the smaller bowls are more straight sided. This is evident on both the large green and black bowls pictured when compared to the cereal. I am getting several reports of larger bowls with sides straight up like the cereal. One collector compared it to the Cloverleaf bowl made by Hazel Atlas. I have only seen pictures of these bowls, but they also measure 8" according to the reports. You may notice that other Ribbon shapes are the same as Cloverleaf and Ovide which are two other Hazel Atlas patterns. Either some glass designer really liked those shapes or the company reworked moulds to make the new patterns.

The black bowl was turned over to show the pattern that is on the outside. Most black glass has to be turned over to see the pattern due to the opaqueness of the black. I see very little Ribbon for sale at shows. Ribbon is one of the patterns that is not found on the West Coast. I recently talked to one collector who has approximately thirty pieces, but all her items had come from the East by mail order.

Tumblers, sugars and creamers are not yet as difficult to find as bowls, but even they are starting to be in shorter supply.

The candy dish remains the most commonly found piece of Ribbon. That fact and the inexpensive price make it a perfect gift for non-collectors. It is also usable!

Shakers are the only pieces in pink that have been reported to me. If you have any other pieces, I would like to hear from you.

| | Green | Black | | Green | Black |
|---|---|---|---|---|---|
| Bowl, 4" berry | 9.50 | | Plate, 8" luncheon | 4.50 | 12.50 |
| Bowl, 5" cereal | 15.00 | | Salt and pepper, pr. | 27.50 | 40.00 |
| Bowl, 8" large berry | 24.00 | 30.00 | Saucer | 2.50 | |
| Candy dish and cover | 35.00 | | Sherbet, ftd. | 5.00 | |
| Creamer, ftd. | 14.00 | | Sugar, ftd. | 12.00 | |
| Cup | 5.00 | | Tumbler, 6", 10 oz. | 25.00 | |
| Plate, 6¼" sherbet | 2.50 | | | | |

## RING, "BANDED RINGS" HOCKING GLASS COMPANY, 1927-1933

Colors: Crystal, crystal w/pink, red, blue, orange, yellow, black, silver, etc. rings; green, some pink, "Mayfair" blue and red.

Green Ring can be collected, but not as easily as the crystal or decorated crystal. A reader tells me that for subscribing to *Country Gentleman* in the 1930's, you received a green berry bowl set consisting of an 8" berry and six 5" berry bowls. They must have received few subscriptions for that offer since I have seen few green bowls. Notice the green flat tumbler behind the sherbet on the right. It is the first decorated piece of green Ring I have seen.

Pink seems to be found only in pitcher and tumbler sets. A Wisconsin collector reports that the pink pitchers are very plentiful in his part of the country. Pink pitchers do not seem to be commonly found anywhere else. Tumblers were not mentioned in that letter; so, perhaps, only the pitchers were premium items.

Most Ring admirers start by collecting one particular color "scheme." Colored rings in a particular order on crystal are what I am calling a "scheme." Some collectors have been known to call it other things. Printable words include headache and "pain in the butt." There is a predominant "scheme" involving black, yellow, red and orange colored rings in that order. I have tried to show you that arrangement here. Those other varieties drive the perfectionists crazy!

Crystal with platinum (silver) bands is another widely gathered form of this pattern. Worn trims harass collectors of this decoration. The colored rings do not seem to have that problem. It probably is because the rings do not decorate the rims - or painted trims proved more durable than platinum!

| | Crystal | Decor., Green | | Crystal | Decor., Green |
|---|---|---|---|---|---|
| Bowl, 5" berry | 3.50 | 5.00 | Plate, 11¾", sandwich | 6.50 | 11.00 |
| Bowl, 7" soup | 8.50 | 12.50 | ***Salt and pepper, pr., 3" | 17.00 | 35.00 |
| Bowl, 5¼", divided | 9.50 | | Sandwich server, center handle | 16.00 | 25.00 |
| Bowl, 8" large berry | 7.00 | 10.00 | Saucer | 1.50 | 2.00 |
| Butter tub or ice tub | 17.50 | 30.00 | Sherbet, low (for 6½" plate) | 5.00 | 12.00 |
| Cocktail shaker | 18.00 | 24.00 | Sherbet, 4¾" ftd. | 5.00 | 9.00 |
| ** Cup | 4..50 | 5.00 | Sugar, ftd. | 4.50 | 5.50 |
| Creamer, ftd. | 4.50 | 6.00 | Tumbler, 3", 4 oz. | 3.50 | 6.00 |
| Decanter and stopper | 22.00 | 35.00 | Tumbler, 3½", 5 oz. | 4.50 | 6.50 |
| Goblet, 7¼", 9 oz. | 7.50 | 14.00 | Tumbler, 4", 8 oz., old fashion | 10.00 | 15.00 |
| Goblet, 3¾", 3½ oz. cocktail | 11.00 | 16.00 | Tumbler, 4¼", 9 oz. | 4.50 | 10.00 |
| Goblet, 4½", 3½ oz., wine | 13.00 | 18.00 | * Tumbler, 4¾", 10 oz | 7.50 | |
| Ice bucket | 14.00 | 22.50 | Tumbler, 5⅛", 12 oz. | 5.50 | 8.50 |
| Pitcher, 8", 60 oz. | 15.00 | 20.00 | Tumbler, 3½" ftd. juice | 5.50 | 7.50 |
| * Pitcher, 8½", 80 oz. | 18.00 | 30.00 | Tumbler, 5½" ftd. water | 5.50 | 8.50 |
| Plate, 6¼" sherbet | 2.00 | 2..50 | Tumbler, 6½", ftd. iced tea | 7.00 | 13.00 |
| Plate, 6½", off-center ring | 3.00 | 5.50 | Vase, 8" | 16.00 | 32.00 |
| ** Plate, 8" luncheon | 2.50 | 4.50 | Whiskey, 2", 1½ oz. | 5.00 | 8.50 |

* Also found in pink. Priced as green.
** Red $17.50. Blue $27.50
*** Green $55.00

**Please refer to Foreword for pricing information**

169

# ROCK CRYSTAL, "EARLY AMERICAN ROCK CRYSTAL" McKEE GLASS COMPANY,
## 1920's and 1930's in colors

Colors: Four shades of green, aquamarine, vaseline, yellow, amber, pink and frosted pink, red slag, dark red, red, amberina red, crystal, frosted crystal, crystal with goofus decoration, crystal with gold decoration, amethyst, milk glass, blue frosted or "Jap" blue and cobalt blue.

Collecting Rock Crystal for eighteen years came to an end in our household last spring. We bought new carpet for our house in Kentucky. After six days of packing glass to make the carpet installation easier, Cathy decided to "weed out" some of our collections while it was already packed. Crystal and red Rock Crystal, along with Flower Garden pieces from our collections, are now delighting many collectors from coast to coast. When you collect patterns for years and finally decide to sell them, you do have a few regrets. However, as you get older, these regrets do not overshadow the fun and good times you had in collecting!

Much of our red was shipped to the West Coast. Dinner plates in red rarely are offered for sale, and it would have been great to have had more settings than the eight we did. Most of our red matched. We kept amberina or deep red over the years. Cathy was unwilling to part with some pieces such as the lamp! The flat candy shown in front of that lamp in the top photograph was bought years ago from a former employee of McKee. He had many extra candy bottoms and said that they were sold as soup bowls. That was the way he and his wife had used them. I also remember that I could hardly move away from the table after the meal his wife served us! The red center handled bowl, which is 8½" across, must be a candy or nut dish since the handle would be in the way if it were used for a serving bowl.

Our crystal Rock Crystal was more extensive in scope. It will take more than a few shows to sell all of it! At present, we are keeping one of everything to photograph; but eventually, that will also find new homes.

Remember that there are two different sizes of punch bowls. The base opening for our bowl is 5" across and stands 6⅟₁₆" tall. This base fits a punch bowl that is 4³⁄₁₆" across the bottom. The other style base has only a 4⅛" opening but also stands 6⅟₁₆" tall. The bowl to fit this base must be around 3½" across the bottom; but I am only guessing since we do not have a punch bowl to fit it. There should be ¾" difference to make the base fit. No one has sent in measurements for that punch bowl yet.

In the top photograph on page 173 are three styles of ice dishes. The one on the left is a combination of the others with a ring and three dividers outside the ring. The one in the center has only dividers and the one on the right has only a ring. The flat juice has been found in some of the ice dishes, but I suspect the liners may have been plain as were Fostoria's. Ice dishes were made to hold shrimp, crab, or juices with surrounding ice keeping the items cold (without diluting the contents or melting on the table). Icers were mostly found in the upper class homes of that day.

Red, crystal and amber sets can be completed with patience. There are so many different pieces available that you need to determine how much you are willing to spend on a set by choosing what items to purchase. Instead of buying every available tumbler and stem, you can pick up a couple of each or choose which styles you prefer and buy only them. That way even collectors with limited budgets can start crystal or amber. Red takes a deeper pocket!

Rock Crystal can be collected as a simple luncheon set, a dinner set or a complete service with many unusual serving and accessory pieces. In fact, many Rock Crystal pieces are purchased by collectors of other patterns to use as accessory items with their own patterns. Vases, cruets, candlesticks and a multitude of serving pieces are some of the items usually purchased.

| | Crystal | All Other Colors | Red |
|---|---|---|---|
| *Bon bon, 7½" s.e. | 18.00 | 28.00 | 50.00 |
| Bowl, 4" s.e. | 11.00 | 15.00 | 30.00 |
| Bowl, 4½" s.e. | 12.00 | 15.00 | 30.00 |
| Bowl, 5" s.e. | 14.50 | 20.00 | 40.00 |
| **Bowl, 5" finger bowl with 7" plate, p.e. | 19.00 | 30.00 | 60.00 |
| Bowl, 7" pickle or spoon tray | 18.00 | 30.00 | 60.00 |
| Bowl, 7" salad s.e. | 19.00 | 27.50 | 60.00 |
| Bowl, 8" salad s.e. | 23.00 | 27.50 | 68.00 |
| Bowl, 8½" center handle | | | 135.00 |
| Bowl, 9" salad s.e. | 22.50 | 26.00 | 90.00 |
| Bowl, 10½" salad s.e. | 24.00 | 30.00 | 75.00 |
| Bowl, 11½" 2-part relish | 29.00 | 37.50 | 65.00 |
| Bowl, 12" oblong celery | 24.00 | 35.00 | 60.00 |
| ***Bowl, 12½" ftd. center bowl | 65.00 | 85.00 | 275.00 |
| Bowl, 12½", 5 part relish | 43.00 | | |
| Bowl, 13" roll tray | 30.00 | 47.50 | 110.00 |
| Bowl, 14" 6-part relish | 34.00 | 50.00 | |
| Butter dish and cover | 310.00 | | |
| Butter dish bottom | 180.00 | | |
| Butter dish top | 130.00 | | |

   * s.e. McKee designation for scalloped edge
   ** p.e. McKee designation for plain edge
   *** Red Slag-$350.00 Cobalt-$165.00
   **** Cobalt-$185.00
                 **Please refer to Foreword for pricing information**

# ROCK CRYSTAL, "EARLY AMERICAN ROCK CRYSTAL" (Cont.)

| | Crystal | All Other Colors | Red |
|---|---|---|---|
| **** Candelabra, 2-lite pr. | 38.00 | 77.50 | 195.00 |
| Candelabra, 3-lite pr. | 47.50 | 90.00 | 275.00 |
| Candlestick, flat, stemmed pr. | 37.50 | 47.50 | 80.00 |
| Candlestick, 5½" low pr. | 33.00 | 50.00 | 150.00 |
| Candlestick, 8" tall pr. | 68.00 | 90.00 | 350.00 |
| Candy and cover, round | 42.50 | 67.50 | 155.00 |
| Cake stand, 11", 2¾" high, ftd. | 32.00 | 47.50 | 110.00 |
| Comport, 7" | 32.00 | 45.00 | 65.00 |
| Creamer, flat s.e. | 35.00 | | |
| Creamer, 9 oz. ftd. | 19.00 | 30.00 | 65.00 |
| Cruet and stopper, 6 oz. oil | 77.50 | | |
| Cup, 7 oz. | 16.00 | 26.00 | 67.50 |
| Goblet, 7½ oz., 8 oz. low ftd. | 15.00 | 25.00 | 55.00 |
| Goblet, 11 oz. low ftd. iced tea | 18.00 | 28.00 | 65.00 |
| Ice dish (3 styles) | 30.00 | | |
| Jelly, 5" ftd. s.e. | 16.00 | 26.00 | 50.00 |
| Lamp, electric | 155.00 | 275.00 | 625.00 |
| Parfait, 3½ oz. low ftd. | 16.00 | 36.00 | 70.00 |
| Pitcher, qt. s.e. | 155.00 | 210.00 | |
| Pitcher, ½ gal., 7½" high | 97.50 | 185.00 | |
| Pitcher, 9" large covered | 155.00 | 280.00 | 625.00 |
| Pitcher, fancy tankard | 155.00 | 475.00 | 825.00 |
| Plate, 6" bread and butter s.e. | 6.00 | 9.50 | 20.00 |
| Plate, 7½" p.e. & s.e. | 8.00 | 12.00 | 21.00 |
| Plate, 8½" p.e. & s.e. | 9.00 | 12.50 | 30.00 |
| Plate, 9" s.e. | 16.00 | 22.00 | 55.00 |
| Plate, 10½" s.e. | 16.00 | 22.00 | 55.00 |
| Plate, 10½" dinner s.e. (large center design) | 46.00 | 67.50 | 165.00 |
| Plate, 11½" | 40.00 | | |
| Plate, 11½" s.e. | 17.00 | 24.00 | 55.00 |
| Punch bowl and stand, 14" (2 styles) | 495.00 | | |
| Punch bowl stand only (2 styles) | 150.00 | | |
| Salt and pepper (2 styles) pr. | 70.00 | 115.00 | |
| Salt dip | 35.00 | | |
| Sandwich server, center-handled | 26.00 | 40.00 | 130.00 |
| Saucer | 7.50 | 8.50 | 22.00 |
| Sherbet or egg, 3½ oz. ftd. | 16.00 | 24.00 | 60.00 |
| Spooner | 37.50 | | |
| Stemware, 1 oz. ftd. cordial | 18.00 | 38.00 | 60.00 |
| Stemware, 2 oz. wine | 18.00 | 27.50 | 50.00 |
| Stemware, 3 oz. wine | 18.00 | 30.00 | 50.00 |
| Stemware, 3½ oz. ftd. cocktail | 15.00 | 21.00 | 40.00 |
| Stemware, 6 oz. ftd. champagne | 16.00 | 23.00 | 35.00 |
| Stemware, 7 oz. | 16.00 | 24.00 | 50.00 |
| Stemware, 8 oz. large ftd. goblet | 17.50 | 26.00 | 55.00 |
| Sundae, 6 oz. low ftd. | 12.00 | 18.00 | 35.00 |
| Sugar, 10 oz. open | 15.00 | 22.00 | 38.00 |
| Sugar, lid | 30.00 | 42.50 | 98.00 |
| Syrup with lid | 130.00 | | |
| Tray, 5⅜" x 7⅜", ⅞" high | 60.00 | | |
| Tumbler, 2½ oz. whiskey | 16.00 | 23.00 | 55.00 |
| Tumbler, 5 oz. juice | 16.00 | 25.00 | 55.00 |
| Tumbler, 5 oz. old fashioned | 16.00 | 25.00 | 55.00 |
| Tumbler, 9 oz. concave or straight | 18.00 | 26.00 | 50.00 |
| Tumbler, 12 oz. concave or straight | 23.00 | 35.00 | 65.00 |
| Vase, cornucopia | 58.00 | 80.00 | |
| Vase, 11" ftd. | 55.00 | 90.00 | 155.00 |

# ROSE CAMEO BELMONT TUMBLER COMPANY, 1931

Color: Green.

Rose Cameo is still one of the mystery patterns of Depression Glass. Mystery surrounds the manufacturer, although Belmont Tumbler Company had a 1931 patent on Rose Cameo. Glass shards of Rose Cameo have been found in "digs" at a factory site of Hazel Atlas. Maybe time will unravel this mystery. Of course, a yellow Cloverleaf shaker was dug up at the site of Akro Agate's factory in Clarksburg, West Virginia; and we know that Akro had nothing to do with making Cloverleaf. (Did you know some glass collectors dabble in archaeology in pursuit of glass?)

The straight sided bowl has been set upright to show its different shape from the cereal.

Rose Cameo is not confusing new collectors as it once did. Cameo, with its dancing girl, and this cameo encircled rose were often mixed up in bygone times. In the past I have made some excellent buys when these mistakes were made. The best one was an unlisted Rose Cameo ice tub for $8.00 that turned out to be Cameo. An informed collecting public rarely makes those mistakes today.

The difference in two styles of tumblers is recognized by noticing the flaring of the rims. One does not flare.

|  | Green |
|---|---|
| Bowl, 4½" berry | 8.50 |
| Bowl, 5" cereal | 14.00 |
| Bowl, 6" straight sides | 17.50 |
| Plate, 7" salad | 11.00 |
| Sherbet | 11.00 |
| Tumbler, 5" ftd. (2 styles) | 16.50 |

---

# ROSEMARY, "DUTCH ROSE" FEDERAL GLASS COMPANY 1935-1937

Colors: Amber, green, pink; some iridized.

The story of Rosemary's becoming a separate pattern redesigned from Federal's Mayfair can be read on page 122. Superfluous to say, Rosemary's existence came about inadvertently because of Hocking's previous patent to the Mayfair name.

Rosemary's cereal bowls, cream soups, grill plates and tumblers are seldom seen. I might add for new collectors that grill plates are the divided plates usually associated with diners or grills (restaurants) in this time. Food was kept from running together by those raised divisions. These are especially tough to find in pink. Pink is the most difficult set to assemble with amber being the easiest. However, a full setting of amber cereals, cream soups, tumblers and grill plates will take you some time to find. I can't remember when I have seen an amber cereal or a green cream soup! They are missing in my inventory for photography!

Note that the sugar has no handles and is often mislabeled as a sherbet. There is no sherbet known in Rosemary! Those sugars would serve as large sherbets and dessert lovers could get an extra helping if you used it that way.

You will find Rosemary an intriguing pattern whether you are a beginning collector or a collector looking for a new set to collect. Try finding this in pink if you wish a challenge!

|  | Amber | Green | Pink |
|---|---|---|---|
| Bowl, 5" berry | 5.50 | 8.50 | 9.50 |
| Bowl, 5" cream soup | 14.00 | 19.00 | 22.00 |
| Bowl, 6" cereal | 26.00 | 29.00 | 33.00 |
| Bowl, 10" oval vegetable | 14.00 | 26.00 | 27.00 |
| Creamer, ftd. | 8.50 | 12.50 | 15.00 |
| Cup | 5.50 | 9.50 | 10.00 |
| Plate, 6¾" salad | 5.50 | 8.50 | 9.00 |
| Plate, dinner | 9.00 | 12.50 | 16.00 |
| Plate, grill | 7.50 | 12.50 | 18.00 |
| Platter, 12" oval | 15.00 | 20.00 | 28.00 |
| Saucer | 4.50 | 5.00 | 6.00 |
| Sugar, ftd. | 8.50 | 12.50 | 17.00 |
| Tumbler, 4¼", 9 oz. | 28.00 | 28.00 | 42.00 |

**Please refer to Foreword for pricing information**

# ROULETTE, "MANY WINDOWS" HOCKING GLASS COMPANY, 1935-1939

Colors: Green, pink and crystal.

The name "Many Windows" was given this pattern before Roulette was found to be the real pattern name. I assume that was from the windowed effect the design makes as it encircles each piece. Several collectors have told me they prefer that descriptive term instead of the real name! Whatever floats your boat!

Basic green pieces abound in cups, saucers, sherbets and luncheon plates. Finding the sandwich plate, pitcher and fruit bowl will take more time as they are all becoming scarce. After obtaining those items, then comes the fun of looking for the six different tumblers! Juice tumblers and the old fashioned are the most elusive of all. I still have not found a juice tumbler for my photograph.

Pink is found only as a pitcher and tumblers. Pink tumblers are easier to find than green ones. All five sizes of pink flat tumblers are pictured, but I have never seen a pink footed tumbler.

Crystal tumbler and pitcher sets are rarely found; a few have surfaced which were decorated with colored stripes. In fact, this striped effect gives an "Art Deco" look. I am more impressed with these decorated crystal pitchers than with any other Roulette items I have seen!

|  | Crystal | Pink, Green |
|---|---|---|
| Bowl, 9" fruit | 9.50 | 13.00 |
| Cup | 36.00 | 6.50 |
| Pitcher, 8", 65 oz. | 25.00 | 35.00 |
| Plate, 6" sherbet | 3.50 | 4.50 |
| Plate, 8½" luncheon | 5.00 | 6.00 |
| Plate, 12" sandwich | 11.00 | 12.50 |
| Saucer | 1.50 | 3.50 |
| Sherbet | 3.50 | 5.50 |
| Tumbler, 3¼", 5 oz. juice | 7.00 | 20.00 |
| Tumbler, 3¼", 7½ oz. old fashioned | 23.00 | 37.50 |
| Tumbler, 4⅛", 9 oz. water | 13.00 | 22.00 |
| Tumbler, 5⅛", 12 oz. iced tea | 16.00 | 25.00 |
| Tumbler, 5½", 10 oz. ftd. | 14.00 | 25.00 |
| Whiskey, 2½", 1½ oz. | 8.00 | 14.00 |

# "ROUND ROBIN" MANUFACTURER UNKNOWN, Probably early 1930's

Colors: Green, iridescent and crystal.

Round Robin is another one of the smaller patterns whose manufacturer has remained undiscovered. The domino tray is the surprising piece in this small pattern. Hocking's Cameo is the only other pattern in Depression Glass to offer a sugar cube tray. This tray has only been found in green. For new readers, the domino tray held the creamer in the center ring with sugar cubes surrounding it. Sugar cubes were made by a famous sugar company, and the tray became synonymous with this name.

Sherbets and berry bowls are the hardest pieces to locate outside the domino tray. Sherbets are particularly hard to find in green, but plentiful in iridescent.

Some crystal Round Robin is found today. Crystal was sprayed and baked to achieve iridized pieces. Obviously, not all the crystal was sprayed, since we see it occasionally.

The Round Robin cup is one of the few footed ones found in Depression Glass.

|  | Green | Iridescent |
|---|---|---|
| Bowl, 4" berry | 5.00 | 5.00 |
| Cup, ftd. | 5.00 | 5.50 |
| Creamer, ftd. | 7.50 | 6.50 |
| Domino tray | 32.00 |  |
| Plate, 6" sherbet | 2.50 | 2.50 |
| Plate, 8" luncheon | 4.00 | 4.00 |
| Plate, 12" sandwich | 7.50 | 7.00 |
| Saucer | 2.00 | 2.00 |
| Sherbet | 5.00 | 5.50 |
| Sugar | 6.50 | 6.00 |

**Please refer to Foreword for pricing information**

# ROXANA, HAZEL ATLAS GLASS COMPANY, 1932

Colors: "Golden Topaz," crystal and some white.

Thanks to some Michigan collectors, you can now see how Roxana was obtained in that area. If you ate Star Brand Oats, you were able to receive one piece of "Golden Topaz" table glassware in every package. This may also explain why the deep 4½" bowl and the 5½" plate are so hard to find. They were not packed as a premium in these oats! I am assuming that the plate shown on the ad is the 6" one to go with the sherbet. In any case, if you collect Roxana, maybe you should plan a vacation to that region!

For years I have listed a saucer in Roxana; and no one has ever written to say that what I was listing as a saucer is actually a 5½" plate! All seven known pieces are shown; I also included a gold decorated plate in hopes it would "show off" the pattern a little better in the photograph. This delicate pattern is difficult to capture on film since the light shade of yellow has a tendency to disappear under bright lights. Notice that the pattern also tended to disappear in the original advertisement! Well, we do recognize shapes!

Roxana was only listed in Hazel Atlas catalogues for one year. It is a limited pattern when compared to thousands of pieces made over the years in many other patterns. Unfortunately, there are so few pieces available that most collectors avoid it. Only the 4½" bowl has been found in white.

|  | Yellow | White |
|---|---|---|
| Bowl, 4½" x 2⅜" | 9.50 | 13.00 |
| Bowl, 5" berry | 8.50 | |
| Bowl, 6" cereal | 13.00 | |
| Plate, 5½" | 7.50 | |
| Plate, 6" sherbet | 6.50 | |
| Sherbet, ftd. | 8.50 | |
| Tumbler, 4¼", 9 oz. | 16.00 | |

**Please refer to Foreword for pricing information**

ONE OF THESE PIECES OF
**GOLDEN TOPAZ**
GLASSWARE
IN EVERY PACKAGE

The cost of the ware is included in the price of the package and we hereby authorize your grocer to show it to you

STAR A STAR
BRAND

NEW PROCESS
OATS
WITH GOLDEN TOPAZ
TABLE GLASSWARE
PACKED FOR
SYMONS BROS. & CO.
SAGINAW, JACKSON, ALMA

# ROYAL LACE HAZEL ATLAS GLASS COMPANY, 1934-1941

Colors: Cobalt blue, crystal, green, pink; some amethyst.

Royal Lace in cobalt blue has always been one of the most desirable patterns in Depression Glass. There is something to that color that lights up collectors' eyes. No matter how expensive it becomes, there is one more collector willing to pay the price to get that one piece he doesn't have in his set!

I bought a collection of blue Royal Lace in Dallas last year. The lady could not believe the prices it was bringing since she had not bought any pieces for several years. One of her purchases had been the nut dish for $18.00 from an advertisement out of the *Daze*. (See ad in back of this book.) You can see this nut dish in the foreground of the bottom picture. It is the same piece as the straight side candleholder without the candle cup in the center.

There are five different pitchers made in Royal Lace: a) 48 oz. straight side; b) 64 oz., 8", no ice lip; c) 68 oz., 8", w/ice lip; d) 86 oz., 8", no ice lip; e) 96 oz., 8½", w/ice lip. The ten ounce difference in the last two listed is caused by the spout on the pitcher without lip dipping below the top edge of the pitcher. This causes the liquid to run out before you get to the top. All spouted pitchers will vary in ounce capacity depending upon how the spout tilts.

Crystal and pink pitchers can be found in all five styles. Green can only be found in four styles. There is no 68 oz. with ice lip in green. There are four styles found in blue. There have been no blue 86 oz. without ice lip found.

More water tumblers (9 oz.) without panels are found than with the panel. These paneled tumblers are more pronounced on crystal than any other color. Most collectors prefer the plain style to match their other tumblers.

The 4⅞",10 oz. tumblers are still the most difficult tumbler to find; but supplies of iced teas and juice tumblers are also drying up. This is true for all colors. Many collectors only purchase water tumblers and the straight sided pitcher. Even though so many of this style pitcher and water tumblers were made, demand continues to drive up the price! Prices would skyrocket if most collectors bought all four sizes of tumblers! The prices for tumblers would surprise even the old folks (over twenty years) of collecting. A twenty year collector told me at a show in Texas that prices for his pattern had increased two thousand percent since he had started collecting it.

Green Royal Lace is coming back "in favor" again. Collecting green runs in cycles for some reason; but so has cobalt blue. The prices get so high that everyone stops buying for a while. When collectors realize that the law of supply and demand takes precedent over all else, they start to buy again, thus pushing the prices higher until everyone stops buying because the prices are too high. Then the same cycle begins all over!

Collectors prefer all glass sherbets to the ones found in metal holders, which makes for higher prices on them. Be sure to check the inside rims for mould roughness and nicks. That inner rim is why mint condition pieces cost more. Even stacking bowls and plates will cause damage to these rims if not carefully done. That is why you see so many dealers placing paper plates between their merchandise. A mint piece can rapidly deteriorate from careless handling of shoppers, "lid bangers" as they are known in the business. Sunday afternoons at many shows sometimes seem to be a contest of people seeing who can lift the most lids without buying a piece of glass. Respect the glass! If your bifocals cause distance discrepancies as mine do, don't lift lids and bang them back down unless you're examining the piece with the clear thought of buying it. Dealers will probably stand up and applaud when they read this!

|  | Crystal | Pink | Green | Blue |
|---|---|---|---|---|
| Bowl, 4¾" cream soup | 11.00 | 19.00 | 28.00 | 35.00 |
| Bowl, 5" berry | 14.00 | 25.00 | 28.00 | 46.00 |
| Bowl, 10" round berry | 17.50 | 24.00 | 28.00 | 58.00 |
| Bowl, 10", 3-legged straight edge | 18.00 | 32.00 | 40.00 | 60.00 |
| Bowl, 10", 3-legged rolled edge | 150.00 | 45.00 | 70.00 | 285.00 |
| Bowl, 10", 3-legged ruffled edge | 25.00 | 45.00 | 60.00 | 425.00 |
| Bowl, 11" oval vegetable | 20.00 | 30.00 | 30.00 | 55.00 |
| Butter dish and cover | 65.00 | 140.00 | 260.00 | 550.00 |
| Butter dish bottom | 42.50 | 90.00 | 170.00 | 357.50 |
| Butter dish top | 27.50 | 50.00 | 90.00 | 192.50 |
| Candlestick, straight edge pr. | 30.00 | 42.00 | 60.00 | 98.00 |
| Candlestick, rolled edge pr. | 45.00 | 50.00 | 65.00 | 190.00 |
| Candlestick ruffled edge pr. | 28.00 | 50.00 | 60.00 | 195.00 |
| Cookie jar and cover | 30.00 | 48.00 | 75.00 | 350.00 |
| Cream, ftd. | 12.00 | 18.00 | 25.00 | 5500 |
| Cup | 7.00 | 13.00 | 20.00 | 32.00 |
| Nut bowl | 150.00 | 350.00 | 350.00 | 1,000.00 |
| Pitcher, 48 oz., straight sides | 40.00 | 65.00 | 98.00 | 150.00 |

|  | Crystal | Pink | Green | Blue |
|---|---|---|---|---|
| Pitcher, 64 oz., 8", w/o/l | 45.00 | 65.00 | 98.00 | 210.00 |
| Pitcher, 8", 68 oz., w/lip | 50.00 | 70.00 |  | 220.00 |
| Pitcher, 8", 86 oz., w/o/l | 50.00 | 70.00 | 125.00 |  |
| Pitcher, 8½", 96 oz., w/lip | 60.00 | 80.00 | 130.00 | 250.00 |
| Plate, 6", sherbet | 5.00 | 8.00 | 10.00 | 12.00 |
| Plate, 8½" luncheon | 8.00 | 13.00 | 14.00 | 30.00 |
| Plate, 9⅞" dinner | 12.50 | 18.00 | 25.00 | 32.00 |
| Plate, 9⅞" grill | 9.50 | 17.00 | 25.00 | 30.00 |
| Platter, 13" oval | 18.00 | 30.00 | 38.00 | 47.00 |
| Salt and pepper, pr. | 40.00 | 58.00 | 120.00 | 250.00 |
| Saucer | 5.00 | 7.00 | 9.00 | 12.50 |
| Sherbet, ftd. | 9.50 | 16.00 | 24.00 | 38.00 |
| * Sherbet in metal holder | 3.50 |  |  | 25.00 |
| Sugar | 8.50 | 15.00 | 22.00 | 25.00 |
| Sugar lid | 16.00 | 38.00 | 42.00 | 125.00 |
| Tumbler, 3½", 5 oz. | 13.50 | 23.00 | 28.00 | 38.50 |
| Tumbler, 4⅛", 9 oz. | 12.00 | 16.00 | 28.00 | 35.00 |
| Tumbler, 4⅞", 10 oz. | 22.00 | 55.00 | 58.00 | 100.00 |
| Tumbler, 5⅜", 12 oz. | 22.00 | 45.00 | 48.00 | 75.00 |

** Toddy or cider set: includes cookie jar metal lid, metal tray, 8 roly-poly cups and ladle — 195.00

* Amethyst $35.00        **Amethyst $150.00

# ROYAL RUBY ANCHOR HOCKING GLASS COMPANY, 1938-1940

Color: Ruby red.

Anchor Hocking introduced Royal Ruby color in 1938 expanding use of their many existing patterns. I am trying to include all pieces of Royal Ruby introduced before 1940 in my list, but I am sure I will be adding others as additional information is uncovered. Pieces of Royal Ruby made after 1940 are included in my book *Collectible Glassware from the 40's, 50's, 60's…*

The catalogue page reproduced on page 183 is from one of Anchor Hocking's first catalogues after the introduction of Royal Ruby. It shows both Oyster and Pearl and Coronation as two of the first patterns used to launch this Royal Ruby campaign. Remember that introductory pieces of Royal Ruby have been found in many of Anchor Hocking's lines including Colonial, Ring and Miss America. There are others, but my idea is to show regular lines that were issued and can be collected.

| | Royal Ruby | | Royal Ruby |
|---|---|---|---|
| Bonbon, 6½" | 8.50 | Creamer, ftd. | 9.00 |
| Bowl, 3¾" berry (Old Cafe) | 5.50 | Cup (Coronation) | 6.50 |
| Bowl, 4½", handled (Coronation) | 6.50 | Cup (Old Cafe) | 8.00 |
| Bowl, 4⅞", smooth (Sandwich) | 12.50 | Cup, round | 5.50 |
| Bowl, 5¼" heart-shaped, 1-handled (Oys & Prl) | 12.00 | Goblet, ball stem | 10.00 |
| Bowl, 5¼", scalloped (Sandwich) | 20.00 | Jewel box, 4¼", crys. w/Ruby cov. | 12.50 |
| Bowl, 5½" cereal (Old Cafe) | 10.00 | Lamp (Old Cafe) | 25.00 |
| Bowl, 5½", 1-handled (Oys & Prl) | 12.00 | Marmalade, 5⅛", crys. w/Ruby cov. | 7.50 |
| Bowl, 6½" deep-handled (Oys & Prl) | 19.00 | Plate, 8½", luncheon (Coronation) | 8.00 |
| Bowl, 6½", handled (Coronation) | 12.00 | Plate, 9⅛", dinner, round | 11.00 |
| Bowl, 6½", scalloped (Sandwich) | 27.50 | Plate, 13½" sandwich (Oys & Prl) | 40.00 |
| Bowl, 8", handled (Coronation) | 15.00 | Puff box, 4⅝", crys. w/Ruby cov. | 9.00 |
| Bowl, 8", scalloped (Sandwich) | 37.50 | Relish tray insert (Manhattan) | 4.50 |
| Bowl, 9", closed handles (Old Cafe) | 14.00 | Saucer, round | 2.50 |
| Bowl, 10½" deep fruit (Oys & Prl) | 45.00 | Sherbet, low ftd. (Old Cafe) | 10.00 |
| Candle holder, 3½" pr. (Oys & Prl) | 45.00 | Sugar, ftd. | 7.50 |
| Candle holder, 4½" pr. (Queen Mary) | 40.00 | Sugar, lid | 11.00 |
| Candy dish, 8" mint, low (Old Cafe) | 11.00 | Tray, 6" x 4½" | 12.50 |
| Candy jar, 5½", crys. w/Ruby cov. (Old Cafe) | 14.00 | Tumbler, 3" juice (Old Cafe) | 8.00 |
| Cigarette box/card holder, 6⅛" x 4" crys. w/Ruby top | 55.00 | Tumbler, 4" water (Old Cafe) | 16.00 |
| | | Vase, 7¼" (Old Cafe) | 16.00 |
| | | Vase, 9", two styles | 16.00 |

# FLOWER VASES

### CRYSTAL
### ROSE
### "ROYAL RUBY"

4¾" Vase
**5010**—Crystal
4 doz. ctn.—30 lbs.

7" Vase
**1942**—Crystal
2 doz. ctn.—43 lbs.

8¾" Vase
**R597**—Rose
1 doz. ctn.—28 lbs.

9" Vase
**A53**—Royal Ruby
2 doz. ctn.—36 lbs.

# CONSOLE SETS
## (Candle Holders and Console Bowls and Plates)

### PROMOTE CONSOLE SETS
Display Sets but price and sell both sets and individual pieces.

**IN "ROYAL RUBY"**
**A881**—3½" Candle Holder
2 doz. ctn.—14 lbs.
**A889**—10½" Console Bowl
1 doz. ctn.—30 lbs.
**A890**—13½" Console Plate
1 doz. ctn.—28 lbs.

**IN "POLISHED CRYSTAL"**
**881**—3½" Candle Holder
2 doz. ctn.—14 lbs.
**889**—10½" Console Bowl
1 doz. ctn.—30 lbs.
**890**—13½" Sandwich Plate
1 doz. ctn.—29 lbs.

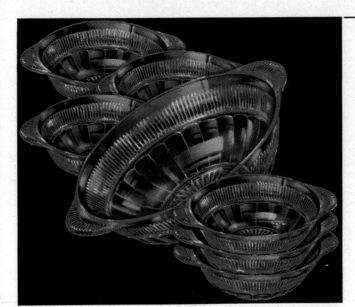

# 7-Pc. Dessert Set

### BULK PACKED
### IN "ROYAL RUBY" GLASS

**A4400/8**—7-Piece Set

Bulk Packed:

1 Ctn., 1 doz. A4478—8" Bowl
(Weight 16 lbs.)

1 Ctn., 6 doz. A4474—4½" Dessert
(Weight 26 lbs.)

Minimum 12 Sets in 2 cartons—42 lbs.

# "S" PATTERN, "STIPPLED ROSE BAND" MacBETH-EVANS GLASS COMPANY, 1930-1933

Colors: Crystal; crystal w/trims of silver, blue, green, amber; pink; some amber, green, fired-on red, Monax, and light yellow.

Decorated "S" Pattern, whether it be platinum trimmed crystal, or pastel banded crystal, catches more collector's attention than does the plain crystal. You can find crystal, but you might have to mix some platinum trimmed with it to create a set. They blend well. Collectors have never yet found a dinner plate in crystal. The problem with collecting the pastel banded crystal is that there is not enough of the decorated glassware to meet demand! You can find amber, blue or green banded crystal; you might follow an ever growing trend in collecting and mix colors.

Color variances in amber make some of it more yellow than amber. As in most yellow Depression Glass patterns, consistently matching colors is a problem. The differences are almost as distinct as they are in Hocking's Princess; however, amber "S" Pattern collectors do have a dinner plate to use that is not yet found in crystal.

A pink or green pitcher and tumbler set still turns up occasionally, but the demand for these has greatly diminished. Years ago, there were a large group of pitcher collectors; rare pitchers sold fast. Today, there are few pitcher collectors still active and most of these already own the hard to find pitchers. A rare piece of glass has to have someone who wishes to own it before it will sell. No matter how rare an item is, it takes demand to make it sell. It is simple economics; no demand means no sale, and rarity can be hanged! Too, in those days rare pieces only sold in the $200.00-500.00 range. Today, some pitchers are commanding prices of $1500.00-5000.00. That also makes a big difference when you are talking to collectors toying with the idea of collecting pitchers. I will say that one of the most stunning collections I ever saw displayed was of pitchers!

Fired-on red items and the red items shaped like red American Sweetheart both fit the rare category, but like the pink and green pitchers, there are few collectors who are excited by them.

| | Crystal | Yellow, Amber, Crystal W/ Trims | | | Crystal | Yellow, Amber, Crystal W/Trims |
|---|---|---|---|---|---|---|
| * Bowl, 5½" cereal | 4.00 | 5.50 | Plate, grill | | 6.50 | 8.00 |
| Bowl, 8½" large berry | 9.50 | 14.50 | Plate, 11¾" heavy cake | | 38.00 | 40.00 |
| * Creamer, thick or thin | 6.00 | 7.00 | *** Plate, 13" heavy cake | | 58.00 | 65.00 |
| * Cup, thick or thin | 3.50 | 4.50 | Saucer | | 2.00 | 2.50 |
| Pitcher, 80 oz. (like "Dogwood") | | | Sherbet, low ftd. | | 4.50 | 7.00 |
| (green or pink 500.00) | 50.00 | 95.00 | * Sugar, thick and thin | | 5.50 | 6.50 |
| Pitcher, 80 oz. (like "American | | | Tumbler, 3½", 5 oz. | | 4.50 | 6.00 |
| Sweetheart") | 60.00 | | Tumbler, 4", 9 oz. (green or | | | |
| Plate, 6" sherbet (Monax 8.00) | 2.50 | 3.00 | pink 50.00) | | 5.00 | 6.50 |
| ** Plate, 8¼" luncheon | 4.50 | 5.00 | Tumbler, 4¾, 10 oz. | | 5.00 | 7.50 |
| Plate, 9¼" dinner | | 7.50 | Tumbler, 5", 12 oz. | | 9.00 | 13.00 |

* Fired-on red items will run approximately twice price of amber     **Red-$40.00; Monax-$10.00     ***Amber-$77.50

# SANDWICH INDIANA GLASS COMPANY, 1920's-1980's

Colors: Crystal late 1920's-today; teal blue 1950's-1980's; milk white mid 1950's; amber late 1920's-1980's; red 1933,1969- early 1970's; Smokey Blue 1976-1977; pink, green 1920's-early 1930's.

Collecting Indiana's Sandwich pattern excites some people. Most dealers and even more collectors avoid it like a disease because of the company's total disregard of protecting old Indiana patterns by continually reissuing them. The pink and green shown here is from the Depression era, but Indiana has made a darker green in recent years.

I can vouch for six items in red Sandwich dating from 1933, i.e., cups, saucers, luncheon plates, water goblets, creamers and sugars. However, in 1969, Tiara Home Products marketed red pitchers, 9 oz. goblets, cups, saucers, wines, wine decanters, 13" serving trays, creamers, sugars, salad and dinner plates. Today, there is no difference in pricing the red unless you have some red marked 1933 Chicago World's Fair. Crystal was made as early as the late 1920's, but few people can tell it apart from the Tiara issues of the last 20 years. You, alone, will have to decide how seriously you want to collect Indiana's Sandwich. Decanter stoppers are difficult to find as indicated by their conspicuous absence in the photograph. Yes, the pattern is attractive! I am just not certain this pattern has much investment potential!

| | Amber Crystal | Teal Blue | Red | Pink/ Green | | Amber Crystal | Teal Blue | Red | Pink/ Green |
|---|---|---|---|---|---|---|---|---|---|
| Ash trays(club, spade, heart, diamond shapes, ea.) | 3.25 | | | | Decanter and stopper | 22.00 | | 80.00 | 110.00 |
| Basket, 10" high | 35.00 | | | | Goblet, 9 oz. | 13.00 | | 45.00 | |
| Bowl, 4¼" berry | 3.50 | | | | Mayonnaise, ftd. | 13.00 | | | 30.00 |
| Bowl, 6" | 4.00 | | | | Pitcher, 68 oz. | 22.00 | | 130.00 | |
| Bowl, 6", hexagonal | 5.00 | 14.00 | | | Plate, 6" sherbet | 3.00 | 7.00 | | |
| Bowl, 8½" | 11.00 | | | | Plate, 7" bread and butter | 4.00 | | | |
| Bowl, 9" console | 16.00 | | | 38.00 | Plate, 8" oval, indent for cup | 5.50 | 12.00 | | |
| Bowl, 11½" console | 18.50 | | | 48.00 | Plate, 8⅜" luncheon | 4.75 | | 18.00 | |
| Butter dish and cover, domed | 22.00 | *155.00 | | | Plate, 10½" dinner | 8.00 | | | 18.00 |
| Butter dish bottom | 6.00 | 42.50 | | | Plate, 13" sandwich | 12.75 | 24.00 | 35.00 | 24.00 |
| Butter dish top | 16.00 | 112.50 | | | Puff box | 16.00 | | | |
| Candlesticks, 3½" pr. | 16.00 | | | 42.00 | Salt and pepper pr. | 17.50 | | | |
| Candlesticks 7" pr. | 26.00 | | | | Sandwich server, center | 18.00 | | 45.00 | 27.50 |
| Creamer | 9.00 | | 45.00 | | Saucer | 2.50 | 4.50 | 7.00 | |
| Celery, 10½" | 16.00 | | | | Sherbet, 3¼" | 5.50 | 12.00 | | |
| Creamer and sugar on diamond shaped tray | 16.00 | 32.00 | | | Sugar, large | 9.00 | | 45.00 | |
| | | | | | Sugar lid for large size | 13.00 | | | |
| Cruet, 6½ oz. and stopper | 26.00 | 135.00 | | 155.00 | Tumbler, 3 oz. ftd. cocktail | 7.50 | | | |
| Cup | 3.50 | 8.50 | 26.00 | | Tumbler, 8 oz. ftd. water | 9.00 | | | |
| | | | | | Tumbler, 12 oz. ftd. iced tea | 10.00 | | | |
| *Beware recent vintage sell $22.00 | | | | | Wine, 3", 4 oz. | 6.00 | | 12.50 | 22.50 |

# SHARON, "CABBAGE ROSE" FEDERAL GLASS COMPANY, 1935-1939

Colors: Pink, green, amber; some crystal. *(See Reproduction Section)*

Sharon prices are on the rise again. Of course, that seems to be true of all major patterns right now. That has not been the case in recent years, but the last couple have seen prices on rarely found items and collectable patterns increase dramatically. Sharon is another Depression pattern that has suffered loss of collectors' interest in the past because of many reproductions. Due to education of the differences between old and new, Sharon has new life! It was not that people stopped collecting as much as new collectors did not start. Without new collectors, basic pieces stop selling and dealers stop buying them. It becomes a vicious cycle with only the rarely found and under priced pieces selling. Now, every dealer who stopped buying, is crying that he can't find enough Sharon to meet today's demand! This rising market is a great sign, unless you are an author trying to keep up with it!

The pink cheese dish continues to climb in price. The cheese and butter top are the same piece. The bottoms are different. The butter bottom is a 1½" deep bowl with a ledge while the cheese bottom is a salad plate with a raised band on top of it. The lid fits inside this raised band! Amber cheese dishes can be found without too much searching. There is no cheese dish in the original green.

Besides the cheese dish, thick iced teas and jam dishes are the only other pink pieces difficult to locate. The jam dish is like the butter bottom except it has no indentation for the top. It differs from the 1⅞" deep soup bowl by standing only 1½" tall.

Hard to find green pieces include the pitchers and tumblers. Surprisingly enough, the green pitcher without ice lip is rarer than the one with an ice lip.

There are two styles of flat tumblers. Liking thick or thin tumblers is a preferential decision; but scarcity enters into price. The heavy tumblers are easier to find in green; and the price reflects that. In amber and pink, the heavy iced teas are more rarely seen.

Amber footed teas are the most scarce of all Sharon tumblers. Fewer collectors of amber Sharon make the true price of these tumblers a mystery. Many collectors just do without them at today's prices; that attitude may make it hard for prices to go much higher! Amber Sharon pitchers are more difficult to find than the pink; but prices do not indicate that. There are twenty times more collectors looking for pink, so demand pushes up the price.

|  | Amber | Pink | Green |
|---|---|---|---|
| Bowl, 5" berry | 8.50 | 12.00 | 14.00 |
| Bowl, 5" cream soup | 26.00 | 40.00 | 45.00 |
| Bowl, 6" cereal | 19.00 | 22.50 | 24.00 |
| Bowl, 7¾" flat soup, 1⅞" deep | 47.50 | 45.00 | |
| Bowl, 8½" large berry | 6.00 | 28.00 | 30.00 |
| Bowl, 9½" oval vegetable | 20.00 | 28.00 | 30.00 |
| Bowl, 10½" fruit | 21.00 | 35.00 | 35.00 |
| Butter dish and cover | 46.00 | 50.00 | 80.00 |
| Butter dish bottom | 23.00 | 25.00 | 35.00 |
| Butter dish top | 23.00 | 25.00 | 45.00 |
| * Cake plate, 11½" ftd. | 24.00 | 38.00 | 55.00 |
| Candy jar and cover | 45.00 | 50.00 | 160.00 |
| Cheese dish and cover | 180.00 | 800.00 | |
| Creamer, ftd. | 14.00 | 18.00 | 20.00 |
| Cup | 9.00 | 14.00 | 18.00 |
| Jam dish, 7½" | 35.00 | 165.00 | 40.00 |
| Pitcher, 80 oz. with ice lip | 125.00 | 140.00 | 375.00 |
| Pitcher, 80 oz. without ice lip | 120.00 | 135.00 | 400.00 |
| Plate, 6" bread and butter | 5.00 | 7.50 | 8.00 |
| ** Plate, 7½" salad | 15.00 | 22.50 | 22.50 |
| Plate, 9½" dinner | 11.00 | 18.00 | 21.00 |
| Platter, 12½" oval | 18.00 | 28.00 | 28.00 |
| Salt and pepper, pr. | 39.00 | 47.50 | 65.00 |
| Saucer | 6.50 | 11.00 | 11.00 |
| Sherbet, ftd. | 12.00 | 15.00 | 32.00 |
| Sugar | 9.00 | 14.00 | 15.00 |
| Sugar lid | 22.00 | 28.00 | 36.00 |
| Tumbler, 4⅛", 9 oz. thick | 25.00 | 35.00 | 60.00 |
| Tumbler, 4⅛", 9 oz. thin | 25.00 | 37.50 | 65.00 |
| Tumbler, 5¼", 12 oz. thin | 50.00 | 40.00 | 92.00 |
| Tumbler, 5¼", 12 oz. thick | 60.00 | 75.00 | 88.00 |
| *** Tumbler, 6½", 15 oz. ftd. | 100.00 | 45.00 | |

\* Crystal $5.00
\*\* Crystal $13.50
\*\*\* Crystal $15.00

# "SHIPS" or "SAILBOAT" also known as "SPORTSMAN SERIES"

## HAZEL ATLAS GLASS COMPANY, LATE 1930's

Colors: Cobalt blue w/white, yellow and red decoration.

Judging from the number of phone calls and letters "Ships" shot glasses are still causing confusion for some collectors; so, I will try to explain them again. The "Ships" shot glass is shown in the top picture on page 189. It is the diminutive (2¼", 2 oz.) tumbler in the far right front. It is not the heavy bottomed tumbler shown on the left front that holds 4 oz. and is 3¼" tall. I have letters from people who purchased the 4 oz. tumbler believing it to be a shot glass! You will notice there's a great difference in price between the true 2 oz. shot and the 4 oz. tumbler!

The supply of the "Ships" decorated Moderntone is not ample. Look for unworn white, not beige, decorations on these pieces. Prices are for mint pieces. Worn and discolored items should fetch much less if someone will even want to buy them.

We have found one yellow "Ships" old fashioned tumbler that is not a discoloration. It really is "raincoat" yellow rather than white! Note the pieces with red "Ships" or even a crystal tumbler with a blue boat. You can expand this pattern to your heart's content or until your pocketbook cries enough!

Pictured below are other items in the "Sportsman Series." The "Polo" series sells well in our "horse country" of Kentucky. People who collect Dutch related paraphernalia enjoy the "Windmills." There are "Nursery Rhymes," dogs, fish and whatever sports interest you – skiing, boating, fishing, golfing, dancing, or horse riding; you can surely find a beverage set to your liking!

In the bottom photo on page 189, are the cocktail shaker, ice tub and tumblers that Cathy likes to refer to as "fancy" ships. The cloud formation differs. Also shown here are some accessory pieces that can go with this Ships pattern (that has its beginnings on the Moderntone blank). None of these are in the Hazel Atlas listing below; so I will put prices for these in parentheses as I mention them.

The round metal tray ($50.00) was bought years ago with a pitcher and tumbler set on it. These accessory items are fun to look for and you never know what will pop up. The square or round ash trays ($45.00) and the three sectional box ($150.00) on the left may have been manufactured by the same company since the designs are very similar. I have seen that box priced as high as $225.00. The ash tray with the metal ship ($85.00) is more than likely Hazel Atlas. The smaller glass tray ($75.00), which has a tumbler with a sailor and matching anchor and rope design, and the larger glass tray ($100.00), which has a matching tumbler, are rarely seen. The crystal ash tray with light blue ship ($12.50) was a piece bought solely because it had a ship. I have seen higher asking prices; but these are prices for which the items will sell!

| | Blue/White | | Blue/White | | Blue/White |
|---|---|---|---|---|---|
| Cup (Plain) "Moderntone" | 11.00 | Plate, 8", salad | 21.00 | Tumbler, 5 oz., 3¾", juice | 11.00 |
| Cocktail mixer w/stirrer | 25.00 | Plate, 9", dinner | 27.50 | Tumbler, 6 oz., roly poly | 9.50 |
| Cocktail shaker | 30.00 | Saucer | 16.00 | Tumbler, 8 oz., 3⅜", old fashion | 15.00 |
| Ice bowl | 30.00 | Tumbler, 2 oz., 2¼" shot glass | 145.00 | Tumbler, 9 oz., 3¾", straight water | 14.00 |
| Pitcher w/o lip, 82 oz. | 47.50 | Tumbler, 3½", whiskey | 25.00 | Tumbler, 9 oz., 4⅝", water | 11.0 |
| Pitcher w/lip, 86 oz. | 45.00 | Tumbler, 4 oz., heavy bottom | 25.00 | Tumbler, 10½ oz., 4⅞", iced tea | 14.00 |
| Plate, 5⅞", bread & butter | 20.00 | Tumbler, 4 oz., 3¼" heavy bottom | 25.00 | Tumbler, 12 oz., iced tea | 20.00 |

# SIERRA, "PINWHEEL" JEANNETTE GLASS COMPANY, 1931-1933

Colors: Green, pink and some ultramarine.

Sierra, meaning sawtooth, is certainly a fitting name for this pattern, don't you agree? Sierra pitchers, tumblers and oval vegetable bowls have all but disappeared in both pink and green. You could locate these pieces in pink a few years ago with persistent shopping, but finding them now, at any price, is a major task! I was able to round up all but a green saucer and tumbler for the photograph. Some enthusiastic Sierra collectors have said that obtaining the green oval vegetable is the most difficult assignment; but finding six or eight tumblers takes about the same amount of searching and a lot more money! Thankfully, most collectors can settle for only one oval bowl in their sets.

Sugar bowls are more difficult to find than the lids. It is the pointed edges on the sugar bowl (which chip so easily) that make this bowl so hard to get in mint condition. That is the one blemish in collecting any Sierra. The points have to be carefully inspected or you will often miss a "chigger bite" off one of these edges.

You need to look carefully at all pink Sierra butter dishes. You might run into the Adam/Sierra combination. Be sure to read about this under Adam.

Frequently, the wrong cup is placed on Sierra saucers. You always have to be on your toes when you are buying! That cup, pitcher and tumblers all have smooth edges instead of the serrated edges of the other pieces. Can you imagine the problems in drinking from a cup or tumbler without smooth edges?

There have been three Sierra ultramarine cups found, but no one has seen a saucer - yet! An ultramarine cereal bowl has been confirmed from a reader. These have to be experimental or more would be surfacing! Possibly a trial run of Sierra was made at the time Jeannette was making Doric and Pansy or Swirl in that color.

| | Pink | Green | | Pink | Green |
|---|---|---|---|---|---|
| Bowl, 5½" cereal | 11.00 | 12.50 | Platter, 11" oval | 38.00 | 42.00 |
| Bowl, 8½" large berry | 26.00 | 26.00 | Salt and pepper, pr. | 37.50 | 37.50 |
| Bowl, 9¼" oval vegetable | 38.00 | 88.00 | Saucer | 6.00 | 7.00 |
| Butter dish and cover | 60.00 | 65.00 | Serving tray, 10¼", 2 handles | 14.00 | 17.00 |
| Creamer | 18.00 | 20.00 | Sugar | 16.00 | 22.00 |
| Cup | 11.00 | 14.00 | Sugar cover | 15.00 | 15.00 |
| Pitcher, 6½", 32 oz. | 67.50 | 98.00 | Tumbler, 4½", 9 oz. ftd. | 42.00 | 67.50 |
| Plate, 9" dinner | 16.00 | 19.00 | | | |

---

# SPIRAL HOCKING GLASS COMPANY, 1928-1930

Colors: Green, crystal and pink.

I have always included a Twisted Optic piece in my Spiral pictures for comparison to the Spiral. Can you spot it this time? Remember that Spiral swirls go to the left or clockwise while Twisted Optic spirals go to the right or counterclockwise.

Unfortunately, on a few pieces, whether the pattern spirals are placed inside or outside the design affects the left or right handed spiraling! This time the Twisted Optic piece is the covered candy on the left. You should be able to see spirals going counterclockwise on that lid!

The Spiral platter is not frequently found. Notice that it is like the Cameo platter in shape. It has closed or tabbed handles as do many patterns made by Hocking. You might also notice that the ice tub, creamer and sugar are all shaped like Cameo. A luncheon set can be acquired rather inexpensively with the only problem being finding it!

Green Spiral is the color normally found, but there is some pink available. You might even find an occasional piece in crystal.

The Spiral center-handled server has a solid handle and the Twisted Optic center-handled server has an open handle if you have trouble distinguishing those from each other.

| | Green | | Green |
|---|---|---|---|
| Bowl, 4¾" berry | 5.00 | Preserve and cover | 30.00 |
| Bowl, 7" mixing | 8.50 | Salt and pepper, pr. | 32.50 |
| Bowl, 8" large berry | 12.50 | Sandwich server, center handle | 22.50 |
| Creamer, flat or ftd. | 7.50 | Saucer | 2.00 |
| Cup | 5.00 | Sherbet | 4.00 |
| Ice or butter tub | 26.00 | Sugar, flat or ftd. | 7.50 |
| Pitcher, 7⅝", 58 oz. | 30.00 | Tumbler, 3", 5 oz. juice | 4.50 |
| Plate, 6" sherbet | 2.00 | Tumbler, 5", 9 oz. water | 7.50 |
| Plate, 8" luncheon | 3.50 | Tumbler, 5⅞" ftd. | 14.00 |
| Platter, 12" | 25.00 | | |

**Please refer to Foreword for pricing information**

# STARLIGHT HAZEL ATLAS GLASS COMPANY, 1938-1940

Colors: Crystal, pink; some white, cobalt.

Crystal Starlight prices are finally awakening after years of being dormant. This small pattern has never been collected by large numbers, but enough new collectors are buying to show some shortcomings in supplies. Problems finding sherbets, cereals and the large salad bowls are just beginning. There are not many of the 13" sandwich plates either. The 5½" cereal is handled and measures 6" including the handles.

Starlight is another one of the smaller sets that can be collected without loans having to be obtained. The only difficulty (twenty years into Depression Glass mania) comes in finding it. The pink and blue bowls make nice accessory pieces that can be used alongside the crystal. As with other Hazel Atlas sets, a punch bowl was made by putting a bowl in a metal holder and extending the metal to accommodate cups. The one pictured was bought for $40.00; but it is the only one I have seen sell!

I have often wondered why Starlight shakers are found with a one hole shaker top. I have now found out! It was a specially designed top made to keep the salt "moisture proof." Shakers with these tops are often found in Florida and other southern areas where the humid air has caused shaker holes to clog. Did you realize we've only "shaken" salt since the turn of the century. Prior to that, you pinched it from salt dips. One of these moisture proof shakers is pictured here with the original label.

|  | Crystal, White | Pink |
|---|---|---|
| Bowl, 5½" cereal, closed handles | 6.50 | 8.50 |
| * Bowl, 8½", closed handles | 9.00 | 15.00 |
| Bowl, 11½" salad | 17.50 | |
| Bowl, 12", 2¾" deep | 24.00 | |
| Creamer, oval | 5.00 | |
| Cup | 4.00 | |
| Plate, 6" bread and butter | 3.00 | |
| Plate, 8½" luncheon | 5.00 | |
| Plate, 9" dinner | 7.50 | |
| Plate, 13" sandwich | 12.50 | 14.00 |
| Relish dish | 13.50 | |
| Salt and pepper, pr. | 22.50 | |
| Saucer | 2.00 | |
| Sherbet | 12.00 | |
| Sugar, oval | 5.00 | |

\* Cobalt $30.00

---

# STRAWBERRY U.S. GLASS COMPANY, Early 1930's

Colors: Pink, green, crystal; some iridized.

Strawberry and Cherryberry are now split into two separate patterns. See page 32 for the Cherryberry listing.

Green Strawberry is in more demand than the pink. A small problem exists in color shadings of the green. Notice the way green varies in the photograph. Under sunlight or direct light, these color changes are more vivid. Green or pink can be collected in a set; however, as with other U. S. Glass patterns, there are no cups, saucers or dinner sized plates.

The iridescent Strawberry pitcher and tumblers are quite rare! Carnival collectors cherish this iridescent pitcher more highly than Depression glass collectors. The one main concern is that it have full, vivid color and not fade out toward the bottom, as many do.

Crystal is priced with iridescent because it is so rare. There are few crystal Strawberry collectors; that is good since so little of it is found! Strawberry sugar covers are another item missing from most collections as is the 2" deep bowl. Some collectors have mistakenly called the sugar with missing lid a spooner. It is a sugar bowl without handles that is often seen in older glassware.

Strawberry is another of those U.S. Glass patterns that has very rough mould seams. This occurs on the tumblers, pitchers and even the plates. If mould roughness offends your collecting sensibilities, then this pattern needs to be avoided.

Strawberry also has a plain butter dish bottom that is interchangeable with other U.S. Glass patterns. This is the pattern for which other U.S. Glass pattern butter dish bottoms were taken to use with Strawberry tops. Strawberry butter dishes have always been coveted by collectors.

| | Crystal, Iridescent | Pink, Green | | Crystal, Iridescent | Pink, Green |
|---|---|---|---|---|---|
| Bowl, 4" berry | 6.50 | 8.50 | Olive dish, 5" one-handled | 8.50 | 13.00 |
| Bowl, 6¼", 2" deep | 42.50 | 65.00 | Pickle dish, 8¼" oval | 8.50 | 12.50 |
| Bowl, 6½" deep salad | 15.00 | 18.00 | Pitcher, 7¾" | 155.00 | 140.00 |
| Bowl, 7½" deep berry | 16.00 | 20.00 | Plate, 6" sherbet | 5.00 | 7.00 |
| Butter dish and cover | 135.00 | 150.00 | Plate, 7½" salad | 10.00 | 13.00 |
| Butter dish bottom | 77.50 | 90.00 | Sherbet | 6.50 | 7.50 |
| Butter dish top | 57.50 | 60.00 | Sugar, small open | 12.00 | 17.50 |
| Comport, 5¾" | 14.00 | 19.00 | Sugar large | 22.00 | 32.00 |
| Creamer, small | 12.00 | 17.50 | Sugar cover | 36.00 | 48.00 |
| Creamer, 4⅝" large | 22.50 | 33.00 | Tumbler, 3⅝", 8 oz. | 19.00 | 30.00 |

193

# SUNFLOWER JEANNETTE GLASS COMPANY, 1930's

Colors: Pink, green, some Delphite; some opaque colors.

   Sunflower cake plates are the piece most often seen in this pattern. I'll relate a story that happened in my shop several years ago when we were selling these cake plates for $6.00. A famous antique lecturer was in town for an "exclusive" antique show. People were charged $35.00 for admission on preview night and they could have one item appraised "free" with that admission. Days later a lady brought a Sunflower cake plate in to sell. Grannie Bear, my Mom, offered her our standard sixty percent of the list price or $3.60. She informed Grannie Bear that it was rare and she could let her have it for $35.00. (I guess she was trying to recoup her admission!) Mom then asked her how many she wished to buy at $6.00 since we had several at the time. The lady was highly incensed and left in a huff. I often wondered just how much she was told this piece was worth!

   Sunflower cake plates were packed in twenty pound bags of flour for several years during the 1930's when everyone bought flour in large quantities because home baking was necessary. A problem that occurs regularly with the green cake plate is that many are found in a deep, dark green that does not match any other pieces of green Sunflower. A pink cake plate is shown against the back of the picture.

   A 7" pink trivet is shown in the center of the photograph. Notice that the edges are slightly upturned and it is three inches smaller than the ever present cake plate. The trivet remains the most elusive piece of Sunflower. Collector demand for the trivet keeps prices increasing steadily. Green is found less often than pink; therefore, prices for green are surpassing prices in pink. Both colors make attractive sets.

   After several collectors told me that Sunflower had a shortage of saucers, I have kept my eyes pealed and they are right! In the last year, I have seen almost twice as many cups as saucers! If you run into a stack of Sunflower saucers, be advised that they might be a good buy!

   The ultramarine ash tray is the only piece I have found in that color. Opaque colors show up occasionally. Only a creamer and a cup have been spotted in Delphite blue. The odd colored creamer and sugar I have always called "mustard" and "mayonnaise," since my editing wife won't let me give the colors the barnyard terms that first come to mind.

|  | Pink | Green |  | Pink | Green |
|---|---|---|---|---|---|
| * Ash Tray, 5", center design only | 9.00 | 12.00 | Saucer | 7.00 | 9.00 |
| Cake Plate, 10", 3 legs | 15.00 | 15.00 | Sugar (opaque 85.00) | 16.00 | 18.00 |
| ** Creamer (opaque 85.00) | 16.00 | 18.00 | Tumbler, 4¾", 8 oz. ftd. | 24.00 | 29.00 |
| Cup (opaque 75.00) | 11.00 | 13.00 | Trivet, 7", 3 legs, turned up edge | 275.00 | 295.00 |
| Plate, 9" dinner | 14.00 | 18.00 |  |  |  |

* Found in ultramarine $25.00     **Delphite $85.00

# SWANKY SWIGS 1930's-early 1940's

I never set up with these at a show that someone doesn't see them and exclaim, "Why, I remember those! We used them when I was a child!" More often than not, they buy one or more for a grandchild.

See *Collectible Glassware from the 40's, 50's, 60's...* for Swankys made later.

| | | | | |
|---|---|---|---|---|
| Top Row | Band No.1 | Red & Black | 3⅜" | 2.00-3.00 |
| | | Red & Blue | 3⅜" | 3.00-4.00 |
| | | Blue | 3⅜" | 3.50-5.00 |
| | Band No.2 | Red & Black | 4¾" | 4.00-5.00 |
| | | Red & Black | 3⅜" | 3.00-4.00 |
| | Band No.3 | Blue & White | 3⅜" | 3.00-4.00 |
| | Circle & Dot: | Blue | 4¾" | 6.00-8.00 |
| | | Blue | 3½" | 5.00-6.00 |
| | | Red, Green | 3½" | 4.00-5.00 |
| | | Black | 3½" | 5.00-6.00 |
| | | Red | 4¾" | 6.00-8.00 |
| | Dot | Black | 4¾" | 7.00-9.00 |
| | | Blue | 3½" | 5.00-6.00 |
| | | | | |
| 2nd Row | Star: | Blue | 4¾" | 5.00-6.00 |
| | | Blue, Red, Green, Black | 3½" | 3.00-4.00 |
| | | Cobalt w/White Stars | 4¾" | 15.00-18.00 |
| | Centennials: | W.Va. Cobalt | 4¾" | 20.00-22.00 |
| | | Texas Cobalt | 4¾" | 25.00-30.00 |
| | | Texas Blue, Black, Green | 3½" | 25.00-30.00 |
| | Checkerboard | Blue, Red | 3½" | 22.50-25.00 |
| | | | | |
| 3rd Row | Checkerboard | Green | 3½" | 25.00-27.50 |
| | Sailboat | Blue | 4½" | 12.00-15.00 |
| | | Blue | 3½" | 10.00-12.00 |
| | | Red, Green | 4½" | 12.00-15.00 |
| | | Green, Lt. Green | 3½" | 10.00-15.00 |
| | Tulip No.1 | Blue, Red | 4½" | 12.50-15.00 |
| | | Blue, Red | 3½" | 3.00-4.00 |
| | | | | |
| 4th Row | Tulip No.1 | Green | 4½" | 12.50-15.00 |
| | | Green, Black | 3½" | 3.00-4.00 |
| | | Green w/Label | 3½" | 8.00-10.00 |
| | *Tulip No.2 | Red, Green, Black | 3½" | 20.00-25.00 |
| | Carnival | Blue, Red | 3½" | 4.00-6.00 |
| | | Green, Yellow | 3½" | 4.00-6.00 |
| | Tulip No. 3 | Dk. Blue, Lt. Blue | 3¾" | 2.50-3.50 |

*West Coast lower price

# SWIRL, "PETAL SWIRL" JEANNETTE GLASS COMPANY, 1937-1938

Colors: Ultramarine, pink, Delphite; some amber and "ice" blue.

An Ultramarine Swirl 10½" rimmed flat soup has been found in the Pittsburgh area! Now that you know there is one, find some others! Almost all pieces of Swirl can be found with two different borders, ruffled and plain. Pink comes mostly with plain borders while ultramarine comes with both. This makes a difference if you order merchandise by mail. It is **your** responsibility to specify what style you want if you place an order. Either style is acceptable to most collectors, but some do not mix shapes in their collections. If you only want plain edged pieces, please tell the dealer before he ships your order. This is not a problem when you can see the merchandise displayed at shows.

As with other Jeannette patterns that appear in ultramarine, there are green tinged pieces as well as the normally found color. This green tint is hard to match, and some collectors avoid this shade. Because of this general avoidance, there are times you can buy the green tint at a super bargain price if you are willing to collect that shade. Who knows? In the future this color may be considered to be best.

Several Ultramarine Swirl pitchers are now in collections, but so far there has not been a pink one spotted. I say, so far, because many collectors of Swirl combine this pattern with Jeannette's "Jennyware" kitchenware line that does have a pink pitcher in it! Others have confused the two patterns because they are similar in style and designed in the same colors. If you find mixing bowls, measuring cups or reamers, then you have crossed over into the kitchenware line and out of the Swirl dinnerware set. See *Kitchen Glassware of the Depression Years* for complete "Jennyware" listings.

As with most patterns, candy and butter dish bottoms are more abundant than are tops in Swirl. Remember that before you buy only the bottom! Unless you are good at remembering color, buying a top or bottom separately can be a problem in matching shades. If you go to a Depression Glass show, it might be wise to take your half with you to match the color.

The pink coaster shown in the right foreground is often found inside a small rubber tire. These tires were advertisements distributed by tire manufactures or neighborhood garages. These small tires have become collectible advertising items. Those with a tire manufacturer's name on the glass insert are more in demand; but those with a non advertising glass insert (such as this coaster) are collected if the miniature tire is embossed with the name of a tire company.

Swirl was made in several experimental colors. A smaller set can be assembled in Delphite blue; it would only have basic pieces and a serving dish or two. Vegetable bowls (9") were made in several experimental colors. Notice the amber and "ice" blue shown in the top photo. Recently, I have seen the ice blue vegetable priced at $100.00 and an amber one at $75.00. I do not know if they sold or not!

| | Pink | Ultra-marine | Delphite | | Pink | Ultra-marine | Delphite |
|---|---|---|---|---|---|---|---|
| Bowl, 5¼" cereal | 10.00 | 14.50 | 13.00 | Plate, 6½" sherbet | 4.50 | 6.50 | 6.00 |
| Bowl, 9" salad | 17.50 | 25.00 | 28.00 | Plate, 7¼" | 6.50 | 12.00 | |
| Bowl, 9" salad, rimmed | 18.00 | 25.00 | | Plate, 8" salad | 8.50 | 13.00 | 9.00 |
| Bowl, 10" ftd., closed | | | | Plate, 9¼" dinner | 12.50 | 16.00 | 12.00 |
|   handles | 24.00 | 28.00 | | Plate, 10½" | | 28.00 | 18.00 |
| Bowl, 10½" ftd. console | 19.00 | 26.00 | | Plate, 12½" sandwich | 12.00 | 25.00 | |
| Butter dish | 180.00 | 245.00 | | Platter, 12" oval | | | 35.00 |
| Butter dish bottom | 32.50 | 40.00 | | Salt and pepper, pr. | | 42.00 | |
| Butter dish top | 147.50 | 205.00 | | Saucer | 3.50 | 5.00 | 5.00 |
| Candle holders, double | | | | Sherbet, low ftd. | 11.00 | 17.50 | |
|   branch pr. | | 45.00 | | Soup, tab handles (lug) | 22.50 | 28.00 | |
| Candle holders, single | | | | Sugar, ftd. | 10.00 | 15.00 | 12.00 |
|   branch pr. | | | 115.00 | Tray, 10½", two-handled | | | 25.00 |
| Candy dish, open, 3 legs | 11.00 | 17.50 | | Tumbler, 4", 9 oz. | 15.00 | 30.00 | |
| Candy dish with cover | 95.00 | 135.00 | | Tumbler, 4⅝", 9 oz. | 16.00 | | |
| Coaster, 1" x 3¼" | 9.50 | 13.00 | | Tumbler, 5⅛", 13 oz. | 40.00 | 95.00 | |
| Creamer, ftd. | 7.50 | 15.00 | 12.00 | Tumbler, 9 oz. ftd. | 17.50 | 35.00 | |
| Cup | 7.00 | 15.00 | 10.00 | Vase, 6½" ftd., ruffled | 16.00 | | |
| Pitcher, 48 oz. ftd. | | 1,525.00 | | Vase, 8½" ftd., two styles | | 26.00 | |

**Please refer to Foreword for pricing information**

# TEA ROOM INDIANA GLASS COMPANY, 1926-1931

Colors: Pink, green, amber and some crystal.

Tea Room is eagerly collected but the days of prices constantly jumping have slowed. This is due in part to the fact that the collectors who helped absorb the small quantity available have finished collections or slowed down in their searches. When a few collectors call every major dealer in the country looking for particular pieces of a pattern no matter what the prices, you should believe someone will come up with those pieces!

There is a club formed by Tea Room and Pyramid collectors. They have their own newsletter. I finally received this information only to discover that new people have taken it over. I have tried to get new information, but no luck - yet.

The major dilemma in collecting Tea Room is finding mint condition pieces. The underneath sides of flat pieces are prone to chip and flake on all the exposed points. There are many points on Tea Room items that need to be looked at when you buy a piece. I once saw an original box of Tea Room that had thirty-two each of cups, saucers and luncheon plates. There were less than a dozen mint condition (as we define it today) pieces out of the ninety-six in the box. These had never been opened so there must have been a mould problem with this pattern originally. Indiana had more than their share of mould problems!

Green Tea Room is more heavily collected than pink; and a few collectors are even beginning to pursue crystal. Crystal pieces are bringing up to seventy-five percent of the pink prices except for the commonly found 9½" ruffled vase and the rarely found pitcher (priced separately below).

For those who have had trouble distinguishing the two styles of banana splits, look at the picture of pink. The flat banana split is in front and the footed banana split is behind it. Both styles of banana splits are very desirable pieces of Tea Room to own in any color!

Amber pitchers and tumblers continue to be found in the Atlanta area. Maybe they really were Coca-Cola premiums as one lady from Marietta, Georgia, once told me. Creamers and sugars appear occasionally in amber. After that, amber has not been seen in any other item. Some interesting lamps are showing up which used tumblers that had been frosted. The regular lamp (shown here in pink) is not as plentiful as it once was. It has been a while since I have seen one in green.

The flat sugar and the marmalade bottom are the same. The marmalade takes a notched lid; the sugar lid is not notched. Finding either of these is not an easy task! The mustard also comes with a plain or notched lid. As the name implies, Tea Room was intended to be used in the "tea rooms" and "ice cream" parlors of the day. That is why you find so many soda fountain type items in this pattern.

Prices are for mint items. These prices are high because mint condition items are difficult to obtain!

| | Green | Pink | | Green | Pink |
|---|---|---|---|---|---|
| Bowl, finger | 47.50 | 37.50 | Salt and pepper, pr. | 55.00 | 50.00 |
| Bowl, 7½" banana split, flat | 80.00 | 78.00 | * Saucer | 28.00 | 28.00 |
| Bowl, 7½" banana split, ftd. | 67.50 | 60.00 | Sherbet, low ftd. | 23.00 | 20.00 |
| Bowl, 8¼" celery | 32.00 | 26.00 | Sherbet, low flared edge | 30.00 | 26.00 |
| Bowl, 8¾" deep salad | 80.00 | 65.00 | Sherbet, tall ftd. | 40.00 | 35.00 |
| Bowl, 9½" oval vegetable | 62.50 | 57.50 | Sugar w/lid, 3" | 100.00 | 95.00 |
| Candlestick, low, pr. | 48.00 | 43.00 | Sugar, 4½" ftd. (amber $75.00) | 17.00 | 16.00 |
| Creamer, 3¼" | 26.00 | 26.00 | Sugar, rectangular | 20.00 | 18.00 |
| Creamer, 4½" ftd. (amber $75.00) | 18.00 | 17.00 | Sugar, flat with cover | 180.00 | 130.00 |
| Creamer, rectangular | 19.00 | 17.00 | Sundae, ftd., ruffled top | 90.00 | 70.00 |
| Creamer & sugar on tray, 4" | 75.00 | 70.00 | Tray, center-handled | 185.00 | 145.00 |
| * Cup | 50.00 | 50.00 | Tray, rectangular sugar & creamer | 50.00 | 40.00 |
| Goblet, 9 oz. | 70.00 | 60.00 | Tumbler, 8 oz., 4³⁄₁₆" flat | 85.00 | 75.00 |
| Ice bucket | 57.50 | 50.00 | Tumbler, 6 oz. ftd. | 35.00 | 35.00 |
| Lamp, 9" electric | 55.00 | 45.00 | Tumbler, 8 oz., 5¼" high, ftd. | | |
| Marmalade, notched lid | 180.00 | 155.00 | (amber $75.00) | 30.00 | 28.00 |
| Mustard, covered | 135.00 | 120.00 | Tumbler, 11 oz. ftd. | 45.00 | 40.00 |
| Parfait | 65.00 | 60.00 | Tumbler, 12 oz. ftd. | 55.00 | 50.00 |
| ** Pitcher, 64 oz. (amber $400.00) | 140.00 | 125.00 | Vase, 6½" ruffled edge | 98.00 | 84.00 |
| Plate, 6½" sherbet | 32.00 | 30.00 | *** Vase, 9½" ruffled edge | 95.00 | 80.00 |
| Plate, 8¼", luncheon | 35.00 | 30.00 | Vase, 9½" straight | 65.00 | 55.00 |
| Plate, 10½", 2-handled | 48.00 | 43.00 | Vase, 11" ruffled edge | 165.00 | 185.00 |
| Relish, divided | 25.00 | 20.00 | Vase, 11" straight | 95.00 | 85.00 |

* Prices for absolutely mint pieces
** Crystal-$350.00
*** Crystal-$15.00

**Please refer to Foreword for pricing information**

199

## THISTLE MacBETH-EVANS, 1929-1930

Colors: Pink, green; some yellow and crystal.

Thistle and Fire-King blue are "beloved" patterns of the photographer who spends hours of his time to record our Depression glass. Yes, my tongue is in my cheek! When he sees us unpacking either of these patterns he utters "certain unprintable words" and inquires if we really want a pattern to show this time! Rarely do we capture either of these patterns satisfactorily. Photography lights cause the pattern to do a vanishing act. That disappearing act is familiar to Thistle collectors. This pattern has been known to hide very well. All seven pieces that are found in pink are shown here. I have had little luck in finding green even if I am writing this on St. Patrick's Day.

Green is more scarce than pink except for the large fruit bowl that is almost nonexistent in pink. I have owned the one shown here for twenty years, and I have only seen one other in all that time.

Thistle mould shapes are the same as Dogwood; however, there is only a thin style cup found in Thistle. The grill plate has the pattern on the edge only, which makes me wonder if that style of grill plate was meant to go with the thin Dogwood style. The overall pattern may have been sold with the thicker Dogwood! No creamer and sugar have ever been found in Thistle!

Those thick butter dishes, pitchers, tumblers and other heavy moulded pieces with Thistle designs are new! They are being made by Mosser Glass Company in Cambridge, Ohio. They are not a part of this pattern, but copies of a much older pattern glass. If you have a piece of Thistle not in the photograph, then you probably do not have a piece of MacBeth-Evans' Thistle pattern.

|  | Pink | Green |
|---|---|---|
| Bowl, 5½" cereal | 20.00 | 22.00 |
| Bowl, 10¼" large fruit | 255.00 | 165.00 |
| Cup, thin | 19.00 | 24.00 |
| Plate, 8" luncheon | 14.00 | 18.00 |
| Plate, 10¼" grill | 17.50 | 22.00 |
| Plate, 13" heavy cake | 110.00 | 130.00 |
| Saucer | 9.50 | 9.50 |

## TULIP DELL GLASS COMPANY, early 1930's

Color: Amber, amethyst, blue, crystal, green.

Tulip is one of the smaller patterns that I have had numerous requests to include in my book. For you persistent collectors, here it is! Basic pieces are available with searching, but there is a problem in finding other pieces in this pattern as you can see by my photographs on page 201 and 202.

Amethyst and blue are the colors most collected, but green and amber have their devotees too. In the last two years of buying, I have noticed that the scalloped rims tend to have damage. Many people selling this pattern do not know what it is, but because it is blue or amethyst, the price is usually not inexpensive. That price doesn't reflect the damaged pieces either. Points can be missing on plates and the price is still firm! Turn the plate over and examine it from the bottom. I have discovered a piece of Tulip can look and feel mint on the surface and still have damage underneath.

The little whiskey (shown in amethyst), the ice tub, and oval bowl are all scarce. You may find pieces of Tulip that I do not have listed; please keep me informed on this newly listed pattern!

I have priced the crystal with the amber and green since you will not see much of it.

|  | Amethyst, Blue | Amber, Crystal, Green |
|---|---|---|
| Bow, 6" | 10.00 | 8.00 |
| Bowl, oval, oblong, 13¼" | 27.50 | 20.00 |
| Creamer | 12.50 | 10.00 |
| Cup | 10.00 | 8.00 |
| Ice tub, 4¾" wide, 2⅝" deep | 20.00 | 16.00 |
| Plate, 6" | 5.00 | 4.00 |
| Plate, 7¼" | 7.50 | 6.00 |
| Plate, 9" | 15.00 | 12.00 |
| Saucer | 2.50 | 2.00 |
| Sherbet, 3¾", flat | 8.00 | 6.00 |
| Sugar | 12.50 | 10.00 |
| Tumbler, whiskey | 12.50 | 10.00 |

**Please refer to Foreword for pricing information**

# TWISTED OPTIC IMPERIAL GLASS COMPANY, 1927-1930

Colors: Pink, green, amber; some blue and canary yellow.

All the pieces shown belong to Twisted Optic. You can see an additional green piece under Spiral placed there to help in differentiating these two patterns that are often confused. If you find a Spiral piece in some color besides pink or green, then it is most likely Twisted Optic since colored Spiral is only found in pink or green. You should understand that many glass companies made spiraling patterns besides Hocking and Imperial! There were many smaller glass factories that never issued catalogues and others that were in business for so short a duration that records were never kept or have long since disappeared.

Twisted Optic spirals to the right and Spiral's go to the left!

There are a couple of Twisted Optic fans who will not rest until I make additional listings to this pattern! The following pieces have been added: three vases, three bowls, a basket, a powder jar, cologne bottle and four different candy jars. I will try to get measurements on each candy jar for the next edition. According to one collector, the candy lids are all interchangeable. Thanks for all this new information!

| | *All Colors | | *All Colors |
|---|---|---|---|
| Basket, 10", tall | 40.00 | Pitcher, 64 oz. | 30.00 |
| Bowl, 4¾" cream soup | 11.00 | Plate, 6" sherbet | 2.00 |
| Bowl, 5" cereal | 5.50 | Plate, 7" salad | 3.00 |
| Bowl, 7" salad | 10.00 | Plate, 7½" x 9" oval with indent | 5.00 |
| Bowl, 9" | 15.00 | Plate, 8" luncheon | 3.50 |
| Bowl, 10½", console | 20.00 | Plate, 10", sandwich | 9.00 |
| Bowl, 11½", 4¼" tall | 22.50 | Powder jar w/lid | 30.00 |
| Candlesticks, 3" pr. | 18.00 | Preserve (same as candy with slotted lid) | 27.50 |
| Candlesticks, 8", pr. | 27.50 | Sandwich server, open center handle | 20.00 |
| Candy jar w/cover, flat | 25.00 | Sandwich server, two-handled | 12.00 |
| Candy jar w/cover, flat, flange edge | 30.00 | Saucer | 2.00 |
| Candy jar w/cover, ftd., flange edge | 30.00 | Sherbet | 6.00 |
| Candy jar w/cover, ftd., short, fat | 35.00 | Sugar | 6.50 |
| Candy jar w/cover, ftd., tall | 35.00 | Tumbler, 4½", 9 oz. | 6.00 |
| Cologne bottle w/stopper | 35.00 | Tumbler, 5¼", 12 oz. | 8.00 |
| Creamer | 7.50 | Vase, 7¼", 2 hndl, rolled edge | 20.00 |
| Cup | 4.00 | Vase, 8", 2 hndl, fan | 30.00 |
| Mayonnaise | 20.00 | Vase, 8", 2 hndl, straight edge | 25.00 |

*Blue, Canary Yellow 50% more

# U.S. SWIRL U.S. GLASS COMPANY, Late 1920's

Colors: Pink, green, iridescent and crystal.

U.S. Swirl has been difficult for me to find in pink. Notice the lone pink shaker in the photograph. Maybe the pink is as hard to find as iridescent and crystal. I keep running into green pieces; happily, that is what most collectors of this pattern want.

Recently, several iridescent butter dishes have been uncovered, but that is the only piece being found in that color. A few crystal sherbets are turning up, but I haven't seen a rush to find additional pieces in crystal either. The tumbler listing 3⅝" corresponds with the only known size of Aunt Polly and Cherryberry/Strawberry tumblers, but the 12 oz. tumbler has only been found in this U.S. Glass Company pattern.

U.S. Swirl has the plain butter bottom that is interchangeable with all the other patterns made by U.S. Glass. The butter dish in this pattern is the one that many Strawberry collectors have purchased over the years to borrow the bottom for their Strawberry tops. This plundering has stressed the search for butters in this pattern, particularly in pink.

I still need a green creamer. If you have an extra one, let me hear from you!

| | Green | Pink | | Green | Pink |
|---|---|---|---|---|---|
| Bowl, 4⅜", berry | 5.50 | 6.50 | Pitcher, 8", 48 oz. | 45.00 | 45.00 |
| Bowl, 5½", 1 handle | 9.50 | 10.50 | Plate, 6⅛", sherbet | 2.50 | 2.50 |
| Bowl, 7⅞, large berry | 15.00 | 16.00 | Plate, 7⅞", salad | 5.50 | 6.50 |
| Bowl, 8¼", oval | 24.00 | 24.00 | Salt and pepper, pr. | 42.50 | 42.50 |
| Butter and cover | 67.50 | 72.50 | Sherbet, 3¼" | 4.50 | 5.00 |
| Butter bottom | 45.00 | 55.50 | Sugar w/lid | 32.00 | 32.00 |
| Butter top | 22.50 | 17.50 | Tumbler, 3⅝", 8 oz. | 10.00 | 10.00 |
| Candy w/cover, 2-handled | 27.50 | 32.00 | Tumbler, 4¾", 12 oz. | 12.00 | 14.00 |
| Creamer | 14.00 | 16.00 | Vase, 6½" | 16.00 | 19.00 |

**Please refer to Foreword for pricing information**

# "VICTORY" DIAMOND GLASS-WARE COMPANY, 1929-1932

Colors: Amber, pink, green; some cobalt blue and black.

Prices for Victory can be found on the next page. I squeezed in an additional page of Tulip pattern and got my format a little out of kilter. At least, you can see a photograph of cobalt blue Victory below. It has been a while since I have been able to show you that color. The last time I had a set for sell, many of the pieces sold to collectors of cobalt blue rather than Victory collectors. Many of these collectors rather politely asked what the pattern was, but I had the feeling that they really did not care what it was called - only that it was an attractive blue color!

That same collecting concept applies to black Victory, but not to the same extent that it does with cobalt blue. Collectors of black glass are more plentiful than collectors of black Victory. Flat black pieces have to be turned over to see the pattern; and unless you have a strong light, the same is true for cobalt blue pieces.

Sets of Victory can be completed in pink and green with much searching. Amber, cobalt blue and black will take more hunting and require more luck.

The Victory gravy boat and platter are the most desirable pieces to own in any color. I have only seen one amber set which was purchased years ago in Pennsylvania. The cobalt blue one pictured previously has long been sold and I haven't seen another one in five years! A green gravy and platter can be seen on the bottom of page 206.

Goblets, cereal and soup bowls, as well as oval vegetable bowls will keep you looking long and hard, no matter which color you choose. Various collectors have notified me that the candlesticks are also scarce.

There are several styles of decorations besides the 22K gold trimmed pieces shown on page 206. There are floral decorations and even a black decorated design that is very "Art Deco" looking. I have only seen this "Art Deco" design on pink and green. I have observed more floral decorated console sets (bowl and candlesticks) than anything. Complete sets of floral decorated ware may not be available. I assume that whole sets can be found with gold trim. At least gold decorated pink and green sets can be found. The black pieces decorated with gold may only be found in luncheon and console sets (bowl and candlesticks).

|  | Amber, Pink, Green | Black, Blue |
|---|---|---|
| Bon bon, 7" | 11.00 | 20.00 |
| Bowl, 6½" cereal | 11.00 | 27.00 |
| Bowl, 8½" flat soup | 17.50 | 40.00 |
| Bowl, 9" oval vegetable | 32.00 | 77.50 |
| Bowl, 11" rolled edge | 28.00 | 50.00 |
| Bowl, 12" console | 33.00 | 65.00 |
| Bowl, 12½" flat edge | 30.00 | 65.00 |
| Candlesticks, 3" pr. | 30.00 | 90.00 |
| Cheese & cracker set, 12" indented plate & compote | 40.00 | |
| Comport, 6" tall, 6¾" diameter | 15.00 | |
| Creamer | 15.00 | 45.00 |
| Cup | 9.00 | 32.00 |
| Goblet, 5", 7 oz. | 19.00 | |
| Gravy boat and platter | 160.00 | 300.00 |
| Mayonnaise set: 3½" tall, 5½" across, 8½" indented plate, w/ladle | 42.00 | 98.00 |
| Plate, 6" bread and butter | 6.00 | 16.00 |
| Plate, 7" salad | 7.00 | 18.00 |
| Plate, 8" luncheon | 7.00 | 28.00 |
| Plate, 9" dinner | 19.00 | 38.00 |
| Platter, 12" | 28.00 | 70.00 |
| Sandwich server, center handle | 29.00 | 70.00 |
| Saucer | 4.00 | 11.00 |
| Sherbet, ftd. | 13.00 | 26.00 |
| Sugar | 15.00 | 45.00 |

# VITROCK, "FLOWER RIM" HOCKING GLASS COMPANY, 1934-1937

Colors: White and white w/fired-on colors, usually red or green.

I didn't receive as many letters on the Kresge's store window display of Vitrock as I did on the Old Colony. Then again, there are not as many collectors of Vitrock either! This mid 1930's store display photograph was found in Anchor Hocking's files. Vitrock was Hocking's venture into the "milk glass" market. Note the emphasis that Vitrock "Will not craze or check" on the display sign. Crazing was a major flaw for many pottery wares of the time.

Platters and cream soups are pieces that are nearly impossible to find. I said in the last book that in looking at a poor overexposed copy of the photo while writing, I did not see any cream soups in this introductory display! Several readers said to look in the upper left hand side of the photo and they were right. You can check it out on page 208. (I still can't find them in this photocopy I am provided for writing purposes.)

In this very durable line, only "Flower Rim" pattern and Lake Como were made into dinnerware sets. At the time, Vitrock vied with Hazel Atlas' "Platonite"; and by all the evidence left today, "Platonite" won.

Vitrock is better known for its kitchenware line of reamers, measuring cups and mixing bowls manufactured in this white color. Notice that the Vitrock Kitchenware items are also shown in this display of "The NEW Material." I now understand why those large Vitrock mixing bowls are so hard to find. They sold for a quarter when a working man's wages were in the range of a $1.00 a day!

You can see more Vitrock in my book *Kitchen Glassware of the Depression Years*. Some collectors are gathering patterns that can "cross-over" into other fields. This is a very good example of a pattern that fits into both collecting areas. Hazel Atlas did the same with their Platonite. It made good business sense to sell other accessory items that matched your everyday dishes.

Vitrock fired-on colors make decorative accessory pieces for special occasions. You can find fired-on blue as well as the three colors shown!

| | White | | White |
|---|---|---|---|
| Bowl, 4" berry | 4.50 | Plate, 7¼" salad | 2.50 |
| Bowl, 5½" cream soup | 15.00 | Plate, 8¾" luncheon | 4.50 |
| Bowl, 6" fruit | 5.50 | Plate, 9" soup | 13.00 |
| Bowl, 7½" cereal | 6.00 | Plate, 10" dinner | 8.50 |
| Bowl, 9½" vegetable | 12.00 | Platter, 11½" | 26.00 |
| Creamer, oval | 4.50 | Saucer | 2.50 |
| Cup | 3.50 | Sugar | 4.50 |

# WATERFORD, "WAFFLE" HOCKING GLASS COMPANY, 1938-1944

Colors: Crystal, pink; some yellow, white; Forest Green 1950's.

Right now, there are more collectors looking for crystal Waterford than for pink. The major reason is supply. The quantity of pink is nearly exhausted unless you find someone willing to sell you a set that was accumulated over the years. Price of hard to find pink Waterford pieces is not a concern with collectors. Most would like to see some cereal bowls, a pitcher or butter dish sitting on a table or shelf for sale! I am not encountering pink Waterford at Depression glass shows either. Of these three pieces, the cereal is the most elusive. It has always been hard to find, and worse, hard to find **mint!**

A crystal Waterford collection can be completed; but there are pieces in crystal that are also scarce today. Cereal bowls and even water goblets are evaporating. Some plates are less available than you can believe for this once bountiful pattern. Be sure to check the inside rims for roughness on this pattern. A little roughness is normal; don't let that keep you from owning a hard to find piece. Because of the scalloped rim design, Waterford does chip.

There is a "look-alike" footed cup that is sometimes sold as a Waterford punch cup. This cup, and the larger lamps that are often displayed as Waterford, are only similar to Waterford. Waterford has a flattened (not rounded) "diamond" shape on each section of the design. There is also a large, pink pitcher with an indented, circular design in each diamond that is not Waterford. This pitcher was made by Hocking, but has more of a "bullseye" look. These only sell for $20.00; do not pay Waterford prices for one!

You may find a few pieces of white Waterford and some "Dusty Rose" and "Springtime Green" on ash trays which sell at crystal prices. Examples of these rose and green colors can be seen in Oyster and Pearl on page 151. Forest Green 13¾" plates in Waterford were made in the 1950's promotion; these are usually found in the $12.50 range. Some crystal has also been found trimmed in red. No, you can not remove it to match the plain crystal.

Advertising ash trays, such as the "Post Cereals" shown below, are now selling for $12.00 to $15.00 depending upon the desirability of the advertising on the piece! An advertisement for Anchor Hocking itself will fetch $25.00.

The items listed below with Miss America style in parentheses are Waterford patterned pieces that have the same mould shapes as Miss America. You can see some of these in the seventh edition of this book or in the first *Very Rare Glassware of the Depression Years*. It seems likely that the first designs for Waterford were patterned on the shapes of Miss America that had been discontinued the year before Waterford was introduced. For some unknown reason, a newly designed shape was chosen and these experimental (?) pieces have been found in small quantities. It is unlikely that a full set could be found, but one never knows!

Those yellow and amber goblets shown below are compliments of Anchor Hocking's photographer from items stored in their morgue. I haven't seen yellow ones for sale, but amber ones have been sitting in a shop in my area for $15.00 for over two years. As dusty as they are getting, someone will mistake the color someday!

| | Crystal | Pink |
|---|---|---|
| * Ash tray, 4" | 7.50 | |
| Bowl, 4¾" berry | 6.50 | 13.00 |
| Bowl, 5½" cereal | 17.00 | 25.00 |
| Bowl, 8¼" large berry | 10.00 | 16.00 |
| Butter dish and cover | 25.00 | 200.00 |
| Butter dish bottom | 6.00 | 27.50 |
| Butter dish top | 19.00 | 178.50 |
| Coaster, 4" | 3.50 | |
| Creamer, oval | 5.00 | 10.00 |
| Creamer (Miss America style) | 35.00 | |
| Cup | 6.50 | 14.00 |
| Cup (Miss America style) | | 35.00 |
| Goblets, 5¼", 5⅝" | 16.00 | |
| Goblet, 5½" (Miss America style) | 35.00 | 80.00 |
| Lamp, 4" spherical base | 26.00 | |
| Pitcher, 42 oz. tilted juice | 24.00 | |
| Pitcher, 80 oz. tilted ice lip | 32.00 | 135.00 |
| Plate, 6" sherbet | 3.00 | 6.00 |

\* With ads $15.00

| | Crystal | Pink |
|---|---|---|
| Plate, 7⅛" salad | 6.00 | 8.00 |
| Plate, 9⅝" dinner | 11.00 | 18.00 |
| Plate, 10¼" handled cake | 10.00 | 16.00 |
| Plate, 13¾" sandwich | 10.00 | 25.00 |
| Relish, 13¾", 5-part | 16.00 | |
| Salt and pepper, 2 types | 8.50 | |
| Saucer | 3.00 | 6.00 |
| Sherbet, ftd. | 4.00 | 11.00 |
| Sherbet, ftd., scalloped base | 4.00 | |
| Sugar | 5.00 | 10.00 |
| Sugar cover, oval | 5.00 | 24.00 |
| Sugar (Miss America style) | 35.00 | |
| Tumbler, 3½", 5 oz. juice (Miss America style) | | 60.00 |
| Tumbler, 4⅞", 10 oz. ftd. | 12.00 | 19.00 |

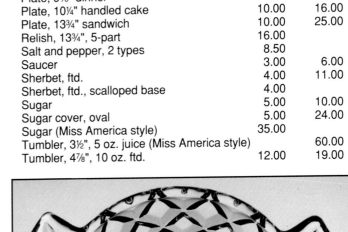

# WINDSOR, "WINDSOR DIAMOND" JEANNETTE GLASS COMPANY, 1936-1946

Colors: Pink, green, crystal; some Delphite, amberina red and ice blue.

Windsor has many crystal items found in unusual shapes that are not found in color. There are numerous collectors of pink and green, but few presently collect crystal. Color was discontinued about 1940, but some crystal pieces were made as late as 1946. A restyled Windsor butter and sugar were later transferred to Holiday when that pattern was introduced in 1947. I have placed the butter dish and the other style lid on the right in the photo below. There are two styles of sugars and lids. In that photograph, the crystal sugar bowl (shaped like Holiday) has no lip for the lid to rest against; at the top of page 213, the pink sugar represents the style with lip. The pink sugar and lid without the lip are hard to find.

Notice the flashed red cup edge at the bottom of this page. I had not seen one before with this treatment. Have you? Was it a special promotion?

Relish trays can be found with or without tab handles. Trays without handles can be found in crystal. Pink trays without handles are much in demand! There are also two styles of sandwich plates. The normally found one is 10¼" and has open handles. The newly discovered tray is 10" and has closed handles. This was the first report I have had on this item. It remains to be seen how difficult it is to find. Since I have never specified open or closed handles in my listings, collectors may have assumed I was talking about whichever one they had.

Green Windsor tumblers are elusive. Even the water tumbler (which is commonly found in pink), is scarce. As with many patterns there is a lot of mould roughness on seams of tumblers; and Windsor tumblers have a tendency to chip on the sides. Check these seams out carefully before you buy! There are color variances in green; be aware of that if you see a piece that looks darker than you are used to seeing!

The pink 13⅝" plate is often found as a beverage set with a pitcher and six water tumblers. That may have been a premium item since so many pitchers and water tumblers are available today.

The 10½" pointed edge bowl is hard to find in pink. This same bowl in crystal, along with the comport, make up a punch bowl and stand. The upended comport fits inside the base of this bowl to keep it from sliding off the base. In recent years, there have been newly made comports in crystal and sprayed-on, multi-colored ones that have a beaded edge. The recent crystal will not work as a punch stand because of the beaded edge. This beaded edge comport was made in the late 1950's in Jeannette's Shell Pink, one of the patterns shown in *Collectible Glassware from the 40's, 50's, 60's....*

You can see an unusual piece of Windsor in my first *Very Rare Glassware of the Depression Years*. It is a yellow (vaseline) powder jar that has a Cube top and Windsor bottom. A pink powder jar with Windsor top and Cube bottom has also been reported!

A new style pink ash tray and a tab handled berry bowl can be seen in the *Very Rare Glassware of the Depression Years, Second Series*. While looking there, check out the blue Windsor butter dish!

I hope you enjoy the additional photographs of Windsor! I have been accused by Windsor advocates of slacking off this "book ending" pattern!

# WINDSOR, "WINDSOR DIAMOND" JEANNETTE GLASS COMPANY, 1936-1946

|  | Crystal | Pink | Green |
|---|---|---|---|
| * Ash tray, 5¾" | 13.50 | 36.00 | 44.00 |
| Bowl, 4¾" berry | 4.00 | 8.50 | 10.00 |
| Bowl, 5" pointed edge | 5.00 | 16.00 | |
| Bowl, 5" cream soup | 6.00 | 19.00 | 25.00 |
| Bowls, 5⅛, 5⅜" cereal | 8.50 | 19.00 | 20.00 |
| Bowl, 7⅛", three legs | 7.50 | 24.00 | |
| Bowl, 8" pointed edge | 9.00 | 38.00 | |
| Bowl, 8", 2-handled | 7.00 | 15.00 | 20.00 |
| Bowl, 8½" large berry | 6.50 | 16.00 | 17.00 |
| Bowl, 9½" oval vegetable | 7.00 | 19.00 | 23.00 |
| Bowl, 10½" salad | 9.00 | | |
| Bowl, 10½" pointed edge | 23.00 | 110.00 | |
| Bowl, 12½" fruit console | 24.00 | 98.00 | |
| Bowl, 7" x 11¾" boat shape | 16.00 | 30.00 | 32.00 |
| Butter dish ( two styles) | 26.00 | 48.00 | 80.00 |
| Cake plate, 10¾" ftd. | 8.50 | 20.00 | 21.00 |
| Candlesticks, 3" Pr. | 20.00 | 80.00 | |
| Candy jar and cover | 16.00 | | |
| Coaster, 3¼" | 3.50 | 12.50 | 16.00 |
| Comport | 8.50 | | |
| ** Creamer | 4.50 | 11.00 | 12.00 |
| Creamer (shaped as "Holiday") | 7.50 | | |
| ** Cup | 3.50 | 9.50 | 11.00 |
| Pitcher, 4½", 16 oz. | 20.00 | 110.00 | |
| *** Pitcher, 6¾", 52 oz. | 13.00 | 26.00 | 50.00 |
| Plate, 6" sherbet | 2.50 | 5.00 | 8.00 |
| Plate, 7" salad | 4.50 | 16.00 | 18.00 |

|  | Crystal | Pink | Green |
|---|---|---|---|
| ** Plate, 9" dinner | 5.00 | 23.00 | 21.00 |
| Plate, 10", sandwich, closed hndl. | | 20.00 | |
| Plate, 10¼", sandwich open hndl. | 6.00 | 16.00 | 16.00 |
| Plate, 13⅝" chop | 9.50 | 45.00 | 45.00 |
| Platter, 11½" oval | 6.00 | 19.00 | 20.00 |
| ****Powder jar | 15.00 | 55.00 | |
| Relish platter, 11½" divided | 10.00 | 180.00 | |
| Salt and pepper, pr. | 16.00 | 36.00 | 48.00 |
| Saucer (ice blue $15.00) | 2.50 | 5.00 | 6.00 |
| Sherbet, ftd. | 3.50 | 11.00 | 14.00 |
| Sugar & cover | 8.00 | 25.00 | 30.00 |
| Sugar & cover (like "Holiday") | 12.00 | 95.00 | |
| Tray, 4", square, w/handles | 5.00 | 10.00 | 12.00 |
| Tray, 4", square, wo/handles | 6.00 | 35.00 | |
| Tray, 4⅛" x 9", w/handles | 4.00 | 10.00 | 16.00 |
| Tray, 4⅛" x 9", wo/handles | 9.00 | 48.00 | |
| Tray, 8½" x 9¾", w/handles | 6.50 | 24.00 | 35.00 |
| Tray, 8½" x 9¾", wo/handles | 13.00 | 80.00 | 40.00 |
| ** Tumbler, 3¼", 5 oz. | 8.00 | 24.00 | 32.00 |
| ** Tumbler, 4", 9 oz. (red 50.00) | 6.00 | 18.00 | 28.00 |
| Tumbler, 5", 12 oz. | 8.00 | 25.00 | 45.00 |
| Tumbler, 4⅝", 11 oz. | 7.50 | | |
| Tumbler, 4" ftd. | 7.00 | | |
| Tumbler, 5" ftd., 11 oz. | 10.00 | | |
| Tumbler, 7¼" ftd. | 15.00 | | |

*Delphite-$40.00      **Blue-$55.00      ***Red-$400.00      ****Yellow-$150.00; Blue-$175.00

**Please refer to Foreword for pricing information**

# REPRODUCTIONS

## NEW "ADAM" PRIVATELY PRODUCED OUT OF KOREA THROUGH ST. LOUIS IMPORTING COMPANY
### ONLY THE ADAM BUTTER DISH HAS BEEN REPRODUCED!

The new Adam butter is being offered at $6.00 wholesale. Identification of the new is easy.

*Top*: Notice the veins in the leaves.

**New:** Large leaf veins do not join or touch in center of leaf.

**Old:** Large leaf veins all touch or join center vein on the old.

A further note in the original Adam butter dish: the veins of all the leaves at the center of the design are very clear cut and precisely moulded: in the new, these center leaf veins are very indistinct – and almost invisible in one leaf of the center design.

*Bottom*: Place butter dish bottom upside down for observation.

**New:** Four (4) "Arrowhead-like" points line up in northwest, northeast, southeast and southwest directions of compass. There are very bad mould lines and a very glossy light pink color on the butter dishes I have examined; but these have been improved.

**Old:** Four (4) "Arrowhead-like" points line up in north, east, south and west directions of compass.

---

## NEW "AVOCADO" INDIANA GLASS COMPANY Tiara Exclusives Line, 1974…

Colors: Pink, frosted pink, yellow, blue, red, amethyst and green.

In 1979 a green Avocado pitcher was produced. It is darker than the original green and was a limited hostess gift item. Yellow pieces that are beginning to show up are all new! Yellow was never made originally!

The original pink Indiana made was a delicate pretty pink. The new tends to be more orange than the original color. The other colors shown pose little threat since these colors were not made originally.

I understand that Tiara sales counselors told potential clientele that their newly made glass is collectible because it was made from old moulds. I don't share this view. I feel it's like saying that since you were married in your grandmother's wedding dress, you will have the same happy marriage for the fifty-seven years she did. All you can truly say is that you were married in her dress. I think all you can say about the new Avocado is that it was made from the old moulds. TIME, SCARCITY and PEOPLE'S WHIMS determine collectability in so far as I'm able to determine it. It's taken nearly fifty years or more for people to turn to collecting Depression Glass – and that's done, in part, because EVERYONE "remembers" it; they had some in their home at one time or another; it has universal appeal. Who is to say what will be collectible in the next hundred years. If we all knew, we could all get rich!

If you like the new Tiara products, then by all means buy them; but don't do so DEPENDING upon their being collectible just because they are made in the image of the old! You have an equal chance, I feel, of going to Las Vegas and DEPENDING upon getting rich at the blackjack table.

---

## NEW "CAMEO"

Colors: Green, pink, cobalt blue (shakers); yellow, green and pink (child's dishes).

Although the photographer I left this shaker with opted to shoot the side without the dancing girl, I trust you can still see how very weak the pattern is on this reproduction. It was made by Mosser originally, but is now being made overseas. Also, you can see how much glass remains in the bottom of the shaker; and, of course, the new tops all make this easy to spot at the market. These were to be bought wholesale at around $6.00 but did not sell well. A new IMPORTER is making shakers in pink, cobalt blue and a terrible green color. These, too, are weakly patterned! They were never originally made in the blue, but **beware of PINK**!

Children's dishes in Cameo pose no problem to collectors since they were never made originally. These are "scale models" of the larger size. This type of production I have no quarrel with as they are not made to "dupe" anyone.

# NEW "CHERRY BLOSSOM"

Colors: Pink, green, blue, delphite, cobalt, red and iridized colors.

**Please use information provided only for the piece described. Do not apply information on tumbler for pitcher, etc. Realize that with so many different importers now involved there are more variations than I can possibly analyze for you. Know your dealer and make sure that he knows what he is doing also!**

Several different people have gotten into the act of making reproduction Cherry Blossom. We've even enjoyed some reproductions of those reproductions! All the items pictured on the next page are extremely easy to spot as reproductions once you know what to look for with the possible exception of the 13" divided platter pictured at the back. It's too heavy, weighing 2¾ pounds, and has a thick, ⅜" of glass in the bottom; but the design isn't too bad! The edges of the leaves aren't smooth; but neither are they serrated like old leaves.

There are many differences between old and new scalloped bottom, AOP Cherry pitchers. The easiest way to tell the difference is to turn the pitcher over. The branch crossing the bottom of my old Cherry pitchers **looks** like a branch. It's knobby and gnarled and has several leaves and cherry stems directly attached to it. The new pitcher just has a bald strip of glass cutting the bottom of the pitcher in half. Further, the old Cherry pitchers have a plain glass background for the cherries and leaves in the bottom of the pitcher. In the new pitchers, there's a rough, filled in, straw-like background. You see no plain glass.

As for the new tumblers, the easiest way to tell old from new is to look at the ring dividing the patterned portion of the glass from the plain glass lip. The old tumblers have three indented rings dividing the pattern from the plain glass rim. The new has only one. Again, the pattern at the bottom of the new tumblers is brief and practically nonexistent in the center curve of the glass bottom. The pattern, what there is, on the new tumblers, mostly hugs the center of the foot.

**2 handled tray - old:** 1⅝ lbs.; ³⁄₁₆" glass in bottom; leaves and cherries east/west from north/south handles; leaves have real spine and serrated edges; cherry stems end in triangle of glass. **new:** 2⅛ lbs.; ¼" glass in bottom; leaves and cherries north/south with the handles; canal type leaves (but uneven edges; cherry stem ends before canal shaped line).

**cake plate - new:** color too light pink, leaves have too many parallel veins that give them a "feathery" look; arches at plate edge don't line up with lines on inside of the rim to which the feet are attached.

**8½" bowl - new:** crude leaves with smooth edges; veins in parallel lines.

**cereal bowl - new:** wrong shape, looks like 8½" bowl, small 2" center. **old:** large center, 2½" inside ring, nearly 3½" if you count the outer rim before the sides turn up.

**plate - new:** center shown close up; smooth edged leaves, fish spine type center leaf portion; weighs 1 pound plus; feels thicker at edge with mould offset lines clearly visible. **old:** center leaves look like real leaves with spines, veins and serrated edges; weighs ¾ pound; clean edges; no mould offset.

**cup - new:** area in bottom left free of design; canal centered leaves; smooth, thick top to cup handle (old has triangle grasp point).

**saucer - new:** off set mould line edge; canal leaf center.

The Cherry child's cup (with a slightly lop-sided handle) having the cherries hanging upside down when the cup was held in the right hand appeared in 1973. After I reported this error, it was quickly corrected by re-inverting the inverted mould. These later cups were thus improved in design but slightly off color. The saucers tended to have slightly off center designs, too. Next came the "child's butter dish" that was never made by Jeannette. It was essentially the child's cup without a handle turned upside down over the saucer and having a little glob of glass added as a knob for lifting purposes. A blue one is pictured on bottom of page 217.

Pictured are some of the colors of butter dishes made so far. Shakers were begun in 1977 and some were dated '77 on the bottom. Shortly afterward, the non dated variety appeared. How can you tell new shakers from old – should you get the one in a million chances to do so?

First, look at the tops. New tops could indicate new shakers. Next, notice the protruding edges beneath the tops. In the new they are squared off juts rather than the nicely rounded scallops on the old (which are pictured under Cherry Blossom pattern). The design on the newer shakers is often weak in spots. Finally, notice how far up inside the shakers the solid glass (next to the foot) remains. The newer shakers have almost twice as much glass in that area. They appear to be ¼ full of glass before you ever add the salt!

In 1989, a new distributor began making reproduction glass in the Far East. He's making shakers in cobalt blue, pink, and an ugly green, that is no problem to spot! These shakers are similar in quality to those made before, but the present pink color is good; yet the quality and design of each batch could vary greatly. Realize that only two original pairs of pink shakers have been found and those were discovered before any reproductions were made in 1977!

Butter dishes are naturally more deceptive in pink and green since those were the only original colors. The major flaw in the new butter is that there is one band encircling the bottom edge of the butter top; there are two bands very close together along the skirt of the old top.

# NEW "MADRID" CALLED "RECOLLECTION" Currently being made.

I hope you have already read about Recollection Madrid on page 118. The current rage of Indiana Glass is to make Madrid in teal after making it in **blue, pink and crystal.** This teal is a very greenish color that was never made originally, so there is no problem of it being confused with old! The teal color is being sold through all kinds of outlets ranging from better department stores to discount catalogues. In the past few months we have received several ads stating that this is genuine Depression glass made from old moulds. None of this is made from old glass moulds unless you consider 1976 old. Most of the pieces are from moulds that were never made originally.

The blue was a big seller for Indiana according to reports I am receiving around the country. It is a brighter, more fluorescent blue than the originally found color.

Look at the top picture! None of these items were ever made in the old pattern Madrid. The new grill plate has one division splitting the plate in half, but the old had three sections. A goblet or vase was never made. The vase is sold with a candle making it a "hurricane lamp." The heavy tumbler was placed on top of a candlestick to make this vase/hurricane lamp. That candlestick gets a workout. It was attached to a plate to make a pedestaled cake stand and to a butter dish to make a preserve stand. That's a clever idea, actually. You would not believe the mail generated by these two pieces!

The shakers are short and heavy and you can see both original styles pictured on page 119. The latest item I have seen is a heavy 11 oz. flat tumbler being sold for $7.99 in a set of four or six called "On the Rocks." The biggest giveaway to this newer pink glass is the pale, washed out color.

The only concerns in the new pink pieces are the cups, saucers and oval vegetable bowl. These three pieces were made in pink in the 1930's. None of the others shown were ever made in the 1930's in pink; so realize that when you see the butter dish, dinner plate, soup bowl, or sugar and creamer. These are new items! Once you have learned what this washed-out pink looks like by seeing these items out for sale, the color will be a clue when you see other pieces. My suggestion is to avoid pink Madrid except for the pitcher and tumblers.

The most difficult piece for new collectors to tell new from old is the candlestick. The new ones all have raised ridges inside to hold the candle more firmly. All old ones do not have these ridges. You may even find new candlesticks in black.

---

# NEW "MAYFAIR"

Colors: Pink, green, blue, cobalt (shot glasses), 1977... Pink, green, amethyst, cobalt blue, red (cookie jars), 1982... Cobalt blue, pink, amethyst, red and green (odd shade), shakers 1988...

Only the pink shot glass need cause any concern to collectors because the glass wasn't made in those other colors originally. At first glance the color of the newer shots is often too light pink or too orange. Dead giveaway is the stems of the flower design, however. In the old that stem branched to form an "A" shape; in the new, you have a single stem. Further, in the new design, the leaf is hollow with the veins moulded in. In the old, the leaf is moulded in and the veining is left hollow. In the center of the flower on the old, dots (anther) cluster entirely to one side and are rather distinct. Nothing like that occurs in the new design.

As for the cookie jars, at cursory glance the base of the cookie has a very indistinct design. It will feel smooth to the touch it's so faint. In the old cookie jars, there's a distinct pattern that feels like raised embossing to the touch. Next, turn the bottom upside down. The new bottom is perfectly smooth. The old bottom contains a **1¾" mould circle rim** that is raised enough to catch your fingernail in it. There are other distinctions as well; but that is the **quickest** and **easiest** way to tell old from new.

In the Mayfair cookie lid, the new design (parallel to the straight side of the lid) at the edge curves gracefully toward the center "V" shape (rather like bird wings in flight); in the old, that edge is a flat straight line going into the "V" (like airplane wings sticking straight out from the side of the plane as you face it head on).

The green color of the cookie, as you can see from the picture, is not the pretty, yellow/green color of true green Mayfair. It also doesn't "glow" under black light as the old green does.

The corner ridges on the old shaker rise one half way to the top and then smooth out. The new shaker corner ridges rise to the top and are quite pronounced. The measurement differences are listed below, but the **diameter of the opening is the critical and easiest way to tell old from new!**

|  | OLD | NEW |
|---|---|---|
| Diameter of opening | ¾" | ⅝" |
| Diameter of lid | ⅞" | ¾" |
| Height | 4¹⁄₁₆" | 4" |

So, you see, none of these reproductions give us any trouble; they're all easily spotted by those of us now "in the know!"

# REPRODUCTIONS   (Continued)

## NEW "MISS AMERICA"

Colors: Crystal, green, pink, ice blue, red amberina, cobalt blue.

The new butter dish in "Miss America" design is probably the best of the newer products; yet there are three distinct differences to be found between the original butter top and the newly made one. Since the value of the butter dish lies in the top, it seems more profitable to examine it. **There is a new importer who is making reproductions of the reproductions.** Unfortunately, these newer models vary greatly from one batch to the next. The only noticeable thing I have seen on these butters is how the top knob sticks up away from the butter caused by a longer than usual stem on the knob. All the other characteristics still hold true, but the paragraph in bold below is the best way to tell old from new!

In the new butter dishes pictured, notice that the panels reaching the edge of the butter bottom tend to have a pronounced curving, skirt-like edge. In the original dish, there is much less curving at the edge of these panels.

Second, pick up the top of the new dish and feel up inside it. If the butter top knob is filled with glass so that it is convex (curved outward), the dish is new; the old inside knob area is concave (curved inward).

**Finally, from the underside, look through the top toward the knob. In the original butter dish you would see a perfectly formed multi-sided star; in the newer version, you see distorted rays with no visible points.** Shakers have been made in green, pink, cobalt blue and crystal. The latest batch of **shakers are becoming more difficult to distinguish from the old!** The new distributor's copies are creating havoc with new collectors and dealers alike. The measurements given below for shakers **do not** hold true for **all** the latest reproductions. It is impossible to know which generation of shaker reproductions that you will find, so you have to be careful on these! Know your dealer and **if the price is too good to be true,** there is likely a good reason! **It's NEW!**

The shakers will have new tops; but since some old shakers have been given new tops, that isn't conclusive at all. Unscrew the lid. Old shakers have a very neatly formed ridge of glass on which to screw the lid. It overlaps a little and has rounded off ends. Old shakers stand 3⅜" tall without the lid. **Most new** ones stand 3¼" tall. Old shakers have almost a forefinger's depth inside (female finger) or a fraction shy of 2½". **Most new** shakers have an inside depth of 2", about the second digit bend of a female's finger. (I'm doing finger depths since most of you will have those with you at the flea market, rather than a tape measure). In men, the old shaker's depth covers my knuckle; the new shakers leaves my knuckle exposed. **Most** new shakers simply have more glass on the inside of the shaker – something you can spot from twelve feet away! The hobs are more rounded on the newer shaker, particularly near the stem and seams; in the old shaker these areas remained pointedly sharp!

New Miss America tumblers have ½" of glass in the bottom, have a smooth edge on the bottom of the glass with no mold rim and show only two distinct mold marks on the sides of the glass. Old tumblers have only ¼" of glass in the bottom, have a distinct mold line rimming the bottom of the tumbler and have four distinct mold marks up the sides of the tumbler. The new green tumbler doesn't "glow" under black light as did the old.

New Miss America pitchers (without ice lip only) are all perfectly smooth rimmed at the top edge above the handle. All old pitchers that I have seen have a "hump" in the top rim of the glass above the handle area, rather like a camel's hump. The very bottom diamonds next to the foot in the new pitchers "squash" into elongated diamonds. In the old pitchers, these get noticeably smaller, but they retain their diamond shape.

## NEW "SHARON" Privately Produced 1976…(continued page 222)

Colors: Blue, dark green, light green, pink, cobalt blue, burnt umber.

A blue Sharon butter turned up in 1976 and turned my phone line to a liquid fire! The color is Mayfair blue – a fluke and dead giveaway as far as real Sharon is concerned.

When found in similar colors to the old, pink and green, you can immediately tell that the new version has more glass in the top where it changes from pattern to clear glass, a thick, defined ring of glass as opposed to a thin, barely defined ring of glass in the old. The knob of the new dish tends to stick up more. In the old butter dish there's barely room to fit your finger to grasp the knob. The new butter dish has a sharply defined ridge of glass in the bottom around which the top sits. The old butter has such a slight rim that the top easily scoots off the bottom.

In 1977 a "cheese dish" appeared having the same top as the butter and having all the flaws inherent in that top which were discussed in detail above. However, the bottom of this dish was all wrong. It's about half way between a flat plate and a butter dish bottom, **bowl** shaped; and it is over thick, giving it an awkward appearance. The real cheese bottom was a salad **plate** with a rim for holding the top. These "round bottom cheese dishes" are but a parody of the old and are easily spotted. We removed the top from one in the picture so you could see its heaviness and its bowl shape.

# REPRODUCTIONS (Continued)

## NEW "SHARON" (Continued)

Some of the latest reproductions in Sharon are a too-light pink creamer and sugar with lid. They are pictured with the "Made in Taiwan" label. These retail for around $15.00 for the pair and are also easy to spot as reproductions. I'll just mention the most obvious differences. Turn the creamer so you are looking directly at the spout. In the old creamer the mold line runs dead center of that spout; in the new, the mold line runs decidedly to the left of center spout.

On the sugar, the leaves and roses are "off" but not enough to DESCRIBE it to new collectors. Therefore, look at the center design, both sides, at the stars located at the very bottom of the motif. A thin leaf stem should run directly from that center star upward on BOTH sides. In this new sugar, the stem only runs from one; it stops way short of the star on one side; OR look inside the sugar bowl at where the handle attaches to the bottom of the bowl; in the new bowl, this attachment looks like a perfect circle; in the old, its an upside down "v" shaped tear drop.

As for the sugar lid, the knob of the new lid is perfectly smooth as you grasp its edges. The old knob has a mold seam running mid circumference. You could tell these two lids apart blind folded!

While there is a hair's difference between the height, mouth opening diameter, and inside depth of the old Sharon shakers and those newly produced, I won't attempt to upset you with those sixteenth and thirty seconds of a degree of difference. Suffice it to say that in physical shape, they are very close. However, as concerns design, they're miles apart.

The old shakers have true appearing roses. The flowers really LOOK like roses. On the new shakers, they look like poorly drawn circles with wobbly concentric rings. The leaves are not as clearly defined on the new shakers as the old. However, forgetting all that, in the old shakers, the first design you see below the lid is a ROSE BUD. It's angled like a rocket shooting off into outer space with three leaves at the base of the bud (where the rocket fuel would burn out). In the new shakers, this "bud" has become four paddles of a windmill. It's the difference between this and this.

Candy dishes have been made in pink and green. These candy jars are among the easiest items to discern old from new. Pick up the lid and look from the bottom side. On the old there is a 2" circle knob ring; on the new the ring is only ½". This shows from the top also but it is difficult to measure with the knob in the center. There are other major differences but this one will not be mould corrected easily. The bottoms are also simple to distinguish. The base diameter of the old is 3¼" and the new only 3". On the example I have quality of the new is rough, poorly shaped and molded, but I do not know if that will hold true for all reproductions of the candy. **I hope so!**

# Collectible Glassware from the 40's, 50's, 60's...

## by Gene Florence

Now that you have seen a copy of Gene Florence's popular *Collector's Encyclopedia of Depression Glass* you will be glad to know that there is another book devoted to the newest glass collectible market since the ever popular Depression Glass! That is the glass made during the 40's, 50's & 60's. It is this glass that collectors are now turning toward. *Collectible Glassware from the 40's, 50's, 60's...* is formated in the same easy-to-use style as our *Collector's Encyclopedia of Depression Glass* with large color photographs, complete with prices and descriptions of thousands of pieces. Today's collectors are expanding their attention to glass made during the 40's, 50's & 60's. If its popularity continues at its present trend, it will become the glass collectible of the 90's. This is the only book on the market today that deals exclusively with this field. It should quickly become the standard reference for this area of collectible and a bestseller in the field of antiques and collectibles. Having this new book will be like having a companion volume to the *Collector's Encyclopedia of Depression Glass*. This new volume picks up where the *Depression Glass* book leaves off. So get a copy and start buying the glass while it is still available and prices are low.

No dealer, glass collector or investor can afford not to own this book.

8½ x 11, 144 Pages, hardbound ................................................................ $19.95

---

# Books By Gene Florence

# Schroeder's ANTIQUES Price Guide

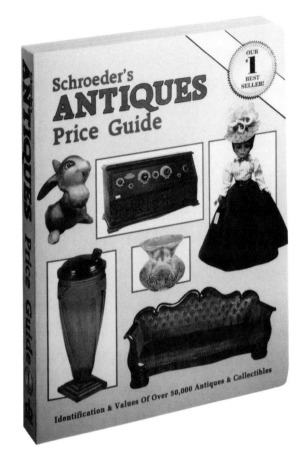

Schroeder's Antiques Price Guide is the #1 best-selling antiques & collectibles value guide on the market today, and here's why . . . More than 300 authors, well-known dealers, and top-notch collectors work together with our editors to bring you accurate information regarding pricing and identification. More than 45,000 items in almost 500 categories are listed along with hundreds of sharp original photos that illustrate not only the rare and unusual, but the common, popular collectibles as well. Each large close-up shot shows important details clearly. Every subject is represented with histories and background information, a feature not found in any of our competitors' publications. Our editors keep abreast of newly-developing trends, often adding several new categories a year as the need arises. If it merits the interest of today's collector, you'll find it in *Schroeder's*. And you can feel confident that the information we publish is up to date and accurate. Our advisors thoroughly check each category to spot inconsistencies, listings that may not be entirely reflective of market dealings, and lines too vague to be of merit. Only the best of the lot remains for publication. Without doubt, you'll find *Schroeder's Antiques Price Guide* the only one to buy for reliable information and values.

**8½ x 11", 608 Pages**                    **$12.95**

**COLLECTOR BOOKS**

*A Division of Schroeder Publishing Co., Inc.*